A COMPEND OF
LUTHER'S THEOLOGY

A COMPEND OF
LUTHER'S THEOLOGY

Edited by

HUGH THOMSON KERR, Jr., Ph.D.

Associate Professor of Systematic Theology
Princeton Theological Seminary

THE WESTMINSTER PRESS · PHILADELPHIA

FOREWORD

THERE is virtual unanimity among historians and theologians as to the unique importance and significance of Martin Luther. He was not only the outstanding hero of the Protestant Reformation, but his influence was such that subsequent history cannot be understood without taking him into consideration. Even those who do not subscribe to his views are forced to admit that he brought about a transformation, if not a reformation, in life and thought as well as in religion. Those who may be theologically offended, for instance, by his doctrine of " justification by faith alone," can, on the other hand, find occasion for rejoicing by proclaiming him the champion of individual responsibility and freedom of thought. Surely he is one of the pivotal personalities of history, and he has always been acknowledged as such. His appeal is universal, and if books about him mean anything he grows in importance with the passing years. That is why he belongs not only to one branch of Protestantism, but, we may say, to Christian theology. The Lutherans have, of course, regarded him as their patron saint, and their praise has always been generous and unstinted. But he is by no means praised only by those who have taken his name. Calvin could say of him, " Although he were to call me a devil, I should still not the less hold him in such honour that I must acknowledge him to be an illustrious servant of God," [1] and while the two Reformers never met, Calvin always treasured his friendship with Luther. Professor Hugh Watt, of Edinburgh, regards Luther as the representative Churchman of the sixteenth century, saying of him, " We can only stand in wonder before his genius and his courage, and in gratitude before his re-discovery and proclamation of the great central truths of the Christian faith." [2] Even John Wesley,

[1] Letter to Bullinger, Nov. 25, 1544.
[2] *Representative Churchmen of Twenty Centuries*, p. 212.

who criticized Luther severely at some points, recalled with reverence the effect of Luther's *Commentary on Romans* upon his Christian experience, and he speaks of him as " a man highly favoured of God, and a blessed instrument in his hand." [3]

It has been well said, however, that while it is not necessary for us to praise famous men, it is necessary for us to know them. If it is true that Luther is the acknowledged father of Protestantism, it is also true that those who ought to know him best and at first hand are often quite ignorant of his basic ideas, his theology. The nailing of the Ninety-Five Theses on the church door at Wittenberg in 1517 and his classic reply at Marburg, " Here I stand; I cannot do otherwise, so help me God," are two of the scattered items of his life that have become common knowledge. His greatest hymn, " A Mighty Fortress Is Our God," has sung itself into the hearts of countless multitudes who have caught in these stirring lines something of the rhythm and majesty of Luther's passion. But Christian ministers and preachers, theological students, and others interested in the message of the Church ought to have at their command some deeper insight into Luther than isolated events in his life or the lines of a hymn. And the sad fact is that Luther himself is not well known, certainly not much read.

Some years ago when it seemed that a Compend of Calvin's immortal *Institutes of the Christian Religion* might prove serviceable for those who wished a firsthand introduction to the thought and theology of the great Genevan Reformer, the work was undertaken because theological students and ministers themselves confessed their ignorance about this book which is certainly one of the classics of the Christian faith. Since that effort,[4] which has been met with some appreciation, it began to appear that what had been done for Calvin might also be done for Luther. Six years of teaching systematic theology and numerous conversations with ministers of all denominations seem to indicate that students and pastors do not read Luther except in secondary sources and general Church histories. Usually they recognize a gap in their theological preparation at this point and regret the fact that there is no single

---

[3] *Journal*, Vol. II, p. 107 (Everyman Edition).
[4] *A Compend of the Institutes of the Christian Religion by John Calvin*. Presbyterian Board of Christian Education, Philadelphia, 1939.

volume of Luther's theology in his own words to which they could turn. Further inquiries among the Lutherans, who would be expected to know Luther well, showed that even here the knowledge of Luther was somewhat shallow and traditional. The purpose of this Compend, therefore, is to offer an introduction to the theology of Martin Luther for those who find it difficult or impossible to make any prolonged or systematic study of the Reformer's many writings.

There are in the main two good reasons why Luther is so much neglected. In the first place, it is difficult to know what to read. Those who follow the German, an ever decreasing number in our theological schools, have at hand several editions of Luther's works, the most authoritative being the so-called Weimar, or Kaiser, edition in eighty very large and ponderous volumes. To confront a busy pastor or overburdened student with such a library of source material is, however, no great service, and it may in fact prejudice him against Luther before he begins. Such editions obviously are not for those who wish to run as they read. There are, of course, shorter editions and single volumes of one kind and another which are available in English as well as in the original German. The Philadelphia edition of Luther in six volumes, edited by Professor Henry E. Jacobs, of the Mount Airy Lutheran Theological Seminary, has provided in recent years the best and most adequate translation of the representative writings. An earlier collection, known as the J. N. Lenker Edition of Luther's works, in fourteen volumes, contains among other things the best selection in English of Luther's sermons. There are also several single volumes of Luther's commentaries, catechisms, hymns, et cetera. But all these sources are not always available to the student or minister, and even when they are accessible in libraries, the list is too long and the obstacles to easy reading are too great. One simply does not know where to begin.

Another reason for the neglect of Luther lies in the fact that, unlike Calvin, for example, he was not and never claimed to be a systematic theologian. There is unfortunately no single work or volume of Luther's that can be regarded as giving the substance of his theology. The three most celebrated treatises, directly related to the Reformation movement, *To the Christian Nobility*, *The*

Babylonian Captivity, On Christian Liberty, have been gathered together into a volume under the title, *The Primary Works of Luther,* but these three essays by no means give a well-rounded picture of Luther's mind or theology. To be sure, we have at hand the Augsburg Confession which is regarded as the definitive doctrinal standard in every branch of the Lutheran Church, but this symbol, Lutheran as it is, was written, not by Luther, but by his colleague Philip Melanchthon. Luther himself wrote a number of essays on the Apostles' Creed and composed two catechisms, but these are somewhat arbitrarily arranged and exhibit a rather mechanical and artificial construction. Although of great educational value and still in wide use, the catechisms can only suggest the breadth and scope of Luther's theology since they are restricted to the Ten Commandments, the Creed, the Lord's Prayer, and the Sacraments.

Nevertheless, it is not strictly true to say that Luther did not have a systematic mind, or that he was not interested in doctrine or theology. Sometimes a contrast is made between Luther and Calvin to the effect that Luther was the preacher of the Reformation while Calvin was the systematic theologian. Both Reformers would have repudiated such a characterization. Calvin was as much a preacher as a theologian, and while Luther wrote no systematic theology, nearly every essay and a great number of his sermons are systematic and certainly doctrinal in method and content. But Luther was not particularly interested in systems or previous attempts at systematic theology. He followed none of the Church Fathers, and, indeed, had a rather low opinion of their theological interpretations. In this respect he was quite unlike Calvin, who quoted at length from the Fathers and leaned heavily at times upon their views, especially those of Augustine. Luther was suspicious of all the Fathers simply because the Roman Church found it expedient on many occasions to confirm certain practices which he detested by appealing to tradition and the writings of the Fathers.

In a sermon preached on the first Sunday after Epiphany in 1523, Luther noted that in his day there were three types of theology, all of which he rejected. There was the Scholastic-Aristotelianism of Saint Thomas Aquinas (" If indeed he be a saint," adds Luther), there was the theology of the Church Councils, and there

was the theology of the Church Fathers. Of his own theology he
wrote in one of his many letters, " Jesus Christ, the judge of all, is
witness to my soul that I am conscious of having taught nothing
save Christ and the commandments of God, and, again, that I am
not so obstinate, but that I desire to be instructed, and when I see
my error, to change my opinion." [5] This, then, is Biblical rather
than dogmatic theology, but it is not for that reason less systematic
or without arrangement and sequence.

It may be argued that from a negative point of view Luther's
theology was simply a rebuttal or condemnation of Roman Ca-
tholicism. Certainly much of his writing was aimed at refuting
what he regarded as gross error. But he was no mere theological
iconoclast. He could be positive and forthright, and when all the
polemic is eliminated from his writings there still remains a con-
siderable corpus of affirmative theology. This positive theology, in
the final analysis, is extremely simple. It is concerned with the
elaboration of a few fundamental themes, such as the sin of man,
the grace of God in Christ, the Christian life, the significance of
the Church and sacraments, and the hope of eternal life. On one
occasion at least he set down a much longer list. Speaking about
the teaching function of the Church, he wrote: " The subjects with
which it is necessary to deal in the true Christian Church, and
which we discuss: What is the Law? What is the Gospel? What is
sin? What is grace? What is the gift of the Spirit? What is true
repentance? How true confession is made. What is faith? What is
forgiveness of sins? What is Christian liberty? What is free will?
What is love? What is the Cross? What is hope? What is Baptism?
What is the Mass? What is the Church? What are the Keys? What
is a bishop? What is a deacon? What is the preaching-office? The
true catechism, that is the Ten Commandments, the Lord's Prayer,
the Creed. True Prayer. The Litany. The reading and interpretation of the Scriptures. What are good works? The instruction of
married folk, children, man-servants and maid-servants. Honoring
the government. Children's schools. Visitation of the sick. The care
of the poor and of hospitals. The treatment of the dying." [6]

---

[5] *Luther's Correspondence*, Vol. I, p. 282.
[6] " An Exhortation to the Clergy Assembled at the Diet of Augsburg,"
Works of Martin Luther, Vol. IV, p. 373.

This in itself may be regarded as an adequate system of theology, but although Luther was capable of such documentation, he rarely followed any such scheme, and we must refrain, however great the temptation, from assigning a preconceived system or arrangement of doctrines to his theology. Enough has been said in any case to indicate the difficulty that is met when the attempt is made to understand Luther's theology.

It may be gathered, therefore, that the purpose of this Compend is twofold: to provide a selection of the best and most representative of Luther's theological writings, on the one hand, and to arrange these into a simple sequence, on the other hand, so that Luther's doctrinal emphases will be apparent without doing injustice to his own lack of traditional order.

The Compend does not claim to be a book for Luther research scholars or experts. It cannot hope to take the place of his works in their unabridged and complete versions. It is intended as a manual for introducing the student to the theology of Luther. It is elementary in character and method, and it is not meant to be exhaustive, for it does not attempt to present all the selections that could be cited on any one subject. Many appropriate passages have been sacrificed in the interests of brevity, but it is hoped that what is included is sufficient to give a correct and balanced account of Luther's theology. The multiplication of parallel passages would, perhaps, give some idea of Luther's particular emphases, but they would also detract considerably from the functional value of the Compend. Care has been taken to group the selections in such a way as to suggest a sequence of thought so that the passages will seem to hang together in a unity and not give the impression of a disjointed anthology. One feels that Luther himself would have approved any editorial policy that promised to give utterance to his positive theological affirmations. He had no great admiration for his own books, and on one occasion wrote: " I rather dislike having my books so widely spread, and should prefer to have them all fall into oblivion together, for they are desultory and unpolished, and yet I do want the matters they treat known to all. But not all can separate the gold from the dross in my works." [7] It

[7] *Luther's Correspondence*, Vol. I, p. 364.

may be claimed, therefore, that we have the authority of Luther himself for the Compend, since here an attempt is made to separate gold from dross.

It may be observed by some that no effort has been made to group the selections in their chronological order, and that therefore no provision is made for tracing the development of Luther's doctrines. Moreover, it will be noted that selections from doctrinal, exegetical, practical, and homiletical works are all grouped together without differentiation. Pains have been taken, however, not to detach passages from their original setting or to make Luther say what he had no intention of saying. So far as the chronological order and development of ideas is concerned, there seems to be no good reason why such considerations should be regarded as all-important. The position taken here, not without good grounds, is that in the consideration of Luther's main doctrinal contributions no importance attaches to change and development since these, wherever they occur, are not of a radical character. Reinhold Seeberg in his monumental *History of Doctrines* takes such a position when he says:

" The difference between the ' first form ' and the later forms of Luther's theology are commonly very much exaggerated. If we consider the technical terminology, there is indeed a manifest difference; but if we have in view the actual content and logical results of his ideas, we can scarcely reach any other conclusion than that Luther had before A.D. 1517 already grasped the conceptions and attained the points of view which gave character to his life-work." [8]

Still another authority would be Julius Köstlin, whose two volumes on Luther are still standard after more than sixty years. Köstlin points out that doctrinal discussions occur in sermons and practical polity in doctrinal treatises, and he himself makes no radical distinction between types of writing or their chronological sequence in his excellent survey of Luther's theology.

As to the system into which the selections are grouped in the Compend, it must be said that the outline here presented is only an expedient, and utilized solely in the interests of clarity. Any " system " of theology must be a halting mechanical device. Calvin used the Apostles' Creed, but he took occasion when necessary to depart

---

[8] Vol. II, p. 223 (Eng. tr.).

from it or add to it, since that Creed, for example, has nothing to say about the Bible, revelation, the life and example of Jesus, the Christian life, the sacraments, et cetera. Thomas Aquinas made use of the Scholastic method and one of the criticisms often made of his *Summa Theologica* is that the system overburdened and obscured the theology. Professor A. E. Garvie, of London, has suggested that the best formula for expressing the Christian faith is not the Apostles' Creed but the Apostolic Benediction, since the Christian's view of God is determined by the grace of Jesus Christ. Luther would doubtless have approved this suggestion for he regarded the Person of Christ as the cardinal doctrine of the Christian faith. Any system, however, must be arbitrary, and nothing special is claimed for the one adopted here except that it is simple and basic.

One further note is in order: The Compend lets Luther speak for himself. That he was not always consistent, that he occasionally contradicted himself, that some of his statements strike us as unworthy — all this and more will be apparent to the reader. The greatness of the man can be judged partly by the fact that such features do not mar the majesty of his insight or the serenity of his spirit.

Something has already been said of the contrast that is often made between Luther and Calvin, and certainly the two Reformers as well as the great Churches that sprang from them are very different in temper and character. Philip Schaff, in his *Creeds of Christendom,* lists nine distinctions between the two. He notes that Lutheranism arose out of monarchical Germany, while the Reformed Church grew simultaneously in republican Switzerland and spread thence to France, Holland, England, and Scotland. He notes that Luther was always the dominating personality in Lutheranism, whereas the Reformed Church points with pride to a number of initiators, Calvin, Farel, Beza, Bullinger, Cranmer, Knox, et cetera. Other differences are noted, some of a doctrinal kind, but surely Schaff is right in emphasizing the close affinity between these two men and the Churches that owe their existence to them. The controversy over the Lord's Supper has often been regarded as a radical breach between the two and although Luther's attitude toward Zwingli would seem to confirm this, nevertheless in a comparison of the writings of Luther and Calvin on the great doctrinal questions what strikes one with greater force than their disagreements is the amazing similarity of the two, even to the point of detail in many instances. For example, so far as the authors themselves are concerned, there would seem to be little reason for distinguishing between them by saying that the regnant principle of Luther's theology was justification by faith, while for Calvin it was the sovereignty of God. If there is any truth in such a distinction, it is largely a matter of emphasis and ought not to leave the impression that Luther did not speak of the sovereignty of God or that Calvin did not treat of justification by faith. Calvin has come in for more misrepresentation here than has Luther. The popular, and often misguided, conception of Calvinism, involving total depravity, election, predestination, et cetera, does not comprehend the center and core of Calvin's faith. For him, as for Luther, justification by faith is the heart of the Christian faith, and that is why the subject forms the center of the *Institutes* around which all the other doctrines are grouped. If the sovereignty of God is emphasized, as it obviously is, it is only because the sovereign God is also the God who justifies. In other particulars the harmony between the two Reformers is so close that it would be difficult to detect differences of any kind. They were at one in their scorn of the Roman Church; they were at one in their refusal to be led into subtleties and verbal casuistry; they were at one in their stand upon Scripture as the Word of God and the final authority for faith; they were at one in emphasizing the evangelical doctrines of the Gospel; and they even exhibit the same sense of humor on occasions, as when they both quote the answer of the man who was asked what God was doing before the creation of the world. " He was," we are told, " making hell for over-curious people! "

The one sharp difference which at the present time distinguishes Luther and Calvin more than any other doctrine is their differing conception of the relation of the Christian individual and the Christian Church on the one hand to the civil Government or the State on the other hand. The difference has been expressed in many ways. Schaff says:

" Luther and Melanchthon were chiefly bent upon the purification of doctrine, and established State churches controlled by princes, theologians, and pastors. Calvin and Knox carried the reform into the sphere of government, discipline, and worship, and labored to found a pure and free church of believers. Lutheran congregations in the old world are almost passive, and most of them enjoy not even the right of electing their pastors; while well-organized Reformed congregations have elders and deacons chosen from the people, and a much larger amount of lay agency, especially in the Sunday-School work. Luther first proclaimed the principle of the general priesthood, but in practice it was confined to the civil rulers, and carried out in a wrong way by making them the supreme bishops of the Church, and reducing the Church to a degrading dependence on the State. Luther and his followers carefully abstained from politics, and intrusted the secular princes friendly to the Reformation with the episcopal rights; Calvin and Knox upheld the sole headship of Christ, and endeavored to renovate the civil state on a theocratic basis. This led to serious conflicts and wars, but they resulted in a great advance of civil and religious liberty in Holland, England, and the United States. The essence of Calvinism is the sense of the absolute sovereignty of God and the absolute dependence of man; and this is the best school of moral self-government, which is true freedom. Those who feel most their dependence on God are most independent of men." [9]

Others have gone farther than Schaff and suggested that the Lutheran passivity toward the State has, in effect, made possible the rise of present-day German political tyranny, and they note with point that dictatorship has never arisen on Reformed or Calvinistic soil. Karl Barth, in his letter to the French Protestants in December, 1939, suggests that the difficulty of understanding the apparent duplicity of modern Church life in Germany must be accounted for on the basis of " Martin Luther's error on the relation between

---

[9] *Creeds of Christendom*, Vol. I, p. 218. Schaff adds in a footnote: " The principles of the Republic of the United States can be traced, through the intervening link of Puritanism, to Calvinism, which, with all its theological rigor, has been the chief educator of manly characters and promoter of constitutional freedom in modern times. The inalienable rights of an American citizen are nothing but the Protestant idea of the general priesthood of believers applied to the civil sphere, or developed into the corresponding idea of the general kingship of free men."

the temporal and the spiritual order and power." This, therefore, is a point where there is radical and very important difference between Luther and Calvin, and that is why the long section on *The Christian and the State* is included as a separate section in the Compend. It will be observed that while Luther does on occasion make room for the right of rebellion, the total impression one derives from his discussion is that Christians are subject to the civil government whether it be right or wrong, just or tyrannical, since it is God's instrument for justice and judgment.

This is far too technical and delicate a subject to be expanded farther here, and it is all too easy to make unwarranted generalizations about the Lutheran or Reformed views of the State. If it is true, for example, that there is some connection between Luther and present-day Germany, one must not, on the other hand, overlook the courageous and at times defiant attitude of many German Lutheran Churchmen toward Nazi interference with the rights of the Church. It has been justly said that the only concerted rebuke against Nazism has come from the Lutheran Church. The stand of Pastor Niemöller in Germany and of Bishop Berggrav in Norway gives the lie to those who would roundly accuse the Lutheran Church of indifferentism in matters political. In any case, we see here one of the points where the Reformation intersects the problems of our own day and age. That is why a compend of Luther's theology is no mere academic treatise but a tract for the times, and it is with the conviction of Luther's importance not only for his own age but for ours, that this Compend is presented.

In the preparation of the Compend it has seemed desirable to restrict the selections to translations of representative writings, so that those who read Luther here for the first time and are unable to use the German may have an easy introduction to his thought through volumes available in English which can be consulted for further study and verification. The following editions and texts of Luther's works have been used, and grateful acknowledgment is hereby made to authors and publishing houses for permission to quote from these sources: *Works of Martin Luther,* six volumes, the United Lutheran Publication House, Philadelphia, 1915–1932; *The J. N. Lenker Edition of Luther's Works,* fourteen volumes (numbered, however, in conformity with the Erlangen German edition), The Luther Press, Minneapolis, 1903–1910; *Commentary on Galatians,* translated by Erasmus Middleton, London, 1839; *Commentary on Genesis,* translated by Henry Cole, Edinburgh, 1858, revised in the Lenker edition, 1904; *Commentary on Peter and Jude,* translated by E. H. Gillett, New York, 1859, revised in the Lenker edition, 1904; *Commentary on the Sermon on the Mount,* translated by C. A. Hay, United Lutheran Publication House, Philadelphia, 1892; *The Book of Concord,* edited by H. E. Jacobs, United Lutheran Publication House, Philadelphia, 1908; *Luther's Correspondence and Other Contemporary Letters,* translated and edited by Preserved Smith and C. M. Jacobs, two volumes, United Lutheran Publication House, Philadelphia, 1913, 1918; *Conversations with Luther,* translated and edited by Preserved Smith and H. P. Gallinger, The Pilgrim Press, Boston, 1915; *Luther's Hymns,* edited and annotated by J. F. Lambert, General Council Publication House, Philadelphia, 1917; *The Bondage of the Will,* translated by Henry Cole, London, 1823, revised by E. T. Vaughan, Sovereign Grace Union edition, Wm. B. Eerdmans Publishing Co., Grand Rapids, 1931 (page references in the Compend are to the S. G. U. edition, but the section references are alike for both editions); *The Table-Talk of Martin Luther,* translated by William Hazlitt, revised edition, United Lutheran Publication House, Philadelphia.

HUGH THOMSON KERR, JR.

Princeton Seminary,
Princeton, N. J.
May, 1943.

CONTENTS

V

Man

VI

The Christian Life

VII

The Church

VIII

The Sacraments

IX

Christian Ethics

X

The Christian and the State

XI

Eschatology

I

Revelation and the Bible

1. REASON AND REVELATION
2. THE OLD AND THE NEW TESTAMENTS
3. THE BIBLE AS THE WORD OF GOD
4. THE PRIMACY AND AUTHORITY OF THE BIBLE
5. PRINCIPLES OF INTERPRETATION

Revelation and the Bible

❧

1. REASON AND REVELATION

WHEN it comes to the knowledge of how one may stand before God and attain to eternal life, that is truly not to be achieved by our work or power, nor to originate in our brain. In other things, those pertaining to this temporal life, you may glory in what you know, you may advance the teachings of reason, you may invent ideas of your own; for example: how to make shoes or clothes, how to govern a household, how to manage a herd. In such things exercise your mind to the best of your ability. Cloth or leather of this sort will permit itself to be stretched and cut according to the good pleasure of the tailor or shoemaker. But in spiritual matters, human reasoning certainly is not in order; other intelligence, other skill and power, are requisite here — something to be granted by God himself and revealed through his Word.

What mortal has ever discovered or fathomed the truth that the three persons in the eternal divine essence are one God; that the second person, the Son of God, was obliged to become man, born of a virgin; and that no way of life could be opened for us, save through his crucifixion? Such truth never would have been heard nor preached, would never in all eternity have been published, learned and believed, had not God himself revealed it.

— *Epistle Sermon, Twelfth Sunday After Trinity* (Lenker Edition, *Vol. IX, #12–13*).

The teachings of human experience and reason are far below the divine law. The Scriptures expressly forbid us to follow our own reason, Deuteronomy xii, " Ye shall not do . . . every man whatsoever is right in his own eyes "; for human reason ever strives against the law of God, as Genesis vi. says: " Every thought and imagination of man's heart is only evil continually." Therefore the attempt to establish or defend divine order with human reason, unless that reason has previously been established and enlightened by faith, is just as futile as if I would throw light upon the sun with a lightless lantern, or rest a rock upon a reed. For Isaiah vii. makes reason subject to faith, when it says: " Except ye believe, ye shall not have understanding or reason." It does not say, " Except ye have reason, ye shall not believe." . . .

The wise man says of the wisdom of God: " Wisdom hath overcome the proud with her power." It is most deplorable that we should attempt with our reason to defend God's Word, whereas the Word of God is rather our defence against all our enemies, as St. Paul teaches us. Would he not be a great fool who in the thick of battle sought to protect his helmet and sword with bare hand and unshielded head? It is no different when we essay, with our reason, to defend God's law, which should rather be our weapon.

— " The Papacy at Rome," Works of Martin Luther, *Vol. I, pp. 346 f.*

Philosophy understands naught of divine matters. I don't say that men may not teach and learn philosophy; I approve thereof, so that it be within reason and moderation. Let philosophy remain within her bounds, as God has appointed, and let us make use of her as of a character in a comedy; but to mix her up with divinity may not be endured.

—Table-Talk, *#XLVIII.*

Why do Christians make use of their natural wisdom and understanding, seeing it must be set aside in matters of faith, as not only not understanding them, but also as striving against them?

Answer: The natural wisdom of a human creature in matters of faith, until he be regenerate and born anew, is altogether darkness, knowing nothing in divine cases. But in a faithful person, regenerate and enlightened by the Holy Spirit, through the Word, it is a fair and glorious instrument, and work of God: for even as all God's gifts, natural instruments, and expert faculties, are hurtful to the ungodly, even so are they wholesome and saving to the good and godly.

The understanding, through faith, receives life from faith; that which was dead, is made alive again; like as our bodies, in light day, when it is clear and bright, are better disposed, rise, move, walk, &c., more readily and safely than they do in the dark night, so it is with human reason, which strives not against faith, when enlightened, but rather furthers and advances it.

— Table-Talk, #CCXCIV.

2. THE OLD AND THE NEW TESTAMENTS

The Scriptures of God are divided into two parts — commands and promises. The commands indeed teach things that are good, but the things taught are not done as soon as taught; for the commands show us what we ought to do, but do not give us the power to do it; they are intended to teach a man to know himself, that through them he may recognize his inability to do good and may despair of his powers. That is why they are called and are the Old Testament. For example: " Thou shalt not covet " is a command which convicts us all of being sinners, since no one is able to avoid coveting, however much he may struggle against it. Therefore, in order not to covet, and to fulfil the command, a man is compelled to despair of himself, and to seek elsewhere and from some one else the help which he does not find in himself, as is said in Hosea, " Destruction is thy own, O Israel: thy help is only in Me." And as we fare with this one command, so we fare with all; for it is equally impossible for us to keep any one of them.

But when a man through the commands has learned to know his weakness, and has become troubled as to how he may satisfy the law, since the law must be fulfilled so that not a jot or tittle shall perish, otherwise man will be condemned without hope; then, being truly humbled and reduced to nothing in his own eyes, he finds in himself no means of justification and salvation. Here the second part of the Scriptures stands ready — the promises of God, which declare the glory of God and say, " If you wish to fulfil the law, and not to covet, as the law demands, come, believe in Christ, in Whom grace, righteousness, peace, liberty and all things are promised you; if you believe you shall have all, if you believe not you shall lack all." For what is impossible for you in all the works of the law, many as they are, but all useless, you will accomplish in a short and easy way through faith. For God our Father has made all things depend on faith, so that whoever has faith, shall have all, and whoever has it not, shall have nothing. " For He has concluded all under unbelief, that He might have mercy on all," Romans xi. Thus the promises of God give what the commands of God ask, and fulfil what the law prescribes, that all things may be of God alone, both the commands and the fulfilling of the commands. He alone commands, He also alone fulfils. Therefore the promises of God belong to the New Testament, nay, they are the New Testament.

— " *A Treatise on Christian Liberty,*" Works of Martin Luther, *Vol. II, pp. 317 f.*

All the fathers in the Old Testament, together with all the holy prophets, had the same faith and Gospel as we have, as St. Paul says in I Corinthians x; for they all remained with a strong faith in this oath of God and in Abraham's bosom and were preserved therein. The sole difference is, they believed in the coming and promised Seed; we believe in the Seed that is come and has been given. But it is all the one truth of the promise, and hence also one faith, one Spirit, one Christ, one Lord, now as then, and forever, as Paul says in Hebrews xiii.

But the subsequent giving of the law to the Jews is not on a par with this promise. The law was given in order that by its light they might the better come to know their cursed state and the more fervently and heartily desire the promised Seed; wherein they had an advantage over all the heathen world. But they turned this advantage into a disadvantage; they undertook to keep the law by their own strength, and failed to learn from it their needy and cursed state. They thus shut the door upon themselves, so that the Seed was compelled to pass them by. They still continue in this state, but God grant not for long. Amen.

This was the cause of the quarrel all the prophets had with them.

For the prophets well understood the purpose of the law, namely, that men should thereby know their accursed nature and learn to call upon Christ. Hence they condemned all the good works and everything in the life of the Jews that did not agree with this purpose. Wherefore the Jews waxed wroth with them and put them to death, as men who condemned the service of God, good works, and godly living; even as the hypocrites and graceless saints ever do, of which we might say a great deal.

— "*The Magnificat*," Works of Martin Luther, *Vol. III, pp. 196 f.*

There are some who have a small opinion of the Old Testament, thinking of it as a book that was given to the Jewish people only, and is now out of date, containing only stories of past times. They think that they have enough in the New Testament and pretend to seek in the Old Testament only a spiritual sense. Origen, Jerome, and many persons of high standing have held this view, but Christ says, " Search in the Scriptures, for they give testimony of me," and St. Paul bids Timothy continue in the reading of the Scriptures, and declares, in Romans i, that the Gospel was promised by God in the Scriptures, and in I Corinthians xv, he says that Christ came of the seed of David, died, and rose from the dead, according to the Scriptures; and St. Peter, too, points us back, more than once, to the Scriptures.

They do this in order to teach us that the Scriptures of the Old Testament are not to be despised, but to be read, because they themselves base the New Testament upon them, and prove it by them, and appeal to them, as St. Luke writes, in Acts xvii, saying that they at Thessalonica searched the Scriptures daily to discover whether it agreed with what Paul taught. The ground and proof of the New Testament are surely not to be despised, and therefore the Old Testament is to be highly regarded. And what is the New Testament except an open preaching and proclamation of Christ, appointed by the sayings of the Old Testament and fulfilled by Christ? . . .

Know, then, that the Old Testament is a book of laws, which teaches what men are to do and not to do, and gives, besides, examples and stories of how these laws are kept or broken; just as the New Testament is a Gospel-book, or book of grace, and teaches where one is to get the power to fulfill the law. But in the New Testament there are given, along with the teaching about grace, many other teachings that are laws and commandments for the ruling of the flesh, since in this life the spirit is not perfected and grace alone cannot rule. Just so in the Old Testament there are, beside the laws, certain promises and offers of grace, by which the holy fathers and prophets, under the law, were kept, like us, under the faith of Christ. Nevertheless, just as the peculiar and chief teaching of the New Testament is the proclamation of grace and peace in Christ, through the forgiveness of sins; so the peculiar and chief teaching of the Old Testament is the teaching of laws, the showing of sin, and the furtherance of good. Know that this is what you have to expect in the Old Testament.

— *" Introduction to the Old Testament,"* Works of Martin Luther, *Vol. VI, pp. 367 f.*

Just as the Old Testament is a book in which are written God's laws and commandments, together with the history of those who kept and of those who did not keep them; so the New Testament is a book in which are written the Gospel and the promises of God, together with the history of those who believe and of those who do not believe them. For Gospel is a Greek word, and means in Greek, a good message, good tidings, good news, a good report, which one sings and tells with rejoicing. So, when David overcame the great Goliath, there came among the Jewish people the good report and encouraging news that their terrible enemy had been smitten and they had been rescued and given joy and peace; and they sang and danced and were glad for it.

So the Gospel, too, is a good story and report, sounded forth into all the world by the apostles, telling of a true David who strove with sin, death, and devil, and overcame them, and thereby rescued all those who were captive in sin, afflicted with death, and overpowered by the devil; He made them righteous, gave them life, and saved them, so that they were given peace and brought back to God. For this they sing, and thank and praise God, and are glad forever, if only they believe firmly and are steadfast in faith.

This report and encouraging tidings, or evangelical and divine news, is also called a New Testament, because it is a testament, when a dying man bequeaths his property, after his death, to heirs whom he names, and Christ, before His death commanded and bequeathed this Gospel, to be preached into all the world, and thereby gave to all who believe, as their possession, everything that He had, that is, His life, in which He swallowed up death; His righteousness, by which He blotted out sin; His salvation, with which He overcame everlasting damnation. A poor man, dead in sin and tied for hell, can hear nothing more comforting than this precious and tender message about Christ, and from the bottom of his heart, he must laugh and be glad over it, if he believes it true. . . .

The Gospel, then, is nothing but the preaching about Christ, Son of God and of David, true God and man, who by His death and resurrection has overcome all men's sin, and death and hell, for us who believe in Him. Thus the Gospel can be either a brief or a lengthy message; one can describe it briefly, another at length. He describes it at length, who describes many works and words of Christ, — as do the four Evangelists; he describes it briefly who does not tell of Christ's works, but indicates shortly how by His death and resurrection He has overcome sin, death, and hell for those who believe in Him, as do St. Peter and St. Paul.

— " *Preface to the New Testament*," Works of Martin Luther, *Vol. VI, pp. 439–442.*

It must be understood that all the Apostles present one and the same doctrine; and it is not correct to speak of four Evangelists and four Gospels for all which the Apostles wrote is one Gospel. But *Gospel* means nothing but a proclamation and heralding of the grace and mercy of God through Jesus Christ, merited, and procured through his death. And it is not properly that which is contained in books, and is comprehended in the letter, but rather an oral proclamation and living word, and a voice which echoes through the whole world, and is publicly uttered that it may universally be heard. Neither is it a book of laws, containing in itself many excellent doctrines, as has hitherto been held. For it does not bid us do works whereby we may become righteous, but proclaims to us the grace of God, bestowed freely, and apart from any merit of our own; and it tells how Christ has taken our place, and rendered satisfaction for our sins, and canceled them, and by His own works justifies and saves us.

Whoever sets forth this, by preaching or writing, *he* teaches the true Gospel, as all the Apostles did, especially St. Paul and St. Peter, in their Epistles. So that all, whatever it be, that sets forth Christ, is one and the same Gospel, although one may use a different method, and speak of it in different language from another, for it may perhaps be a brief or extended address, or a brief or extended writing. But yet, if it tends to this point, that Christ is our Saviour, and we through faith on Him, apart from works of our own, are justified and saved, it is still the same Word, and but one Gospel, just as there is also but one faith and one baptism in the whole Christian world.

— Commentary on Peter and Jude, *pp. 9 f.*

3. THE BIBLE AS THE WORD OF GOD

We must make a great difference between God's Word and the word of man. A man's word is a little sound, that flies into the air, and soon vanishes; but the Word of God is greater than heaven and earth, yea, greater than death and hell, for it forms part of the power of God, and endures everlastingly; we should, therefore, diligently study God's Word, and know and assuredly believe that God himself speaks unto us.

— Table-Talk, #*XLIV*.

Let all other doctrine present itself, let all other books be introduced, and see if they have any virtue or power to comfort a single soul in its least tribulation. Truly, no comfort but that of God's word is possible to the soul. But where will we find God's word except in the Scriptures? What do we accomplish by reading other books to the exclusion of the Book? Other books may have power to slay us, indeed, but no book except the holy Scriptures has power to comfort us. No other bears the title here given by Paul (Rom. 15:4) — book of comfort — one that can support the soul in all tribulations, helping it not to despair but to maintain hope. For thereby the soul apprehends God's word and, learning his gracious will, cleaves to it, continuing stedfast in life and death.

He who knows not God's will must doubt, for he is unaware what relation he sustains to God.

— *Epistle Sermon, Second Sunday in Advent* (Lenker Edition, *Vol. VII, #34*).

The Scriptures, although they also were written by men, are not of men nor from men, but from God.

— " *That Doctrines of Men Are to Be Rejected,*" Works of Martin Luther, *Vol. II, p. 455.*

You ask, " What then is this Word of God, and how shall it be used, since there are so many words of God? " I answer, The Apostle explains that in Romans i. The Word is the Gospel of God concerning His Son, Who was made flesh, suffered, rose from the dead, and was glorified through the Spirit Who sanctifies. For to preach Christ means to feed the soul, to make it righteous, to set it free and to save it, if it believe the preaching. For faith alone is the saving and efficacious use of the Word of God, Romans x, " If thou confess with thy mouth that Jesus is Lord, and believe with thy heart that God hath raised Him up from the dead, thou shalt be saved "; and again, " The end of the law is Christ, unto righteousness to every one that believeth "; and, Romans i, " The just shall live by his faith."

— " *A Treatise on Christian Liberty,*" Works of Martin Luther, *Vol. II, p. 315.*

How can we know what is God's Word, and what is right or wrong? . . . You must determine this matter yourself, for your very life depends upon it. Therefore God must speak to your heart: This is God's Word; otherwise you are undecided. . . . And God commands this Word to be told you through men, and especially has he permitted it to be proclaimed and written for you by the Apostles; for St. Peter and St. Paul do not preach their own word, but God's Word, as Paul himself testifies in I Thess. 2:13: " When ye receive the Word of God which ye heard of us, ye received it not as the word of men, but as it is in truth, the Word of God, which effectually worketh also in you that believe." Surely, a person can preach the Word to me, but no one is able to put it into my heart except God alone, who must speak to the heart, or all is vain; for when he is silent, the Word is not spoken. Hence no one shall draw me from the Word which God teaches me.

Of this I must be as certain as two and three make five, for this is so certain, that if all the councils would say otherwise, I know they lie. Again, that a yard is longer than a half a yard is certain, even though all the world denied it, I still know that it cannot be otherwise. Who shall determine this for me? No one but the truth alone, which is so entirely and wholly certain, that no one can deny it. . . .

Hence you must be able to say: God said this, and that God has not said. As soon as you say: A man has said this, or the councils have determined that, then you are building on sand. Hence there is no judge upon the earth in spiritual things concerning Christian doctrine, except the person who has in his heart the true faith, whether it be a man or woman, young or old, maid or servant, learned or unlearned. For God is no respecter of persons, since all are alike precious to him, who live according to his commandments, Acts 10:34, hence they alone have the right to judge.

But if one should come who knew the sense of the Word better than I, then I should close my mouth and keep still, and receive knowledge from him. This is what St. Paul desires in speaking to the Corinthians, I Cor. 14:29–30: " Let the prophets speak two or three, and let the others judge. If anything be revealed to another that sitteth by, let the first hold his peace." That is to say, if the hearer knows and understands more than the preacher, then the preacher should allow him the privilege to speak, and he should hold his peace.

— *Gospel Sermon, Eighth Sunday After Trinity* (Lenker Edition, *Vol. XIII, #8–15*).

4. THE PRIMACY AND AUTHORITY OF THE BIBLE

Those things which have been delivered to us by God in the Sacred Scriptures must be sharply distinguished from those that have been invented by men in the Church, it matters not how eminent they be for saintliness and scholarship.

— " *The Babylonian Captivity of the Church*," Works of Martin Luther, *Vol. II, p. 261*.

The writings of all the holy fathers should be read only for a time, in order that through them we may be led to the Holy Scriptures. As it is, however, we read them only to be absorbed in them and never come to the Scriptures. We are like men who study the sign-posts and never travel the road. The dear fathers wished, by their writings, to lead us to the Scriptures, but we so use them as to be led away from the Scriptures, though the Scriptures alone are our vineyard in which we ought all to work and toil.

— "*An Open Letter to the Christian Nobility*," Works of Martin Luther, *Vol. II, p. 151.*

St. Augustine is quoted as having written in the *Book Against the Letter of the Manicheans*, " I would not believe the Gospel if I did not believe the Church."

Here you see, they say, we are to believe the Church more than the Gospel.

I answer: Even if Augustine had used those words, who gave him authority, that we must believe what he says? What Scripture does he quote to prove the statement? What if he erred here, as we know that he frequently did, as did all the fathers? Should one single sentence of Augustine be so mighty? . . .

Further, if that were St. Augustine's meaning, he would contradict himself; for in very many places he exalts the Holy Scriptures above the opinions of all teachers, above the decrees of all councils and churches, and will have men judge of him and of the teachings of all men according to the Scriptures. Why then do the faithful shepherds pass by those sayings of St. Augustine, plain and clear as they are, and light on this lonely one, which is so obscure and sounds so unlike Augustine as we know him from all his writings? . . .

For St. Augustine's words really are, " I would not have believed the Gospel if the authority of the whole Church had not moved me." Augustine speaks of the whole Church, and says that throughout the world it with one consent preaches the Gospel and not the Letter of the Manicheans; and this unanimous authority of the Church moves him to consider it the true Gospel. . . .

Then we must not understand St. Augustine to say that he would not believe the Gospel unless he were moved thereto by the authority of the whole Church. For that were false and unchristian.

Every man must believe only because it is God's Word, and because he is convinced in his heart that it is true, although an angel from heaven and all the world preached the contrary. His meaning is rather, as he himself says, that he finds the Gospel nowhere except in the Church, and that this external proof can be given heretics that their doctrine is not right, but that that is right which all the world has with one accord accepted.

— " *That Doctrines of Men Are to Be Rejected,*" Works of Martin Luther, *Vol. II, pp. 451–453.*

The teachings of the fathers are useful only to lead us to the Scriptures, as they were led, and then we must hold to the Scriptures alone.

—" *Answer to the Superchristian, Superspiritual, and Superlearned Book of Goat Emser,*" Works of Martin Luther, *Vol. III, p. 337.*

If the Christian faith were to depend on men, and be founded in human words, what were the need for the Holy Scriptures, or why has God given them? Let us throw them under the bench and lay the councils and the fathers on the desk instead! Or, if the fathers were not men, how shall we men be saved? If they were men, they must also have thought, spoken, and acted sometimes as we think, speak and act, and then said, like us, the prayer, " Forgive us our trespasses "; especially since they have not the promise of the Spirit, like the apostles, and must be pupils of the apostles. . . .

Then, too, there is no council or father in which you can find, or from which you can learn, the whole of Christian doctrine. So the Nicene Council deals only with the doctrine that Christ is true God; the Council of Constantinople, that the Holy Ghost is God; the Council of Ephesus, that Christ is not two Persons, but one; the Council of Chalcedon, that Christ has not one nature, but two, deity and humanity. These are the four great, chief councils, and they have nothing more for us than these points, as we shall hear; but this is not the whole doctrine of Christian faith. St. Cyprian discusses how one is to suffer and die, firm in faith, rebaptizes heretics, and rebukes bad morals and the women. St. Hilary defends the Council of Nicæa and its statement that Christ is true God and discusses the Psalms a little. St. Jerome praises virginity and the hermits. St. Chrysostom teaches prayer, fasting, almsgiving, patience, etc. St. Ambrose contains much, but St. Augustine most of all. . . .

In short, you may put them all together, both fathers and councils, and you cannot cull the whole doctrine of Christian faith out of them, though you keep on culling forever. If the Holy Scriptures had not made and preserved the Church, it would not have remained long because of the councils and fathers. As evidence let me ask, " Whence do the fathers and councils get what they teach and discuss? Think you that they were first discovered in their time or that the Holy Ghost was always giving them something new? How did the Church exist before these councils and fathers? Or were there no Christians before the rise of the councils and fathers?

— " *On the Councils and the Churches,*" Works of Martin Luther, *Vol. V, pp. 170–173.*

What else do I contend for but to bring every one to an understanding of the difference between the divine Scripture and human teaching or custom, so that a Christian may not take the one for the other and exchange gold for straw, silver for stubble, wood for precious stones, as St. Paul teaches, I Corinthians iii, likewise St. Augustine in many places.

— " *Answer to the Superchristian, Superspiritual, and Superlearned Book of Goat Emser,*" Works of Martin Luther, *Vol. III, p. 372.*

St. Augustine . . . says, in the letter to St. Jerome, which Gratian also quotes, . . . " I have learned to hold the Scriptures alone inerrant; all others, I so read that, however holy or learned they may be, I do not hold what they teach to be true, unless they prove, from Scripture or reason, that it must be so." Furthermore, in the same section of the *Decretum* is St. Augustine's saying, from the preface to his book *De trinitate,* " Do not follow my writings as Holy Scripture. When you find in Holy Scripture anything that you did not believe before, believe it without doubt; but in my writings, you should hold nothing for certain, concerning which

you were before uncertain, unless I have proved that it is certain."
Many more sayings of this kind are in other passages of his writings. He says, for example, " As I read the books of others, so will
I have mine read."
— *"On the Councils and the Churches,"* Works of Martin Luther, *Vol. V, pp. 147 f.*

In all sciences, the ablest professors are they who have thoroughly mastered the texts. A man, to be a good jurisconsult, should
have every text of the law at his fingers' ends; but in our time, the
attention is applied rather to glosses and commentaries. When I
was young, I read the Bible over and over and over again, and was
so perfectly acquainted with it, that I could, in an instant, have
pointed to any verse that might have been mentioned. I then read
the commentators, but I soon threw them aside, for I found therein
many things my conscience could not approve, as being contrary
to the sacred text. 'Tis always better to see with one's own eyes
than with those of other people.
— Table-Talk #*XXXIII.*

I should prefer all my books to perish that only the Bible might
be read, for other books take up our attention and make us neglect
the Bible.
— Conversations with Luther, *p. 179.*

5. PRINCIPLES OF INTERPRETATION

Not in vain did God have His Scriptures set down in these two
languages alone — the Old Testament in Hebrew, the New in
Greek. The languages, therefore, that God did not despise but chose
above all others for His Word, we too ought to honor above all
others. For St. Paul declared it to be a peculiar glory and distinction of Hebrew that God gave His Word in that language, when he
said in Romans iii, " What profit is there of circumcision? Much
every way: chiefly, because unto them were committed the oracles
of God." King David also boasts in Psalm cxlvii, " He sheweth his
word unto Jacob, his statutes and his judgments unto Israel. He
hath not dealt so with any nation nor made known to them his
judgments." Hence Hebrew is called a sacred language, and St.

Paul terms it in Romans i " the holy scriptures," doubtless because of the holy Word of God contained therein. Similarly, the Greek language may be called sacred, because it was chosen above all others as the language in which the New Testament was to be written and from which, as from a fountain, it flowed by translation into other languages and made them also sacred.

And let us be sure of this: we shall not long preserve the Gospel without the languages. The languages are the sheath in which this sword of the Spirit is contained; they are the casket in which we carry this jewel; they are the vessel in which we hold this wine; they are the larder in which this food is stored; and as the Gospel itself says, they are the baskets in which we bear these loaves and fishes and fragments. . . .

The apostles themselves considered it necessary to put the New Testament into Greek and to bind it fast to that language, doubtless in order to preserve it for us safe and sound as in a sacred ark. For they foresaw all that was to come and now has come to pass, and knew that if it were contained only in men's heads, wild and fearful disorder and confusion, and many various interpretations, fancies and doctrines would arise in the Church, which could be prevented and from which the plain man could be protected only by committing the New Testament to writing and language. Hence it is certain that unless the languages remain the Gospel must finally perish.

— " *To the Councilmen of All Cities in Germany That They Establish and Maintain Christian Schools,*" Works of Martin Luther, *Vol. IV, pp. 114 f.*

No violence is to be done to the words of God, whether by man or angel; but they are to be retained in their simplest meaning wherever possible, and to be understood in their grammatical and literal sense unless the context plainly forbids; lest we give our adversaries occasion to make a mockery of all the Scriptures. Thus Origen was repudiated, in olden times, because he despised the grammatical sense and turned the trees, and all things else written concerning Paradise, into allegories; for it might therefrom be concluded that God did not create trees.

— " *The Babylonian Captivity of the Church,*" Works of Martin Luther, *Vol. II, pp. 189 f.*

I would not have a theologian give himself to allegorizing until he has perfected himself in the grammatical and literal interpretation of the Scriptures; otherwise his theology will bring him into danger, as Origen discovered.

— " *The Babylonian Captivity of the Church,*" Works of Martin Luther, *Vol. II, p. 276.*

Wiles and evasions for the distorting of the Scriptures St. Paul, in Ephesians iv, calls in Greek *kybia* and *panurgia,* that is, " sleight of hand," " jugglers' tricks," " gamesters' tricks," because they toss the words of God to and fro, as the gamesters throw their dice; and because, like the jugglers who give things new noses and change the whole appearance of them, they take from the Scriptures their single, simple, constant sense, and blind our eyes, so that we waver to and fro, hold fast to no sure interpretation, and are like men whom they have bewitched or tricked, while they play with us as gamblers with their dice.

— " *An Argument in Defense of All the Articles of Dr. Martin Luther Wrongly Condemned in the Roman Bull,*" Works of Martin Luther, *Vol. III, pp. 32 f.*

That is the true method of interpretation which puts Scripture alongside of Scripture in a right and proper way; the father who can do this best is the best among them. And all the books of the fathers must be read with discrimination, not taking their word for granted, but looking whether they quote clear texts and explain Scripture by other and clearer Scripture. How should they have overcome the heretics, if they had fought with their own glosses? They would have been regarded as fools and madmen. But when they brought forward clear texts which needed no glosses, so that reason was brought into captivity, the evil spirit himself with all his heresies was completely routed.

— " *Answer to the Superchristian, Superspiritual, and Superlearned Book of Goat Emser,*" Works of Martin Luther, *Vol. III, p. 334.*

The Holy Spirit is the plainest writer and speaker in heaven and earth, and therefore His words cannot have more than one, and that the very simplest, sense, which we call the literal, ordinary, natural, sense. That the things indicated by the simple sense of His simple words should signify something further and different, and therefore one thing should always signify another, is more than a question of words or of language. For the same is true of all other things outside of the Scriptures, since all of God's works and creatures are living signs and words of God, as St. Augustine and all the teachers declare. But we are not on that account to say that the Scriptures or the Word of God have more than one meaning.

A painted picture of a living man signifies a person, without need of a word of explanation. But that does not cause you to say that the word " picture " has a twofold sense, a literal sense, meaning the picture, and a spiritual sense, meaning the living person. Now, although the things described in the Scriptures have a further significance, the Scriptures do not on that account have a twofold sense, but only the one which the words give. Beyond that we can give permission to speculative minds to seek and chase after the various significations of the things mentioned, provided they take care not to go too far or too high, as sometimes happens to the chamois hunters and did happen to Origen. It is much surer and safer to abide by the words in their simple sense; they furnish the real pasture and right dwelling-places for all minds.

— *" Answer to the Superchristian, Superspiritual, and Superlearned Book of Goat Emser,"* Works of Martin Luther, *Vol. III, p. 350.*

To play with allegories in Christian doctrine, is dangerous. The words, now and then, sound well and smoothly, but they are to no purpose. They serve well for such preachers that have not studied much, who know not rightly how to expound the histories and texts, whose leather is too short, and will not stretch. These resort to allegories, wherein nothing is taught certainly on which a man may build; therefore, we should accustom ourselves to remain by the clear and pure text.

— Table-Talk, *#DCCLXV*.

> Look down, O Lord, from heaven behold,
> And let thy pity waken!
> How few the flock within thy fold,
> Neglected and forsaken!

Almost thou'lt seek for faith in vain,
And those who should thy truth maintain
    Thy Word from us have taken.

With frauds which they themselves invent
    Thy truth they have confounded;
Their hearts are not with one consent
    On thy pure doctrine grounded;
And, whilst they gleam with outward show,
They lead thy people to and fro,
    In error's maze astounded.

The silver seven times tried is pure
    From all adulteration;
So, through God's Word, shall men endure
    Each trial and temptation:
Its worth gleams brighter through the cross,
And, purified from human dross,
    It shines through every nation.

Thy truth thou wilt preserve, O Lord,
    From this vile generation;
Make us to lean upon thy Word,
    With calm anticipation.
The wicked walk on every side
When, 'mid thy flock, the vile abide
    In power and exaltation.

— Luther's Hymns, *p. 51*.

II

God

God

1. THE NATURE OF GOD

A GOD is that to which we look for all good and where we resort for help in every time of need; to have a god is simply to trust and believe in one with our whole heart. As I have often said, the confidence and faith of the heart alone make both God and an idol. If your faith and confidence are right, then likewise your God is the true God. On the other hand, if your confidence is false, if it is wrong, then you have not the true God. For the two, faith and God, have inevitable connection. Now, I say, whatever your heart clings to and confides in, that is really your God. . . .

Many a one thinks he has God and entire sufficiency if he has money and riches; in them he trusts and proudly and securely boasts that he cares for no one. He surely has a god, called mammon, Matt. 6:24 — that is, money and riches — on which he fixes his whole heart. This is a universal idol upon earth. He who is in possession of money and riches deems himself secure; he is as happy and fearless as if he were in the midst of paradise. On the other hand, he who has nothing, doubts and despairs as if he had no knowledge of God. Very few persons are found who, cheerful of heart, are not stirred to murmuring and complaint by scantiness of substance. This desire for wealth cleaves to our natures until we are in our graves. In like manner, he who boasts great skill, wisdom, power and influence, and friends and honors, and trusts in them, has also a god, but not the one true God. Notice, again, how presumptuous, secure and proud people are when in the enjoyment of such possessions, and how despondent when without them or deprived of them. Therefore, I repeat that to have a god, truly means to have something in which the heart puts all trust. . . .

Examine your heart diligently and inquire of it, and you will surely find whether or no it cleaves to God alone. Do you possess a heart that expects from him nothing but good, especially when in need and distress, and that renounces and forsakes all that is not God? Then you have the only true God. On the contrary, does your heart cleave to something from which it expects more good and more aid than it does from God, and does it flee, not to him, but from him? Then you have another god, an idol.

— " *Large Catechism* " (Lenker Edition, *Vol. XXIV, pp. 44–48*).

How may these two contrary sayings which the apostle here setteth down, be reconciled together? " Ye knew not God, and ye worshipped God." I answer, all men naturally have this general knowledge, that there is a God, according to that saying, Rom. i. 19: " Forasmuch as that which may be known of God was manifest in them." For God was manifest unto them, in that the invisible things of him did appear by the creation of the world. Moreover, the ceremonies and religions which were, and always remained among all nations, sufficiently witness that all men have had a certain general knowledge of God. But whether they had it by nature, or by the tradition of their forefathers, I will not here dispute.

But here some will object again: If all men knew God, wherefore then doth Paul say, that the Galatians knew not God, before the preaching of the gospel? I answer, there is a double knowledge of God: general and particular. All men have the general knowledge, namely, that there is a God, that he created heaven and earth, that he is just, that he punisheth the wicked. But what God thinketh of us, what his will is towards us, what he will give or what he will do, to the end that we may be delivered from sin and death, and be saved, (which is the true knowledge of God indeed), this they know not. As it may be that I know some man by sight, whom yet, indeed, I know not thoroughly, because I understand not what affection he beareth towards me. So men know naturally that there is a God; but what his will is, or what is not his will, they do not know. For it is written, " There is none that understandeth God," (Rom. iii. 11). And in another place, " No man hath seen God," (John i. 18). That is to say, no man hath known what is the will of God. Now, what doth it avail thee, if thou know that there is a God, and yet art ignorant what is his will towards thee? Here some think one thing, and some another. The Jews imagine this to be the will of God, if they worship him according to the rule of Moses' law; the Turk, if he observe his Alcoran; the monk, if he keep his order and perform his vows. But all these are deceived, and become vain in their own cogitations, as Paul saith, (Rom. i) not knowing what pleaseth or displeaseth God. Therefore, instead of the true and natural God, they worship the dreams and imaginations of their own heart.

This is it that Paul meaneth, when he saith, " When ye knew not God; " that is, when ye knew not the will of God, ye served those which by nature were no gods, that is to say, ye served the dreams and imaginations of your own heart, whereby ye imagined, without the word, that God was to be worshipped with this or that work, with this or that rite or ceremony. For upon this proposition, which all men do naturally hold, namely, that there is a God, hath sprung all idolatry, which, without the knowledge of the Divinity, could never have come into the world. But, because men had this natural knowledge of God, they conceived vain and wicked imaginations of God, without and against the word, which they esteemed and maintained as the very truth itself, and so dreamed that God is such a one, as by nature he is not. So the monk imagineth him to be such a God as forgiveth sins, giveth grace and everlasting life, for the keeping of his rule. This god is nowhere to be found: therefore he serveth not the true God, but that which by nature is no god; to wit, the imagination and idol of his own heart: that is to say, his own false and vain opinion of God, which he dreameth to be an undoubted truth. Now, reason itself will enforce us to confess, that man's opinion is no god. Therefore, whosoever will worship God without his word, serveth not the true God, (as Paul saith), but that which by nature is no god.

— Commentary on Galatians, *pp. 318 f.*

Aristotle . . . does not believe that God presides over human affairs, or if he does, he thinks that God governs the world much as a sleepy maid rocks the baby. But Cicero got much further. I believe that he gathered together whatever of good he found in all the Greek writers. He proves the existence of God from the generation of species, a very strong argument, which has often moved me: a cow always bears a cow, a horse a horse; a cow never bears a horse, nor a horse a cow, nor a goldfinch a siskin. It follows therefore that there must be some power which regulates all this. We have very obvious proof that God exists, in the exact and perpetual movement of the heavenly bodies: we find that the sun rises and sets from year to year in its regular place. We reach the same conclusion from the certainty with which at the appointed time the seasons succeed each other. But those things, which are a part of our daily experience, do not excite our wonder, they are hardly deemed worthy of notice. But if a person should be educated from his youth up in a dark place, and after twenty years released, he would be astonished at the sun and wonder what it was and why it always took a certain course at any given time! But to us it is nothing, because it is so common.

— Conversations with Luther, *pp. 118 f.*

Note this fact carefully, that when you find in the Scriptures the word God's justice, it is not to be understood of the self-existing, imminent justice of God . . . ; but, according to the usage of Holy Writ, it means the revealed grace and mercy of God through Jesus Christ in us by means of which we are considered godly and righteous before him. Hence it is called God's justice or righteousness effected not by us, but by God through grace, just as God's work, God's wisdom, God's strength, God's word, God's mouth, signifies what he works and speaks in us. All this is demonstrated clearly by St. Paul, Rom. 1:16: " I am not ashamed of the Gospel of Christ; for it is the power of God (which works in us and strengthens us) unto salvation to everyone that believeth. For therein is revealed a righteousness of God," as it is written in Hab. 2:4: " The righteous shall live by his faith." Here you see that he speaks of the righteousness of faith and calls the same the righteousness of God, preached in the Gospel, since the Gospel teaches nothing else but that he who believes has grace and is righteous before God and is saved.

In the same manner you should understand Ps. 31:1: "Deliver me in thy righteousness," i.e. by thy grace, which makes me godly and righteous. The word Saviour or Redeemer compels us to accept this as the meaning of the little word "just." For if Christ came with his severe justice he would not save anyone, but condemn all, as they are all sinners and unjust. But now he comes to make not only just and righteous, but also blessed, all who receive him, that he alone as the just one and the Saviour be offered graciously to all sinners out of unmerited kindness and righteousness.

— *Gospel Sermon, First Sunday in Advent* (Lenker Edition, *Vol. X, #37*).

What is it we poor wretched people aim at? We who cannot, as yet, comprehend with our faith the merest sparks of God's promises, the bare glimmering of his commandments and works, — both of which, notwithstanding he himself has confirmed with words and miracles, — weak, impure, corrupt as we are, — presumptuously seek to understand the incomprehensible light of God's wonders.

We must know that he dwells in a light to which human creatures cannot come, and yet we go on, and essay to reach it. We know that his judgments are incomprehensible, and his ways past finding out, (Rom. xi.,) yet we undertake to find them out. We look, with blind eyes like a mole, on the majesty of God, and after that light which is shown neither in words nor miracles, but is only signified; out of curiosity and wilfulness we would behold the highest and greatest light of the celestial sun ere we see the morning star. Let the morning star, as St. Peter says, go first up in our hearts, and we shall then see the sun in his noon-tide splendor.

True, we must teach, as we may, of God's incomprehensible and unsearchable will; but to aim at its perfect comprehension is dangerous work, wherein we stumble, fall, and break our necks. I bridle myself with these words of our Saviour Christ to St. Peter: "Follow thou me: what is it to thee?" &c., for Peter busied himself also about God's works; namely, how he would do with another, how he would do with John? And as he answered Philip, that said, "Show us the Father" — "What," said Christ; "believest thou not that the Father is in me, and I in the Father? He that seeth me, seeth the Father also," &c. For Philip would also willingly have seen the majesty and fellowship of the Father. Solomon, the wise king, says: "What is too high for thee, thereafter inquire thou not." And even did we know all the secret judgments of God, what good and profit would it bring unto us, more than God's promises and commandments?

Let us abstain from such cogitations, seeing we know for certain that they are incomprehensible. Let us not permit ourselves to be so plagued by the devil with that which is impossible. A man might as well busy himself how the kingdom of the earth shall endure upon the waters, and go not down beneath them. Above all things, let us exercise the faith of God's promises, and the works of his commandments; when we have done this, we may well consider whether it is expedient to trouble oneself about impossible things, though it is a very difficult thing to expel such thoughts, so fiercely drives the devil. A man must as vehemently strive against such cogitations as against unbelief, despair, heresies, and such like temptations. For most of us are deceived herewith, not believing they proceed from the devil, who yet himself fell through those very cogitations, assuming to be equal with the Most Highest, and to know all that God knows, and scorning to know what he ought to know, and what was needful for him.

— Table-Talk, #*CXVIII*.

When one asked, where God was before heaven was created? St. Augustine answered: He was in himself. When another asked me the same question, I said: He was building hell for such idle, presumptuous, fluttering and inquisitive spirits as you. After he had created all things, he was everywhere, and yet he was nowhere, for I cannot take hold of him without the Word. But he will be found there where he has engaged to be. The Jews found him at Jerusalem by the throne of grace, (Exod. xxv.) We find him in the Word and faith, in baptism and the sacraments; but in his majesty, he is nowhere to be found.

— Table-Talk, #*LXVII*.

Many philosophers and men of great acumen have also engaged in the endeavor to find out the nature of God; they have written much about Him, one in this way, another in that, yet all have gone blind over their task and failed of the proper insight. And, indeed, it is the greatest thing in heaven and on earth, to know God aright, if that may be granted to one. . . .

How can one know God better than in the works in which He is most Himself? Whoever understands His works aright cannot fail to know His nature and will, His heart and mind.

— " *The Magnificat*," Works of Martin Luther, *Vol. III, p. 167.*

2. THE WORKS OF GOD

" I believe in God the Father Almighty, Maker of heaven and earth." What does this mean? I believe that God has made me, and all creatures; that he has given and still preserves to me my body and soul, eyes, ears, and all my members, my reason and all my senses; also clothing and shoes, meat and drink, house and home, wife and child, land, cattle and all my goods; that he richly and daily provides me with all that I need for this body and life, protects me against all danger and guards and keeps me from all evil; and all this purely out of fatherly, divine goodness and mercy, without merit or worthiness in me; for all of which I am in duty bound to thank and praise, to serve and obey him. This is most certainly true.

— " *Small Catechism* " (Lenker Edition, *Vol. XXIV, p. 23*).

Even as God in the beginning of creation made the world out of nothing, whence He is called the Creator and the Almighty, so His manner of working continues still the same. Even now and unto the end of the world, all His works are such that out of that which is nothing, worthless, despised, wretched and dead, He makes that which is something, precious, honorable, blessed and living. Again, whatever is something, precious, honorable, blessed and living, He makes to be nothing, worthless, despised, wretched and dying.

— " *The Magnificat*," Works of Martin Luther, *Vol. III, p. 127.*

Hilary and Augustine, who are as it were two great lights in the church, believe, that the world was made on a sudden, and all at once, and not *successively,* during the space of *six days.* And Augustine plays upon these six days, in a marvellous manner, in treating of them. He considers them to be mystical days of knowledge, in the angels, and not natural days. . . . But if we cannot fully comprehend the days here mentioned, nor understand why God chose to use these intervals of time, let us rather confess our ignorance in the matter, than wrest the words of Moses away from the circumstances which he is recording to a meaning, which has nothing to do with those circumstances.

With respect, therefore, to this opinion of Augustine, we conclude, that Moses spoke properly and plainly, and neither allegorically nor figuratively: that is, he means, that the world, with all creatures, was created in *six days,* as he himself expresses it. And if we cannot attain unto a comprehension of the *reason why* it was so, let us still remain scholars, and leave all the preceptorship to the Holy Spirit!

— Commentary on Genesis, *pp. 24 f.*

O could a man attain unto such a knowledge of his God, how safely, how quietly, how joyfully, would he fare! He would in truth have God on his side, knowing this of a certainty, that all his fortunes, whatever they might be, had come to him, and still were coming, under the guidance of His most sweet will. The word of Peter stands firm, " He careth for you." What sweeter sound than this word can we hear! Therefore, he says, " Cast all your care upon Him." If we do this not, but rather take our care upon ourselves, what is this but to seek to hinder the care of God, and, besides, to make our life a life of sorrow and labor, troubled with many fears and cares and much unrest! And all to no avail; for we accomplish nothing good thereby, but, as the Preacher saith, it is vanity of vanities, and vexation of spirit. Indeed, that whole book treats of this experience, as written by one who for himself made trial of many things, and found them all only weariness, vanity and vexation of spirit, so that he concludes it is a gift of God that a man may eat and drink and live joyfully with his wife, i.e., when he passes his days without anxiety, and commits his care to God. Therefore, we ought to have no other care for ourselves than this, namely, not to care for ourselves, and rob God of His care for us.

— *"The Fourteen of Consolation,"* Works of Martin Luther, *Vol. I, pp. 154 f.*

Whether we will or no, all our care falls back on God alone, and we are scarcely ever left to care for ourselves. Still, God does now and again leave us to care for ourselves, in order to bring home to us His goodness, and to teach us how great the difference between His care and ours. Hence, He suffers us now and then to be assailed by some slight malady or other ill, dissembling His care for us (for He never ceases to care), and yet at the same time preventing the many evils that threaten us on every side from bursting in upon us all together. Hereby He tries us as His well-beloved children, to see whether we will not trust His care, which extends through all our past life, and learn how vain and powerless a thing is any care of ours. How little, indeed, do we or can we do for ourselves, throughout our life, when we are not able to stop a small pain in one of our limbs, even for the shortest space of time?

— *"The Fourteen of Consolation,"* Works of Martin Luther, *Vol. I, pp. 124 f.*

God says in Jeremiah ix: " Let not the wise man glory in his wisdom, neither let the mighty man glory in his might, let not the rich man glory in his riches: but let him that glorieth glory in this, that he understandeth and knoweth me, that I am the Lord who exercise lovingkindness, judgment, and righteousness, in the earth; for in these things I delight, saith the Lord." . . .

Here we see that He . . . divides all that is in the world into three parts — wisdom, might and riches — and puts them all down by saying none should glory in these things, for none will find Him in them nor does He delight therein. Over against them He sets three others — lovingkindness, judgment, and righteousness. In these things, says He, I am to be found; yea, I exercise them, so nigh am I to them; nor do I exercise them in heaven, but in the earth, where men may find me. And whoever thus understandeth Me may well glory and trust therein. For, if he be not wise, but poor in spirit, My lovingkindness is with him; if he be not mighty, but brought low, My judgment is by his side to save him; if he be not rich, but poor and needy, the more hath he of My righteousness.

— *"The Magnificat,"* Works of Martin Luther, *Vol. III, p. 168.*

3. GOD AND MAN

This is the work of the First Commandment, which commands: " Thou shalt have no other gods," which means: " Since I alone am God, thou shalt place all thy confidence, trust and faith on Me alone, and on no one else." For that is not to have a god, if you call him God only with your lips, or worship him with the knees or bodily gestures; but if you trust Him with the heart, and look to Him for all good, grace and favor, whether in works or sufferings, in life or death, in joy or sorrow; as the Lord Christ says to the heathen woman, John iv: " I say unto thee, they that worship God must worship Him in spirit and in truth." And this faith, faithfulness, confidence deep in the heart, is the true fulfilling of the First Commandment.

— *" Treatise on Good Works,"* Works of Martin Luther, *Vol. I, p. 194.*

If man is to deal with God and receive anything from Him, it must happen in this wise, not that man begin and lay the first stone, but that God alone, without any entreaty or desire of man, must first come and give him a promise. This word of God is the beginning, the foundation, the rock, upon which afterward all works, words and thoughts of man must build. This word man must gratefully accept, and faithfully believe the divine promise, and by no means doubt that it is and comes to pass just as He promises. This trust and faith is the beginning, middle, and end of all works and righteousness. For, because man does God the honor of regarding and confessing Him as true, He becomes to him a gracious God, Who in turn honors him and regards and confesses him as true. Thus it is not possible that man, of his own reason and strength, should by works ascend to heaven and anticipate God, moving Him to be gracious; but God must anticipate all works and thoughts, and make a promise clearly expressed in words, which man then takes and keeps with a good, firm faith.

— *"Treatise on the New Testament,"* Works of Martin Luther, *Vol. I, pp. 297 f.*

The Lord comes to your door. You do not have to seek him. If you are grateful he tarries to speak with you. But if you let him pass by you will have to complain as did the bride in Song of Solomon 5:6: " I opened to my beloved; but my beloved had withdrawn himself, and was gone. . . . I sought him, but I could not find him; I called him, but he gave me no answer." Think not you will find the Lord when he has once gone, though you traverse the world. But while he is near you may seek and find; as Isaiah says (Chap. 55:6), " Seek ye Jehovah while he may be found." If through your neglect he passes by, all seeking then will be vain.

For more than twenty years in my cloister I experienced the meaning of such disappointment. I sought God with great toil and with severe mortification of the body, fasting, watching, singing and praying. In this way I shamefully wasted my time and found not the Lord. The more I sought and the nearer I thought I was to him, the farther away I got. No, God does not permit us to find him so. He must first come and seek us where we are. We may not pursue and overtake him. That is not his will.

— *Epistle Sermon, Twentieth Sunday After Trinity* (Lenker Edition, *Vol. IX, #12*).

We should note that there are two ways of believing. One way is to believe *about* God, as I do when I believe that what is said of God is true; just as I do when I believe what is said about the Turk, the devil or hell. This faith is knowledge or observation rather than faith. The other way is to believe *in* God, as I do when I not only believe that what is said about Him is true, but put my trust in Him, surrender myself to Him and make bold to deal with Him, believing without doubt that He will be to me and do to me just what is said of Him.

— *" A Brief Explanation of the Ten Commandments, the Creed, and the Lord's Prayer,"* Works of Martin Luther, *Vol. II, p. 368.*

If you doubt, or disdain to know that God foreknows and wills all things, not contingently, but necessarily and immutably, how can you believe confidently, trust to, and depend upon His promises? For when He promises, it is necessary that you should be certain that He knows, is able, and willing to perform what He promises; otherwise, you will neither hold Him true nor faithful; which is unbelief, the greatest of wickedness, and a denying of the Most High God!

And how can you be certain and secure, unless you are persuaded that He knows and wills certainly, infallibly, immutably, and necessarily, and will perform what He promises? Nor ought we to be certain only that God wills necessarily and immutably, and will perform, but also to glory in the same; as Paul, (Rom. iii. 4,) " Let God be true, but every man a liar." And again, " For the word of God is not without effect." (Rom. ix. 6.) And in another place, " The foundation of God standeth sure, having this seal, the Lord knoweth them that are His." (2 Tim. ii. 19.) And, " Which God, that cannot lie, promised before the world began." (Titus i. 2.) And, " He that cometh, must believe that God is, and that He is a rewarder of them that hope in Him." (Heb. xi. 6.)

— Bondage of the Will, #XII, pp. 44 f.

Nothing can be more plain to common sense, than that this conclusion is certain, stable, and true: — if it be pre-established from the Scriptures, that God neither errs nor is deceived; then, whatever God *foreknows*, must, of *necessity*, take place. It would be a difficult question indeed, nay, an impossibility, I confess, if you should attempt to establish, both the *prescience* of God, and the " *Free-will* " of man. For what could be more difficult, nay a greater impossibility, than to attempt to prove, that contradictions do not clash; or that a number may, at the same time, be both nine and ten? . . .

But however, natural Reason herself is compelled to confess, that the living and true God must be such an one as, by His own liberty, to impose necessity on us. For He must be a ridiculous God, or idol rather, who did not, to a certainty, foreknow the future, or was liable to be deceived in events, when even the Gentiles ascribed to their gods " fate inevitable." And He would be equally ridiculous, if He could not do and did not all things, or if any thing could be done without Him. If then the prescience and Omnipotence of God be granted, it naturally follows, as an irrefragable consequence that we neither were made by ourselves, nor live by ourselves, nor do any thing by ourselves, but by His Omnipotence. And since He at the first foreknew that we should be such, and since He has made us such, and moves and rules over us as such, how, I ask, can it be pretended, that there is any liberty in us to do, in any respect, otherwise than He at first foreknew and now proceeds in action!

Wherefore, the prescience and Omnipotence of God, are diametrically opposite to our " Free-will." And it must be, that either God is deceived in His prescience and errs in His action, (which is impossible) or we act, and are acted upon, according to His prescience and action. — But by the Omnipotence of God, I mean, not that power by which He *does not* many things that He *could do*, but that *actual power* by which He powerfully *works all in all*, in which sense the Scripture calls Him Omnipotent.

— Bondage of the Will, *#XCII–XCIII, pp. 240–242.*

If a man ask, Why God permits that men be hardened, and fall into everlasting perdition? let him ask again: Why God did not spare his only Son, but gave him for us all, to die the ignominious death of the cross, a more certain sign of his love towards us poor people, than of his wrath against us. Such questions cannot be better solved and answered than by converse questions. True, the malicious devil deceived and seduced Adam; but we ought to consider that, soon after the fall, Adam received the promise of the woman's seed that should crush the serpent's head, and should bless the people on earth. Therefore, we must acknowledge that the goodness and mercy of the Father, who sent his Son to be our Saviour, is immeasurably great towards the wicked ungovernable world. Let, therefore, his good will be acceptable unto thee, oh, man, and speculate not with thy devilish queries, thy whys and thy wherefores, touching God's words and works. For God, who is creator of all creatures, and orders all things according to his unsearchable will and wisdom, is not pleased with such questionings.

Why God sometimes, out of his divine counsels, wonderfully

wise, unsearchable to human reason and understanding, has mercy on this man, and hardens that, it beseems not us to inquire. We should know, undoubtingly, that he does nothing without certain cause and counsel. Truly, if God were to give an account to every one of his works and actions, he were but a poor, simple God.

Our Saviour said to Peter, " What I do thou knowest not now, but thou shalt know hereafter." Hereafter, then, we shall know how graciously our loving God and Father has been affected unto us. In the meantime, though misfortune, misery, and trouble be upon us, we must have this sure confidence in him, that he will not suffer us to be destroyed either in body or soul, but will so deal with us, that all things, be they good or evil, shall redound to our advantage.

— Table-Talk, #LXVI.

When a man begins to discuss predestination, the temptation is like an inextinguishable fire; the more he disputes, the more he despairs. Our Lord God is opposed to this disputation and accordingly he has provided against it baptism, the Word, the sacraments, and various signs. In these we should trust and say: " I am baptized, I believe in Jesus Christ; what does it concern me, whether or not I am predestined? " He has given us ground to stand on, that is, Jesus Christ, and through him we may climb to heaven. He is the one way and the gate to the Father. But when we begin in the devil's name to build first on the roof above, scorning the ground, then we fall! . . . I forget all that Christ and God are, when I get to thinking about this matter, and come to believe that God is a villain. We ought to remain by the Word, in which God is revealed to us and salvation offered, if we believe it. Moreover in trying to understand predestination, we forget God, we cease to praise and begin to blaspheme. In Christ, however, are hid all treasures; without him none may be had. Therefore we should give no place whatever to this argument concerning predestination.

— Conversations with Luther, pp. 135 f.

Into these things God would not have us curiously inquire. He has not given us any special revelation in regard to them, but refers all men here to the words of the Gospel. By them they are to be guided. He would have them hear and learn the Gospel, and believing in it they shall be saved. Therein have all the saints found comfort and assurance in regard to their election to eternal life; not in any special revelation in regard to their predestination, but in faith in Christ. Therefore, where Saint Paul treats of election, in the three chapters preceding this text (Rom. 11:33–36), he would not have any to inquire or search out whether he has been predestinated or not; but he holds forth the Gospel and faith to all men. So he taught before, that we are saved through faith in Christ. He says (Rom. 10:8) : " The word is nigh thee, in thy mouth, and in thy heart," and he explains himself by saying that this word should be proclaimed to all men, that they may believe what he says in verses 12 and 13: " For the same Lord is Lord of all, and is rich unto all that call upon him: for, Whosoever shall call upon the name of the Lord shall be saved."

— *Epistle Sermon, Trinity Sunday* (Lenker Edition, *Vol. IX, #19*).

4. GOD AS TRINITY

This article is so far above the power of the human mind to grasp, or the tongue to express, that God, as the Father of his children, will pardon us when we stammer and lisp as best we can, if only our faith be pure and right. By this term, however, we would say that we believe the divine majesty to be three distinct persons of one true essence.

This is the revelation and knowledge Christians have of God: they not only know him to be one true God, who is independent of and over all creatures, and that there can be no more than this one true God, but they know also what this one true God in his essential, inscrutable essence is.

The reason and wisdom of man may go so far as to reach the conclusion, although feebly, that there must be one eternal divine being, who has created and who preserves and governs all things. Man sees such a beautiful and wonderful creation in the heavens and on the earth, one so wonderfully, regularly and securely preserved and ordered, that he must say: It is impossible that this came into existence by mere chance, or that it originated and controls itself; there must have been a Creator and Lord from whom all these things proceed and by whom they are governed. Thus God may be known by his creatures, as St. Paul says: " For the invisible things of him since the creation of the world are clearly seen, being perceived through the things that are made, even his everlasting power and divinity," Rom. 1:20. This is (*a posteriori*) the knowledge that we have when we contemplate God from without, in his works and government; as one, looking upon a castle or house from without, would draw conclusions as to its lord or keeper.

But from within (*a priori*) no human wisdom has been able to conceive what God is in himself, or in his internal essence. Neither can anyone know or give information of it except it be revealed to him by the Holy Spirit. For no one knoweth, as Paul says (I Cor. 2:11), the things of man save the spirit of man which is in him; even so the things of God none knoweth save the Spirit of God. From without, I may see what you do, but what your intentions are and what you think, I cannot see. Again, neither can you know what I think except I enable you to understand it by word or sign. Much less can we know what God, in his own inner and secret essence is, until the Holy Spirit, who searcheth and knoweth all things, yea, the deep things of God — as Paul says above — reveals it to us: as he does in the declaration of this article, in which he teaches us the existence in the divine majesty of the one undivided essence, but in such manner that there is, first, the person which is called the Father; and of him exists the second person called the Son, born from eternity; and proceeding from both of these is the third, namely, the Holy Spirit. These three persons are not distinct from each other, as individual brothers or sisters are, but they have being in one and the same eternal, undivided and indivisible essence.

This, I say, is not discovered or attained to by human reason. It is revealed from heaven above. Therefore, only Christians can intelligently speak of what the Godhead essentially is, and of his outward manifestation to his creatures, and his will toward men concerning their salvation. For all this is imparted to them by the Holy Spirit, who reveals and proclaims it through the Word. . . .

We know from the testimony of Holy Writ, that we cannot expound the mystery of these divine things by the speculations of reason and a pretense of great wisdom. To explain this, as well as all the articles of our faith, we must have a knowledge higher than any to which the understanding of man can attain. That knowledge of God which the heathen can perceive by reason or deduce from rational premises is but a small part of the knowledge that we should possess. The heathen Aristotle in his best book concludes from a passage in the wisest pagan poet, Homer: There can be no good government in which there is more than one lord; it results as where more than one master or mistress attempts to direct the household servants. So must there be but one lord and regent in every government. This is all rightly true. God has implanted such light and understanding in human nature for the purpose of giving a conception and an illustration of his divine office, the only Lord and Maker of all creatures. But, even knowing this, we have not yet searched out or fathomed the exalted, eternal, divine Godhead essence. For even though I have learned that there is an only divine majesty, who governs all things, I do not thereby know the inner workings of this divine essence himself; this no one can tell me, except, as we have said, in so far as God himself reveals it in his Word. . . .

God's actual divine essence and his will, administration and works — are absolutely beyond all human thought, human understanding or wisdom; in short, that they are and ever will be incomprehensible, inscrutable and altogether hidden to human reason. When reason presumptuously undertakes to solve, to teach and explain these matters, the result is worthless, yea, utter darkness and deception. If anything is to be ascertained, it must be through revelation alone; that is, the Word of God, which was sent from heaven.

— *Epistle Sermon, Trinity Sunday* (Lenker Edition, *Vol. IX, #2–18*).

Rightly did the fathers compose the Creed, or Symbol, in the simple form repeated by Christian children: " I believe in God the Father Almighty, Maker of heaven and earth, and in Jesus Christ his only Son. . . . I believe in the Holy Ghost." This confession we did not devise, nor did the fathers of former times. As the bee collects honey from many fair and gay flowers, so is this Creed collected, in appropriate brevity, from the books of the beloved prophets and apostles — from the entire holy Scriptures — for children and for unlearned Christians. It is fittingly called the " Apostle's Symbol," or " Apostle's Creed." For brevity and clearness it could not have been better arranged, and it has remained in the Church from ancient time. It must either have been composed by the apostles themselves or it was collected from their writings and sermons by their ablest disciples.

It begins " I believe." In whom? " In God the Father." This is the first person in the Godhead. For the sake of clear distinction, the peculiar attribute and office in which each person manifests himself is briefly expressed. With the first it is the work of creation. True, creation is not the work of one individual person, but of the one divine, eternal essence as such. We must say, God the Father, God the Son and God the Holy Spirit created heaven and earth. Yet that work is more especially predicated of the person of the Father, the first person, for the reason that creation is the only work of the Father in which he has stepped forth out of concealment into observation; it is the first work wrought by the divine Majesty upon the creature. By the word " Father " he is particularly and rightly distinguished from the other persons of the Trinity. It indicates him as the first person, derived from no other, the Son and the Holy Spirit having existence from him.

Continuing, the Creed says, I believe in another who is also God. For to believe is something we owe to no being but God alone. Who is this second person? Jesus Christ, God's only-begotten Son. Christians have so confessed for fifteen hundred years; indeed, such has been the confession of believers since the beginning of the world. Though not employing precisely these words, yet this has been their faith and profession.

The first designation of God the Son makes him the only Son of God. Although angels are called sons of the Lord our God, and even Christians are termed his children, yet no one of these is said to be the " only " or " only-begotten " Son. Such is the effect of Christ's birth from the Father that he is unequaled by any creature, not excepting even the angels. For he is in truth and by nature the Son of God the Father; that is, he is of the same divine, eternal, uncreated essence.

Next comes the enumeration of the acts peculiar to him: " Who was conceived by the Holy Spirit, born of the Virgin Mary, suffered under Pontius Pilate, was crucified, dead and buried. He descended into hell; on the third day he rose again from the dead; he ascended into heaven, and sits at the right hand of God the Father Almighty; from thence he shall come to judge the quick and the dead." The distinct personality of the Son is thus demonstrated by acts peculiar to himself. Not the Father and not the Holy Spirit, but the Son alone, assumed human nature of flesh and blood, like unto ours, to suffer, die, rise again and ascend into heaven.

In the third place we confess, " I believe in the Holy Ghost." Here again a distinct person is named, yet one in divine essence with the Father and the Son; for we must believe in no one but the true God, in obedience to the first commandment: " I am Jehovah thy God . . . Thou shalt have no other gods before me."

Thus briefly this confession comprehends the unity of the divine essence — we accept and worship only one God — and the revealed truth that in the Trinity are three distinct persons. The same distinction is indicated in holy baptism; we are baptized into the faith of one God, yet Christ commands us to baptize " into the name of the Father and of the Son and of the Holy Spirit."

The peculiarity of this third person is the fact that he proceeds from both the Father and the Son. He is therefore called also the Spirit of the Father and the Son; he is poured into the human heart and reveals himself in the gathering of the Church of Christ in all tongues. Through the Word of the Gospel he enlightens and kindles the hearts of men unto one faith, sanctifying, quickening and saving them.

So the Creed confesses three persons as comprehended in one divine essence, each one, however, retaining his distinct personality; and in order that the simple Christian may recognize that there is but one divine essence and one God, who is tri-personal, a special work, peculiar to himself, is ascribed to each person. And such acts, peculiar to each person, are mentioned for the reason that thus a confusion of persons is avoided. To the Father we ascribe the work of creation; to the Son the work of Redemption; to the Holy Spirit the power to forgive sins, to gladden, to strengthen, to transport from death to life eternal.

The thought is not that the Father alone is the Creator, the Son alone Redeemer and the Holy Spirit alone Sanctifier. The creation and preservation of the universe, atonement for sin and its forgiveness, resurrection from the dead and the gift of eternal life — all these are operations of the one Divine Majesty as such. Yet the Father is especially emphasized in the work of creation, which proceeds originally from him as the first person; the Son is emphasized in the redemption he has accomplished in his own person; and the Holy Spirit in the peculiar work of sanctification, which is both his mission and revelation. Such distinction is made for the purpose of affording Christians the unqualified assurance that there is but one God and yet three persons in the one divine essence — truths the sainted fathers have faithfully gathered from the writings of Moses, the prophets and the apostles, and which they have maintained against all heretics.

— *Epistle Sermon, Trinity Sunday* (Lenker Edition, *Vol. IX*, #16–23).

> We all believe in one true God,
>   Maker of the earth and heaven,
> The Father who to us the power
>   To become his sons hath given.
> He will us at all times nourish,
>   Soul and body, guard us, guide us,
> 'Mid all harms will keep and cherish,
>   That no ill shall ever betide us.
> He watches o'er us day and night;
> All things are governed by his might.
>
> And we believe in Jesus Christ,
>   Lord and Son of God confessed,
> From everlasting days with God,
>   In like power and glory blessed.
> By the Holy Ghost conceived,
>   Born of Mary, virgin mother,
> That to lost men who believed
>   He should Saviour be and brother;
> Was crucified, and from the grave,
> Through God, is risen, strong to save.

We in the Holy Ghost believe,
  Who with Son and Father reigneth,
One true God. He, the Comforter,
  Feeble souls with gifts sustaineth.
All his saints, in every nation,
  With one heart this faith receiving,
From all sin obtain salvation,
  From the dust of death reviving.
These sorrows past, there waits in store
For us, the life for evermore.
— Luther's Hymns, *p. 82.*

III

Jesus Christ

❦

Jesus Christ

※

1. THE PERSON OF CHRIST: HUMAN AND DIVINE

I believe in . . . Jesus Christ, His only Son, our Lord, Who was conceived by the Holy Ghost, born of the Virgin Mary, suffered under Pontius Pilate, was crucified, dead, and buried; He descended into hell; the third day He rose again from the dead; He ascended into heaven, and sitteth on the right hand of God the Father Almighty; from thence He shall come to judge the quick and the dead."

This means —

I believe not only that Jesus Christ is the true and only Son of God, begotten from eternity in one eternal, divine nature and substance; but also that all things are made subject to Him by His Father, and that in His humanity He is made Lord of me and of all things which, in His divinity, He, with the Father, has created.

I believe that no one can believe in the Father or come to the Father by his own learning, works or reason, nor by anything that can be named in heaven or on earth, save only in and through Jesus Christ, His only Son — that is, through faith in His name and lordship. . . .

I believe that He bore His cross and passion for my sin and the sin of all believers, and thereby has consecrated all sufferings and every cross, and made them not only harmless, but salutary and highly meritorious.

I believe that He died and was buried to slay entirely and to bury my sin and the sin of all who believe in Him, and that He has destroyed bodily death and made it altogether harmless, nay profitable and salutary.

I believe that He descended into hell to overthrow and take captive the devil and all his power, guile and wickedness, for me and for all who believe in Him, so that henceforth the devil cannot harm me; and that He has redeemed me from the pains of hell, and made them harmless and meritorious.

I believe that He rose on the third day from the dead, to give to me and to all who believe in Him a new life; and that He has thereby quickened us with Him, in grace and in the Spirit, that we may sin no more, but serve Him alone in every grace and virtue.

I believe that He ascended into heaven and received from the Father power and honor above all angels and all creatures, and thus sitteth on the right hand of God — that is, He is King and Lord over all that is God's, in heaven and hell and earth. Therefore, He can help me and all believers in all our necessities against all our adversaries and enemies.

I believe that He will come again from heaven at the last day, to judge those who then are living and those who have died meanwhile, and all men, all angels and devils must come before His judgment-seat and see Him in the flesh; that He will come to redeem me and all who believe in Him from bodily death and all infirmities, to punish our enemies and adversaries eternally, and to redeem us eternally from their power.

— " A Brief Explanation of the Ten Commandments, the Creed, and the Lord's Prayer," Works of Martin Luther, Vol. II, pp. 370– 372.

The history of the Church Universal has confirmed in me the conviction that those who have had and maintained the central article in its integrity, that of Jesus Christ, have remained safely intrenched in their Christian faith. They may, in other matters, not have been free from error and sin, — they were finally preserved, nevertheless. He who steadfastly holds to the doctrine that Jesus

Christ is true God and true man, who died and rose again for us, will acquiesce in and heartily assent to all the other articles of the Christian faith. Paul's saying in Ephesians 1:22, is true — that Christ is the chief treasure, the basis, the foundation, the sum total, to whom all are drawn and under whom all are gathered. And in him are hidden all the treasures of wisdom and knowledge, Col. 2:3. Christ himself says in John 15:5: " He that abideth in me, and I in him, the same beareth much fruit." And in Luke 11:23: " He that is not with me is against me; and he that gathereth not with me scattereth." It is decreed, says Paul (Col. 2:9), that in Christ Jesus should dwell all the fullness of the Godhead bodily or personally. So, he who does not find or receive God in Christ will never find him. He will not find God outside of Christ, even should he mount up above the heavens or descend below hell itself, or go beyond the limits of the world. God declares that here, in Christ's human nature, which he assumed through his birth of the Virgin Mary, shall be his dwelling-place. If thou believest this, it is well for thee; but if not, do what thou wilt, thine unbelief shall change nothing in this respect, and Christ with his believers will be quite safe from thee; as he has been safe all this time from the very powers of the devil and the world.

On the other hand, I have also observed that all errors, heresies, idolatries, offenses, abuses and ungodliness in the Church have arisen primarily because this article, or part, of the Christian faith concerning Jesus Christ, has been either disregarded or abandoned. Clearly and rightly viewed, it is plain that all heresies militate against this precious article concerning Jesus Christ. Simeon says of Christ in Luke 2:34, that he is set for the falling and the rising of many in Israel and for a sign which is spoken against. And Isaiah (8:14) long before preached Christ as " a stone of stumbling and a rock of offense." He who takes offense will surely be offended at this stone, which, as Christ himself testifies in Psalm 118:22, lies in the way of everyone and is rejected of the builders. Also John in his epistle (II John 7) gives no other nor surer sign by which to identify false and antichristian spirits than denial of Jesus Christ. All these have attempted to gain honor for themselves from coping with Christ, and shame is what they have reaped.

Some have attacked Christ's divinity. They have led the attack in various ways. To some he is no more than any other man, and in no sense God. Others have identified him with the Father, holding that the Father suffered for us. There have been those who believed that he may be called God in view of his superiority to all angels, and of the fact that all creatures came into being through him; denying, however, that in essence, nature and eternal existence he is divine equally with the Father.

It is passing strange how those wiseacres have racked their heads in the attempt to obviate the necessity of believing in Christ as God, endeavoring to make reason the rule, measure and master both of this article and the Scriptures. The article, however, has stood immovable, while they all have perished. It is true, however, that the devil has always sowed his seed in the hearts of his children, the unbelievers, until finally Mohammed came, who led the whole eastern world away from Christ.

Others have made his humanity the object of their attack, and wonderful are their performances. The Manicheans claimed that a shadow passed through Mary like a spectre, which possesses neither a true body nor a true soul. Others taught that Christ was without soul, and that the Deity controlled his body in the place of the soul. Still others maintain that he was not Mary's true son according to the process of nature. And the Jews lay claim to special wisdom for contending that he was begotten by Joseph, some among them upholding their views with arguments of unutterable turpitude. These whittle the matter down to a fine point when they argue the impossibility of three persons existing in the Godhead. The three cannot be brothers or kinsmen, they say, and on no other known ground can they be reckoned as equal persons. What acute people who would make the nature of mortal men or of dogs the standard by which they judge the inscrutable, eternal nature of God. The gist of the matter is that the devil's rage never ceases where the love of Christ is preached in harmony with the Apostles' Creed, namely, that he, true God and true man, died for us and rose again; that Christ is the seed of the woman who bruises the serpent's head and into whose heel the serpent in turn thrusts his venomous fang. Hence enmity continues until the final judgment.

— " *Earliest Christian Creeds* " (Lenker Edition, *Vol. XXIV*, *pp. 223–226*).

I, out of my own experience, am able to witness, that Jesus Christ is true God; I know full well and have found what the name of Jesus has done for me. I have often been so near death, that I thought verily now must I die, because I teach his Word to the wicked world, and acknowledge him; but always he mercifully put life into me, refreshed and comforted me. Therefore, let us use diligence only to keep him, and then all is safe, although the devil were ever so wicked and crafty, and the world ever so evil and false. Let whatsoever will or can befall me, I will surely cleave by my sweet Saviour Christ Jesus, for in him am I baptized; I can neither do nor know anything but only what he has taught me.

— Table-Talk, *#CLXXXII*.

If thou look upon this person Christ, thou shalt see sin, death, the wrath of God, hell, the devil, and all evils vanquished and mortified in him. Forasmuch then as Christ reigneth by his grace in the hearts of the faithful, there is no sin, no death, no curse: but where Christ is not known, there all these things do still remain. Therefore all they which believe not, do lack this inestimable benefit and glorious victory. " For this (as St. John saith) is our victory that overcometh the world, even our faith," (I John v. 4). . . .

And here ye see how necessary a thing it is to believe and to confess the article of the divinity of Christ, which, when Arius denied, he must needs also deny the article of our redemption. For to overcome the sin of the world, death, the curse, and the wrath of God in himself, is not the work of any creature, but of the divine power. Therefore he which in himself should overcome these, must needs be truly and naturally God. For against this mighty power of sin, death, and the curse, (which of itself reigneth throughout the world, and in the whole creature) it was necessary to set a more high and mighty power. But besides the sovereign and divine power, no such power can be found. Wherefore, to abolish sin, to destroy death, to take away the curse in himself: and again, to give righteousness, to bring life to light, and to give the blessing, are the works of the divine power only and alone. Now, because the scripture doth attribute all these to Christ, therefore he in himself is life, righteousness, and blessing, which is naturally and substantially God. Wherefore they that deny the divinity of Christ, do lose all Christianity.

— Commentary on Galatians, *pp. 217 f.*

2. THE WORK OF CHRIST: ATONEMENT, RESURRECTION, ASCENSION

The greatest wonder ever on earth is, that the Son of God died the shameful death of the cross. It is astonishing, that the Father should say to his only Son, who by nature is God: Go, let them hang thee on the gallows. The love of the everlasting Father was immeasurably greater towards his only begotten Son than the love of Abraham towards Isaac; for the Father testifies from heaven: " This is my beloved Son, in whom I am well pleased; " yet he was cast away so lamentably, like a worm, a scorn of men, and outcast of the people.

At this the blind understanding of man stumbles, saying, Is this the only begotten Son of the everlasting Father — how, then, deals he so unmercifully with him? he showed himself more kind to Caiaphas, Herod, and Pilate, than towards his only beloved Son. But to us true Christians, it is the greatest comfort; for we therein recognize that the merciful Lord God and Father so loved the poor condemned world, that he spared not his only begotten Son, but gave him up for us all, that whosoever believeth in him should not perish, but have everlasting life.

— Table-Talk, *#CCXXVIII.*

Because an eternal, unchangeable sentence of condemnation has passed upon sin — for God cannot and will not regard sin with favor, but his wrath abides upon it eternally and irrevocably — redemption was not possible without a ransom of such precious worth as to atone for sin, to assume the guilt, pay the price of wrath and thus abolish sin.

This no creature was able to do. There was no remedy except for God's only Son to step into our distress and himself become man, to take upon himself the load of awful and eternal wrath and make his own body and blood a sacrifice for the sin. And so he did, out of the immeasurably great mercy and love towards us, giving himself up and bearing the sentence of unending wrath and death.

So infinitely precious to God is this sacrifice and atonement of his only begotten Son who is one with him in divinity and majesty, that God is reconciled thereby and receives into grace and forgiveness of sins all who believe in this Son. Only by believing may we enjoy the precious atonement of Christ, the forgiveness obtained for us and given us out of profound, inexpressible love. We have nothing to boast of for ourselves, but must ever joyfully thank and praise him who at such priceless cost redeemed us condemned and lost sinners.

— *Epistle Sermon, Twenty-fourth Sunday After Trinity* (Lenker Edition, *Vol. IX, #43–45*).

I beheld once a wolf tearing sheep. When the wolf comes into a sheep-fold, he eats not any until he has killed all, and then he begins to eat, thinking to devour all. Even so it is also with the devil; I have now, thinks he, taken hold on Christ, and in time I will also snap his disciples. But the devil's folly is that he sees not he has to do with the Son of God; he knows not that in the end it will be his bane. It will come to that pass, that the devil must be afraid of a child in the cradle; for when he but hears the name Jesus, uttered in true faith, then he cannot stay. The devil would rather run through the fire, than stay where Christ is; therefore, it is justly said: The seed of the woman shall crush the serpent's head. I believe, indeed, he has so crushed his head, that he can neither abide to hear or see Christ Jesus. I often delight myself with that similitude in Job, of an angle-hook that fishermen cast into the water, putting on the hook a little worm; then comes the fish and snatches at the worm, and gets therewith the hook in his jaws, and the fisher pulls him out of the water. Even so has our Lord God dealt with the devil; God has cast into the world his only Son, as the angle, and upon the hook has put Christ's humanity, as the worm; then comes the devil and snaps at the (man) Christ, and devours him, and therewith he bites the iron hook, that is, the godhead of Christ, which chokes him, and all his power thereby is thrown to the ground. This is called *sapientia divina*, divine wisdom.

— Table-Talk, *#CXCVII.*

Some reflect upon the sufferings of Christ in a way that they become angry at the Jews, sing and lament about poor Judas, and are then satisfied; just like by habit they complain of other persons, and condemn and spend their time with their enemies. Such an exercise may truly be called a meditation not on the sufferings of Christ, but on the wickedness of Judas and the Jews. . . . Others . . . so sympathize with Christ as to weep and lament for him because he was so innocent, like the women who followed Christ from Jerusalem, whom he rebuked, in that they should better weep for themselves and for their children. . . .

They meditate on the Passion of Christ aright, who so view Christ that they become terror-stricken in heart at the sight, and their conscience at once sinks in despair. This terror-stricken feeling should spring forth, so that you see the severe wrath and the unchangeable earnestness of God in regard to sin and sinners, in that he was unwilling that his only and dearly beloved Son should set sinners free unless he paid the costly ransom for them as is mentioned in Isa. 53:8: " For the transgression of my people was he stricken." What happens to the sinner, when the dear child is thus stricken? An earnestness must be present that is inexpressible and unbearable, which a person so immeasurably great goes to meet and suffers and dies for it; and if you reflect upon it real deeply, that God's Son, the eternal wisdom of the Father, himself suffers, you will indeed be terror-stricken; and the more you reflect the deeper will be the impression. . . .

Now bestir yourself to the end: first, not to behold Christ's sufferings any longer; for they have already done their work and terrified you; but press through all difficulties and behold his friendly heart, how full of love it is toward you, which love constrained him to bear the heavy load of your conscience and your sin. Thus will your heart be loving and sweet toward him, and the assurance of your faith be strengthened. Then ascend higher through the heart of Christ to the heart of God, and see that Christ would not have been able to love you if God had not willed it in eternal love, to which Christ is obedient in his love toward you; there you will find the divine, good father heart, and, as Christ says, be thus drawn to the Father through Christ. Then will you understand the saying of Christ in John 3:16: " God so loved the world that he gave his only begotten Son," etc. That means to know God aright, if we apprehend him not by his power and wisdom, which terrify us, but by his goodness and love; there our faith and confidence can then stand unmovable and man is truly thus born anew in God. . . . When your heart is thus established in Christ, and you are an enemy of sin, out of love and not out of fear of punishment, Christ's sufferings should also be an example for your whole life, and you should meditate on the same in a different way.

— *Gospel Sermon, Good Friday* (Lenker Edition, *Vol. XI, #1–16*).

Christ is not only born unto us, but He is also given unto us. Therefore, His resurrection, and all that He wrought by it, are mine, and, as the Apostle exults in exuberant joy, " how hath He not also, with Him, given us all things? " But what is it that He hath wrought by His resurrection? Why, He hath destroyed sin and brought righteousness to light, abolished death and restored life, conquered hell and bestowed on us everlasting glory. These are such inestimably precious blessings that the mind of man dare scarce believe that they have become ours; as it was with Jacob, in Genesis xlv, who, when he heard that his son Joseph was ruler in Egypt, was like one awakened out of deep slumber, and believed them not, until, after telling him all the words of Joseph, they showed him the wagons that Joseph had sent. So difficult, indeed, would it be for us to believe that in Christ such great blessings have been conferred on us unworthy creatures, did He not teach us to believe it, with many words, and by the evidence of our own experience; even as He manifested Himself to His disciples in divers appearances. Such are our " Joseph's wagons." This is indeed a most goodly " wagon," that He is made unto us of God righteousness, and sanctification, and redemption, and wisdom; as the Apostle saith in I Corinthians i. For, I am a sinner; yet am I drawn in His righteousness, which is given me. I am unclean; but His holiness is my sanctification, in which I pleasurably ride. I am an ignorant fool; but His wisdom carries me forward. I have deserved condemnation; but I am set free by His redemption, a wagon in which I sit secure. So that a Christian, if he but believe it, may boast of the merits of Christ and all His blessings, even as if he had won them all himself. So truly are they his own, that he may even dare to look boldly forward to the judgment of God, unbearable though it be. So great a thing is faith, such blessings does it bring us, such glorious sons of God does it make us. For we cannot be sons without inheriting our Father's goods. Let the Christian say, then, with full confidence: " O death, where is thy victory? O death, where is thy sting? The sting of death is sin; and the strength of sin is the law. But thanks be to God, which giveth us the victory through our Lord Jesus Christ." That is to say, the law makes us sinners, and sin makes us guilty of death. Who hath conquered these twain? Was it our righteousness, or our life? Nay: it was Jesus Christ, rising from the dead, condemning sin and death, bestowing on us His merits, and holding His hand over us. And now it is well with us, we keep the law, and vanquish sin and death. For all which be honor, praise, and thanksgiving unto our God for ever and ever. Amen.

— " *The Fourteen of Consolation*," Works of Martin Luther, *Vol. I, pp. 168 f.*

We must consider the ascension of the Lord Jesus Christ. In the first place, it is easily said and understood that the Lord ascended into heaven and sits at the right hand of God. But they are dead words to the understanding if they are not grasped with the heart.

We must, therefore, conceive of his ascension and Lordship as something active, energetic and continuous, and must not imagine that he sits above while we hold the reins of government down here. Nay, he ascended up thither for the reason that there he can best do his work and exercise dominion. Had he remained upon earth in visible form, before the people, he could not have wrought so effectually, for all the people could not have been with him and heard him. Therefore, he inaugurated an expedient which made it possible for him to be in touch with all and reign in all, to preach to all and be heard by all, and to be with all. Therefore, beware lest you imagine within yourself that he has gone, and now is, far away from us. The very opposite is true: While he was on earth, he was far away from us; now he is very near.

Reason cannot comprehend how this can be. Therefore it is an article of faith. Here one must close his eyes and not follow his reason, but lay hold of all by faith. For how can reason grasp the thought that there should be a being like ourselves, who is all-seeing and knows all hearts and gives all men faith and the Spirit; or that he sits above in heaven, and yet is present with us and in us and rules over us? Therefore, strive not to comprehend, but say: This is Scripture and this is God's Word, which is immeasurably higher than all understanding and reason. Cease your reasoning and lay hold of the Scriptures, which testify of this being — how he ascended to heaven and sits at the right hand of God and exercises dominion.

— *Gospel Sermon, Ascension Day* (Lenker Edition, *Vol. XII, #23–25*).

Christ once appeared visible here on earth, and showed his glory, and according to the divine purpose of God finished the work of redemption and the deliverance of mankind. I do not desire he should come once more in the same manner, neither would I he should send an angel unto me. Nay, though an angel should come and appear before mine eyes from heaven, yet it would not add to my belief; for I have of my Saviour Christ Jesus bond and seal; I have his Word, Spirit, and sacrament; thereon I depend, and desire no new revelations. And the more steadfastly to confirm me in this resolution, to hold solely by God's Word, and not to give credit to any visions or revelations, I shall relate the following circumstance: — On Good Friday last, I being in my chamber in fervent prayer, contemplating with myself, how Christ my Saviour on the cross suffered and died for our sins, there suddenly appeared upon the wall a bright vision of our Saviour Christ, with the five wounds, steadfastly looking upon me, as if it had been Christ himself corporally. At first sight, I thought it had been some celestial revelation, but I reflected that it must needs be an illusion and juggling of the devil, for Christ appeared to us in his Word, and in a meaner and more humble form; therefore I spake to the vision thus: Avoid thee, confounded devil: I know no other Christ than he who was crucified, and who in his Word is pictured and presented unto me. Whereupon the image vanished, clearly showing of whom it came.

— Table-Talk, *#CCXXXVI*.

3. JESUS CHRIST THE MEDIATOR

Of first importance, we must hear the Gospel and believe in Christ; believe in him not merely as a Lord to whom honor is due, but as that one who offered himself in place of our sinful nature, who took upon himself all the wrath of God merited by ourselves with our works, and overcame; believe that the fruit of that conquest he did not reserve unto himself, but assigned it to us, for our own; and that all who believe in him as such a conqueror shall thereby surely be redeemed from God's wrath and received into his favor.

So we see how great the need and benefit of Christ is to us, and recognize the fallacy of the position that one may by his own natural powers earn God's grace; yes, recognize it as a device of Satan himself. For if human nature can obtain grace, Christ is unnecessary as an intercessor, a mediator. But, he being essential, human nature can obtain only disgrace; the two are inconsistent — man his own mediator, and Christ the mediator for man.

— *Epistle Sermon, New Year's Day* (Lenker Edition, *Vol. VII, #50*).

Christ is a spiritual priest for the inner man; for He sitteth in heaven, and maketh intercession for us as a priest, teaches us inwardly in the heart, and does everything a priest should do in mediating between God and man, as St. Paul says, Romans iii, and the whole Epistle to the Hebrews.

— " *The Papacy at Rome*," Works of Martin Luther, *Vol. I, p. 367.*

Faith . . . unites the soul with Christ as a bride is united with her bridegroom. And by this mystery, as the Apostle teaches, Christ and the soul become one flesh. And if they are one flesh and there is between them a true marriage, nay, by far the most perfect of all marriages, since human marriages are but frail types of this one true marriage, it follows that all they have they have in common, the good as well as the evil, so that the believing soul can boast of and glory in whatever Christ has as if it were its own, and whatever the soul has Christ claims as His own. Let us compare these and we shall see things that cannot be estimated. Christ is full of

grace, life and salvation; the soul is full of sins, death and condemnation. Now let faith come between them, and it shall come to
pass that sins, death and hell are Christ's, and grace, life and salvation are the soul's. For it behooves Him, if He is a bridegroom, to
take upon Himself the things which are His bride's, and to bestow
upon her the things that are His. For if He gives her His body and
His very self, how shall He not give her all that is His? And if He
takes the body of the bride, how shall He not take all that is hers?

Lo! here we have a pleasant vision not only of communion, but
of a blessed strife and victory and salvation and redemption. For
Christ is God and man in one person, Who has neither sinned nor
died, and is not condemned, and Who cannot sin, die or be condemned; His righteousness, life and salvation are unconquerable,
eternal, omnipotent; and He by the wedding-ring of faith shares
in the sins, death and pains of hell which are His bride's, nay,
makes them His own, and acts as if they were His own, and as if
He Himself had sinned; He suffered, died and descended into hell
that He might overcome them all. Now since it was such a one who
did all this, and death and hell could not swallow Him up, they
were of necessity swallowed up of Him in a mighty duel. For His
righteousness is greater than the sins of all men, His life stronger
than death, His salvation more invincible than hell. Thus the believing soul by the pledge of its faith is free in Christ, its Bridegroom, from all sins, secure against death and against hell, and
is endowed with the eternal righteousness, life and salvation of
Christ, its Bridegroom. So He presents to Himself a glorious bride,
without spot or wrinkle, cleansing her with the washing in the
Word of life, that is, by faith in the Word of life, of righteousness,
and of salvation. Thus He marries her to Himself in faith, in loving kindness, and in mercies, in righteousness and in judgment, as
Hosea ii says.

— "*A Treatise on Christian Liberty,*" Works of Martin Luther,
Vol. II, pp. 320 f.

I have oftentimes proved by experience, and I daily find what a
hard matter it is to believe (especially in the conflict of conscience) "that Christ was given," not for the holy, righteous,
worthy, and such as were his friends, " but for wicked sinners, for

the unworthy, and for his enemies, which have deserved God's wrath and everlasting death."

Let us therefore arm ourselves with these, and such like sentences of the holy scripture, that we may be able to answer the devil (accusing us, and saying, " thou art a sinner, and therefore thou art damned,") in this sort: Because thou sayest, I am a sinner, therefore I will be righteous and saved; Nay, (saith the devil) " thou shalt be damned." No, (say I) for I fly unto Christ, " who hath given himself for my sins; " therefore, Satan, " thou shalt not prevail against me," in that thou goest about to terrify me, in setting forth the greatness of my sins, and so to bring me into heaviness, distrust, despair, hatred, contempt, and blaspheming of God. Yea, rather, in that thou sayest, I am a sinner, thou givest me armour and weapons against thyself, that with thine own sword I may cut thy throat, and tread thee under my feet; for Christ died for sinners. Moreover, thou thyself preachest unto me the glory of God; for thou puttest me in mind of God's fatherly love towards me, wretched and damned sinner; " Who so loved the world, that he gave his only begotten Son, that whosoever believeth in him shall not perish, but have everlasting life," (John iii. 16). And as often as thou objectest that I am a sinner, so often thou callest me to remembrance of the benefit of Christ my Redeemer, upon whose shoulders, and not upon mine, lie all my sins; for the Lord hath " laid all our iniquity upon him," (Isaiah liii. 6). Again, " For the transgressions of his people was he smitten," (chap. liii. 8). Wherefore, when thou sayest I am a sinner, thou dost not terrify me, but comfortest me above measure.

Whoso knoweth this one point of cunning well, shall easily avoid all the engines and snares of the devil, who, by putting man in mind of his sins, driveth him to despair, and destroyeth him, unless he withstand him with this cunning, and with this heavenly wisdom, whereby only sin, death, and the devil, are overcome. But the man that putteth not away the remembrance of his sin, but keepeth it still and tormenteth himself with his own cogitations, thinketh either to help himself by his own strength or policy, or to tarry the time till his conscience may be quieted, falling into Satan's snares, and miserably afflicteth himself, and at length is overcome with the continuance of the temptation; for the devil will never cease to accuse his conscience. . . .

Hold this fast, and suffer not thyself by any means to be drawn away from this most sweet definition of Christ, which rejoiceth even the very angels in heaven: that is to say, that Christ, according to the proper and true definition, is no Moses, no lawgiver, no tyrant, but a mediator for sins, a free giver of grace, righteousness, and life; who gave himself, not for our merits, holiness, righteousness, and godly life, but for our sins.

— Commentary on Galatians, *pp. 20–22.*

> All praise, Lord Jesus Christ, to Thee,
> Who condescendest man to be!
> Of Virgin-mother born on earth,
> The angels celebrate Thy Birth.
> > Kyri' Eleison.

> Th' Eternal Father's only Son
> Accepts a manger for His throne;
> Arrayed in our poor flesh and blood,
> Now comes to us th' eternal Good.
> > Kyri' Eleison.

> The Father's Son, true God of God,
> Now takes this world for His abode,
> And in our human life appears,
> To lift us from this vale of tears!
> > Kyri' Eleison.

> In mercy to our fallen race,
> In poverty He takes His place,
> That heavenly riches we may own,
> And dwell as angels round His Throne!
> > Kyri' Eleison.

> All this for us, Thou, Lord, hast done,
> And thus Thy matchless goodness shown;
> For this all Christendom now sings,
> And thanks eternal to Thee brings.
> > Kyri' Eleison.

— Luther's Hymns, *p. 90.*

IV

The Office and Work of the
Holy Spirit

The Office and Work of the
Holy Spirit

❧

"I BELIEVE in the Holy Spirit; the holy Christian Church; the communion of saints; the forgiveness of sins; the resurrection of the body; and the life everlasting." What does this mean? I believe that I cannot by my own reason or strength believe in Jesus Christ, my Lord, or come to him; but the Holy Spirit has called me by the Gospel, enlightened me with his gifts and sanctified and preserved me in the true faith; even as he calls, gathers, enlightens and sanctifies the whole Christian Church on earth and preserves it in union with Jesus Christ in the one true faith; in which Christian Church he daily and richly forgives me and all believers all our sins, and at the last day will raise up me and all the dead, and will grant me and all believers in Christ everlasting life. This is most certainly true.

— " *Small Catechism* " (Lenker Edition, *Vol. XXIV, p. 24*).

It is testified by Holy Scripture, and the Nicene creed out of Holy Scripture teaches that the Holy Ghost is he who makes alive, and, together with the Father and the Son, is worshipped and glorified.

Therefore the Holy Ghost, of necessity, must be true and everlasting God with the Father and the Son, in one only essence.

For if he were not true and everlasting God, then could not be attributed and given unto him the divine power and honor that he makes alive, and together with the Father and the Son is worshipped and glorified; on this point the Fathers powerfully set themselves against the heretics, upon the strength of the Holy Scripture.

The Holy Ghost is not such a comforter as the world is, where neither truth nor constancy is, but he is a true, an everlasting, and a constant comforter, without deceit and lies; he is one whom no man can deceive. He is called a witness, because he bears witness only of Christ and of none other; without his testimony concerning Christ, there is no true or firm comfort. Therefore all rests on this, that we take sure hold of the text, and say: I believe in Jesus Christ, who died for me; and I know that the Holy Ghost, who is called, and is a witness and a comforter, preaches and witnesses in Christendom of none, but only of Christ, therewith to strengthen and comfort all sad and sorrowful hearts. Thereon will I also remain, depending upon none other for comfort. Our blessed Saviour Christ himself preaches that the Holy Ghost is everlasting and Almighty God. Otherwise he would not have directed his commission thus: Go, and teach all nations, and baptize them in the name of the Father, of the Son, and of the Holy Ghost, and teach them to keep and observe all things whatsoever I have commanded of you. It must needs follow, that the Holy Ghost is true, eternal God, equal in power and might with the Father and the Son, without all end. Likewise Christ says: " And I will pray the Father, and he shall give you another comforter, that he may abide with you for ever; even the Spirit of Truth, whom the world cannot receive, because it seeth him not, neither knoweth him." Mark well this sentence, for herein we find the difference of the three persons distinctly held out unto us: " I will pray the Father, and he shall give you another comforter." Here we have two persons — Christ the Son that prays, and the Father that is prayed unto. Now, if the Father shall give such a comforter, then the Father himself cannot be that comforter; neither can Christ, that prays, be the same; so that very significantly the three persons are here plainly pictured and portrayed unto us. For even as the Father and the Son are two distinct and sundry persons, so the third person of the

Holy Ghost is another distinct person, and yet notwithstanding there is but one only everlasting God.

Now, what the same third person is, Christ teaches (John, xv.) : " But when the Comforter is come, whom I will send unto you from the Father, even the Spirit of Truth, which proceedeth from the Father, he shall testify of me."

In this place, Christ speaks not only of the office and work of the Holy Ghost, but also of his essence and substance, and says: " He proceedeth from the Father; " that is, his proceeding is without beginning, and is everlasting. Therefore the holy prophets attribute and give unto him this title and call him " The Spirit of the Lord."

— Table-Talk, #CCXLIII.

It is a faithful saying that Christ has accomplished everything, has removed sin and overcome every enemy, so that through him we are lords over all things. But the treasure lies yet in one pile; it is not yet distributed nor invested. Consequently, if we are to possess it, the Holy Spirit must come and teach our hearts to believe and say: I, too, am one of those who are to have this treasure. When we feel that God has thus helped us and given the treasure to us, everything goes well, and it cannot be otherwise than that man's heart rejoices in God and lifts itself up, saying: Dear Father, if it is thy will to show toward me such great love and faithfulness, which I cannot fully fathom, then will I also love thee with all my heart and be joyful, and cheerfully do what pleases thee. Thus, the heart does not now look at God with evil eyes, does not imagine he will cast us into hell, as it did before the Holy Spirit came, when it felt none of the goodness, love, or faithfulness of God, but only his wrath and disfavor. Since the Holy Spirit has impressed upon the heart that God is kind and gracious toward it, it believes that God can no more be angry, and grows so happy and so bold that, for God's sake, it performs and suffers everything possible to perform and to suffer.

In this way you are to become acquainted with the Holy Spirit. You may know to what purpose he is given and what his office is, namely, to invest the treasure — Christ and all he has, who is given to us and proclaimed by the Gospel; the Holy Spirit will give him into your heart so that he may be your own. When he has accomplished this, and when you feel Christ in your heart, you will be constrained to cry: Is this the idea, that my works are of no avail but the Holy Spirit must perform all? Why then do I punish myself with works and the Law? Thus all human works and laws vanish, yea, even the law of Moses; for such a being is superior to all law. The Holy Spirit teaches man better than all the books; he teaches him to understand the Scriptures better than he can understand from the teaching of any other; and of his own accord he does everything God wills he should, so the Law dare make no demands upon him.

— *Gospel Sermon, Pentecost Sunday* (Lenker Edition, *Vol. XII, #16–17*).

The Holy Ghost is sent two manner of ways. In the primitive church he was sent in a manifest and visible appearance. So he came upon Christ, at Jordan, in the likeness of a dove, (Matt. iii. 16) and in the likeness of fire upon the apostles and other believers (Acts ii. 3). And this was the first sending of the Holy Ghost: which was necessary in the primitive church; for it was expedient that it should be established by many miracles, because of the unbelievers, as Paul witnesseth. " Strange tongues," saith he, " be for a sign and a token, not to them that believe, but to them that believe not," (I Cor. xiv. 23). But after that the church was gathered together, and confirmed with those miracles, it was not necessary that this visible sending of the Holy Ghost should continue any longer.

Secondly, The Holy Ghost is sent by the word into the hearts of the believers, as here it is said, " God sent the spirit of his Son," etc. This sending is without any visible appearance; to wit, when, by the hearing of the external word, we receive an inward fervency and light, whereby we are changed and become new creatures; whereby also we receive a new judgment, a new feeling, and a new moving. This change, and this new judgment, is no work of reason, or of the power of man, but is the gift and operation of the Holy Ghost, which cometh with the word preached, which purifieth our hearts by faith, and bringeth forth in us spiritual motions. . . .

And although it appear not before the world, that we be renewed in spirit, and have the Holy Ghost, yet notwithstanding our judgment, our speech, and our confession do declare sufficiently, that the Holy Ghost with his gifts is in us. For before we could judge rightly of nothing. We spake not as now we do. We confessed not that all our works were sin and damnable, that Christ was our only merit, both before grace and after, as now we do, in the true knowledge and light of the gospel. Wherefore let this trouble us nothing at all, that the world (whose works we testify to be evil) judgeth us to be most pernicious heretics and seditious persons, destroyers of religion, and troublers of the common peace, possessed of the devil speaking in us, and governing all our actions. Against this perverse and wicked judgment of the world, let this testimony of our conscience be sufficient, whereby we assuredly know that it is the gift of God, that we do not only believe in Jesus Christ, but that we also preach and confess him before the world. As we believe with our heart, so do we speak with our mouth, according to that saying of the Psalmist, " I believed, and therefore have I spoken," (Ps. cxvi. 10).

Moreover we exercise ourselves in the fear of God, and avoid sin as much as we may. If we sin, we sin not of purpose, but of ignorance, and we are sorry for it. We may slip, for the devil lieth in wait for us, both day and night. Also the remnants of sin cleave yet fast in our flesh: therefore, as touching the flesh, we are sinners, yea, after that we have received the Holy Ghost. And there is no great difference betwixt a Christian and a civil honest man. For the works of a Christian in outward shew are but base and simple. He doth his duty according to his vocation, he guideth his family, he tilleth the ground, he giveth counsel, he aideth and succoureth his neighbour. These works the carnal man doth not much esteem, but thinketh them to be common to all men, and such as the heathen may also do. For the world understandeth not the things which are of the spirit of God, and therefore it judgeth perversely of the works of the godly. But the monstrous superstition of hypocrites, and their will-works, they have in great admiration. They count them holy works, and spare no charges in maintaining the same. Contrariwise, the works of the faithful (which, although in outward appearance they seem to be but vile and nothing worth, yet are they good works indeed, and accepted of God, because they are done in faith, with a cheerful heart, and with obedience and thankfulness towards God), these works, I say, they do not only not acknowledge to be good works, but also they despise and condemn them as most wicked and abominable. The world, therefore, believeth nothing less than that we have the Holy Ghost. Notwithstanding, in the time of tribulation or of the cross, and of the confession of our faith, (which is the proper and principal work of those that believe) when we must either forsake wife, children, goods, and life, or else deny Christ, then it appeareth that we make confession of our faith, that we confess Christ and his word, by the power of the Holy Ghost.

We ought not, therefore, to doubt whether the Holy Ghost dwelleth in us or not; but to be assuredly persuaded that we " are the temple of the Holy Ghost," as Paul saith, (I Cor. iii. 16). For if any man feel in himself a love towards the word of God, and willingly heareth, talketh, writeth, and thinketh of Christ, let that man know, that this is not the work of man's will or reason, but the gift of the Holy Ghost: for it is impossible that these things should be done without the Holy Ghost. Contrariwise, where hatred and contempt of the word is, there the devil, the god of this world, reigneth, " blinding men's hearts, and holding them captive, that the light of the glorious gospel of Christ should not shine unto them," (II Cor. iv. 4). Which thing we see at this day in the most part of the common people, which have no love to the word, but contemn it, as though it pertained nothing at all unto them. But whosoever do feel any love or desire to the word, let them acknowledge with thankfulness, that this affection is poured unto them by the Holy Ghost. For we bring not this affection and desire with us, neither can we be taught by any laws how we may obtain it; but this change is plainly and simply the work of the right hand of the Most High. Therefore, when we willingly and gladly hear the word preached, concerning Christ the Son of God, who for us was made man, and became subject to the law, to deliver us from the malediction of the law, hell, death, and damnation; then let us assure ourselves that God, by and with this preaching, sendeth the Holy Ghost into our hearts. Wherefore it is very expedient for the godly to know that they have the Holy Ghost.

— Commentary on Galatians, *pp. 296–298.*

Let us, then, learn to recognize the Holy Spirit — to know that his mission is to present to us the priceless Christ and all his blessings; to reveal them to us through the Gospel and apply them to the heart, making them ours. When our hearts are sensible of this work of the Spirit, naturally we are compelled to say: " If our works avail naught, and the Holy Spirit alone must accomplish our salvation, then why burden ourselves with works and laws? " By the doctrine of the Spirit, all human works and laws are excluded, even the laws of Moses. The Holy Spirit's instruction is superior to that of all books. The Spirit-taught individual understands the Scriptures better than does he who is occupied solely with the Law.

Hence, our only use for books is to strengthen our faith and to show others written testimony to the Spirit's teaching. For we may not keep our faith to ourselves, but must let it shine out; and to establish it the Scriptures are necessary. Be careful, therefore, not to regard the Holy Spirit as a Law-maker, but as proclaiming to your heart the Gospel of Christ and setting you so free from the literal law that not a letter of it remains, except as a medium for preaching the Gospel.

Here we should be intelligent and know that in one sense all is not accomplished when the Holy Spirit is received. The possessor of the Spirit is not at once entirely perfect, pure in all respects, no more sensible of the Law and of sin. We do not preach the doctrine that the Spirit's office is one of complete accomplishment, but rather that it is progressive; he operates continuously and increasingly. Hence, there is not to be found an individual perfect in righteousness and happiness, devoid of sin and sorrow, ever serving all men with pleasure.

The Scriptures make plain the Holy Spirit's office — to liberate from sin and terror. But the work is not then complete. The Christian must, in some measure, still feel sin in his heart and experience the terrors of death; he is affected by whatever disturbs other sinners. While unbelievers are so deep in their sins as to be indifferent, believers are keenly conscious of theirs; but Christians are supported by the Holy Spirit, who consoles and strengthens till his work is fully accomplished. It is terminated when they no longer feel their sins.

So I say we must be prudent; we must take heed we do not arrogantly and presumptuously boast possession of the Holy Spirit, as do certain proud fanatics. The danger is in becoming too secure, in imagining ourselves perfect in all respects. The pious Christian is still flesh and blood like other men; he but strives to resist evil lusts and other sins, and is unwillingly sensible of evil desires. But he who is not a Christian is carelessly secure, wholly unconcerned about his sins.

It is of no significance that we feel evil lusts, provided we endeavor to resist them. One must not go by his feelings and consider himself lost if he have sinful desires. At the same time he must, so long as life lasts, contend with the sins he perceives in himself. He must unceasingly groan to be relieved of them, and must permit the Holy Spirit to operate in him. There is in believers continual groaning after holiness — groaning too deep for expression, as Paul says in Romans 8:26. But Christians have a blessed listener — the Holy Spirit himself. He readily perceives sincere longing after purity, and sends the conscience divine comfort.

There will ever be in us mingled purity and imperfection; we must be conscious both of the Holy Spirit's presence and of our own sins — our imperfections. We are like the sick man in the hands of the physician who is to restore him to health. Let no one think: " Here is a man who possesses the Holy Spirit; consequently he must be perfectly strong, having no imperfections and performing only worthy works." No, think not so; for so long as we live in the flesh here on earth, we cannot attain such a degree of perfection as to be wholly free from weakness and faults. The holy apostles themselves often lamented their temptations and sorrows. Their feelings concealed from them the Holy Spirit's presence, though they were aware of his strengthening and sustaining power in their temptations, a power conveyed through the Word and through faith.

The Holy Spirit is given only to the anxious and distressed heart. Only therein can the Gospel profit us and produce fruit. The gift is too sublime and noble for God to cast it before dogs and swine, who, when by chance they hear the preached message, devour it without knowing to what they do violence. The heart

must recognize and feel its wretchedness and its inability to extri-
cate itself. Before the Holy Spirit can come to the rescue, there
must be a struggle in the heart. Let no one imagine he will receive
the Spirit in any other way.

— *Epistle Sermon, Pentecost Sunday* (Lenker Edition, *Vol.
VIII, #11–16*).

> Come, Holy Spirit, God and Lord!
> Be all Thy graces now outpoured
> On the believer's mind and soul
> To strengthen, save, and make us whole.
> Lord, by the brightness of Thy light,
> Thou in the faith dost men unite
> Of every land and every tongue:
> This to Thy praise, O Lord, be sung.
>   Hallelujah! Hallelujah!
>
> Thou strong Defence, Thou Holy Light,
> Teach us to know our God aright,
> And call Him Father from the heart:
> The Word of life and truth impart:
> That we may love not doctrines strange,
> Nor e'er to other teachers range,
> But Jesus for our Master own,
> And put our trust in Him alone.
>   Hallelujah! Hallelujah!
>
> Thou sacred Ardor, Comfort sweet,
> Help us to wait with ready feet
> And willing heart at Thy command,
> Nor trial fright us from Thy band.
> Lord, make us ready with Thy powers:
> Strengthen the flesh in weaker hours,
> That as good warriors we may force
> Through life and death to Thee our course!
>   Hallelujah! Hallelujah!

— Luther's Hymns, *p. 72.*

V

Man

❦

Man

❦

1. WHAT IS MAN?

MAN has a twofold nature, a spiritual and a bodily. According to the spiritual nature, which men call the soul, he is called a spiritual, or inner, or new man; according to the bodily nature, which men call the flesh, he is called a carnal, or outward, or old man, of whom the Apostle writes, in II Cor. iv, " Though our outward man is corrupted, yet the inward man is renewed day by day." Because of this diversity of nature the Scriptures assert contradictory things of the same man, since these two men in the same man contradict each other, since the flesh lusteth against the spirit and the spirit against the flesh (Gal. v).

— " *A Treatise on Christian Liberty*," Works of Martin Luther, *Vol. II, p. 313.*

The Scriptures assign three parts to man, as St. Paul says in I Thessalonians v, " The God of peace sanctify you wholly, that your whole spirit, and soul, and body may be preserved blameless unto the coming of our Lord Jesus Christ." (There is yet another division of each of these three, and the whole of man, into two parts, which are called spirit and flesh. This is a division not of the nature of man, but of his qualities. The nature of man consists of the three parts — spirit, soul and body; and all of these may be good or evil, that is, they may be spirit or flesh. But we are not now dealing with this division.)

The first part, the spirit, is the highest, deepest and noblest part of man. By it he is enabled to lay hold on things incomprehensible, invisible, and eternal. It is, in brief, the dwelling-place of faith and the Word of God. Of it David speaks in Psalm li, " Lord, create in my inward parts a right spirit " — that is, a straight and upright faith. But of the unbelieving he says, in Psalm lxxviii, " Their heart was not right with God, nor was their spirit faithful to him."

The second part, or the soul, is this same spirit, so far as its nature is concerned, but viewed as performing a different function, namely, giving life to the body and working through the body. In the Scriptures it is frequently put for the life; for the soul may live without the body, but the body has no life apart from the soul. Even in sleep the soul lives and works without ceasing. It is its nature to comprehend not incomprehensible things, but such things as the reason can know and understand. Indeed, reason is the light in this dwelling, and unless the spirit, which is lighted with the brighter light of faith, controls this light of reason, it cannot but be in error. For it is too feeble to deal with things divine. To these two parts of man the Scriptures ascribe many things, such as wisdom and knowledge — wisdom to the spirit, knowledge to the soul; likewise hatred and love, delight and horror, and the like.

The third part is the body with its members. Its work is but to carry out and apply that which the soul knows and the spirit believes.

Let us take an illustration of this from Holy Scripture. In the tabernacle fashioned by Moses there were three separate compartments. The first was called the holy of holies: here was God's dwelling-place, and in it there was no light. The second was called the holy place: here stood a candlestick with seven arms and seven lamps. The third was called the outer court: this lay under the open sky and in the full light of the sun. In this tabernacle we have a figure of the Christian man. His spirit is the holy of holies, where God dwells in the darkness of faith, where no light is; for he believes that which he neither sees nor feels nor comprehends.

His soul is the holy place, with its seven lamps, that is, all manner of reason, discrimination, knowledge and understanding of visible and bodily things. His body is the forecourt, open to all, so that men may see his works and manner of life.

— "*The Magnificat,*" Works of Martin Luther, *Vol. III, pp. 132 f.*

The mere corporeal or animal life of man was designed to resemble, in a great measure, the life of the beasts of the creation. Because, as beasts require food, drink and sleep for the refreshment and restoration of their bodies; so Adam was designed also to use these things, even in his state of innocence. But that which Moses moreover affirms, — that man was so created unto this animal life that he was also " *made* " in the " image " and " after the likeness " of God, — this is a manifest indication of a life different from, and far above, a mere animal life.

Adam was endowed therefore with a twofold life; an animal, and an immortal life. The latter however was not as yet plainly revealed, but held in hope. Had he not fallen by sin therefore, he would have eaten and drunk, and worked, and generated, in all innocence, sinlessness, and happiness.

— Commentary on Genesis, *pp. 83 f.*

2. THE IMAGE OF GOD IN MAN

There is here agitated a whole sea of questions; — as to what that " image " of God was in which Moses here says that man was formed. Augustine has dwelt largely on the explanation of this passage, in his book " On the Trinity." Those divines in general, who retain the *division* and *definition* of Aristotle, follow Augustine. They consider the image of God to be those powers of soul, — memory, mind, or intellect, and will. They affirm, that the image of God consists in these *three* qualities: which image (they say) is found in all men. And their argument is, that as, in divine things, the Word is begotten of the substance of the Father; and as the Holy Spirit is the complacency or good pleasure of the Father; so, in man, from the memory proceeds the word of the heart; which is the mind of the man: which word being uttered, there is developed the will; which will the mind beholds, and with which it is delighted.

These divines affirm, moreover, that "the similitude," after which man was formed, stands in gratuitous gifts. For as a similitude is a certain perfectness of an image; so (they say) the created nature of man is perfected by grace. According to their views, therefore, the " similitude " of God, in man, consists in his memory being adorned with hope, his intellect with faith, and his will with love. It is in this manner (they assert) that man is created in the image of God; — that man has a mind, a memory, and a will. Again, they state the sacred matter thus; — Man is created after the " similitude " of God; that is, his intellect is illuminated by faith, his memory is confirmed by hope and constancy, and his will is adorned with love. . . .

Divines make also other divisions and definitions of the qualities of this " image " of God, in which man was originally created. They hold that memory is the image of the power of God, mind the image of His wisdom, and will the image of His justice. It was after this manner that Augustine, and after him others, bent their minds on the discovery of certain *trinities* of natural qualities or endowments, in man. For they thought that, by this mode of explanation, the image of God in man would be the more clearly seen. These not unpleasing speculations do, indeed, argue deep employment and great acuteness of mental ability, but they by no means aid the right explanation of this " image " of God. . . .

I fear, however, that since this " image of God " has been lost by sin, we can never fully attain to the knowledge of what it was. Memory, mind, and will, we do most certainly possess; but wholly corrupted, and most miserably weakened; nay, (that I may speak with greater plainness,) utterly leprous, and unclean. If these natural endowments therefore constitute the image of God, it will inevitably follow, that Satan also was created in the image of God; for he possesses all these natural qualities; and, to an extent and strength, far beyond our own. For he has a memory and intellect the most powerful, and a will the most obstinate.

The image of God therefore is something far different from all this. It is a peculiar work of God. If there be those however who are yet disposed to contend, that the above natural endowments

and powers do constitute the image of God; they must of necessity
confess, that they are all leprous and unclean. Even as we still call
a leprous man a man, though all the parts of his leprous flesh be
stupefied and dead, as it were, with disease, except that his whole
nature is vehemently excited to lust.

Wherefore that image of God in which Adam was created was a
workmanship the most beautiful, the most excellent, and the most
noble, while as yet no leprosy of sin adhered either to his reason
or to his will. Then all his senses, both internal and external, were
the most perfect and the most pure. His intellect was most clear,
his memory most complete, and his will the most sincere, and ac-
companied with the most charming security, without any fear of
death and without any care or anxiety whatsoever. To these internal perfections of Adam was added a power of body, and of all his
limbs, so beautiful and so excellent, that therein he surpassed all
other animate natural creatures. For I fully believe that, before
his sin, the eyes of Adam were so clear and their sight so acute,
that his powers of vision exceeded those of the lynx. Adam, I believe, being stronger than they, handled lions and bears, whose
strength is so great, as we handle the young of any animal. I believe also that to Adam the sweetness and the virtue of the fruits
which he ate were far beyond our enjoyment of them now.

After the fall, however, death crept in, like a leprosy, over all
the senses. So that now, we cannot reach the comprehension of this
image of God by our intellect, nor even in thought. Adam, moreover, in his innocency, could not have known his wife Eve, but
with the most pure and confident mind towards God; with a will
the most obedient to God, and with a soul the most free from all
impurity of thought. But now, since the sin of the fall, all know
how great is the excitement of the flesh; which is not only furious
in concupiscence, but also in disgust, after it has satisfied its desire. In neither case, therefore, is either the reason, or the will,
sound or whole. Both are fallen and corrupt. And the fury of the
desire is more brutish than human. Is not this our leprosy, then,
grievous and destructive? But of all this Adam knew nothing, before the sin of his fall. His only peculiarity then was, that he had
greater powers, and more acute and exquisite senses, than any
other living creature. But now, how far does the wild boar exceed

man, in the sense of hearing! the eagle, in sight! and the lion, in strength! No one, therefore, can now conceive, even in thought, how far the excellency of man, when first created, surpasses what he is now.

Wherefore I, for my part, understand the image of God to be this; — that Adam possessed it in its moral substance, or nature; — that he not only knew God, and believed Him to be good, but that he lived also a life truly divine; that is, free from the fear of death and of all dangers, and happy in the favour of God. This is apparent in Eve, who, we find, talks with the serpent, devoid of all fear; just as we do with a lamb or a dog. And therefore it is, that God sets before Adam and Eve this, as a punishment, if they should transgress His command; — " In the day that thou eatest of this tree, thou shalt surely die the death." As if He had said, " Adam and Eve, Ye now live in all security. Ye neither see nor fear death. This is My image in which ye now live. Ye live as God lives. But if ye sin ye shall lose this image: Ye shall die."

Hence it is that we see and feel the mighty perils in which we now live; — how many forms and threatenings of death this miserable nature of ours is doomed to experience and endure; in addition to that unclean concupiscence, and those other ragings of sin, and those inordinate emotions and affections, which are engendered in the minds of all men. We are never confident and happy in God: fear and dread in the highest are perpetually trying us. These and like evils are the image of the devil, who has impressed that image upon us. But Adam lived in the highest pleasure, and in the most peaceful security. He feared not fire nor water: nor dreaded any of those other evils with which this life is filled, and which we dread too much continually.

Let them who are disposed to do so, therefore, extenuate *original sin*. It plainly appears, and with awful certainty, both in sins and in the punishment of them, that original sin is great and terrible indeed. Look only at lust. Is it not most mighty, both in concupiscence and in disgust? And what shall we farther say of hatred towards God, and blasphemies of all kinds? These are those sad evidences of the fall, which do indeed prove, that the image of God in us is lost.

Wherefore, when we now attempt to speak of that image, we

speak of a thing unknown; an image which we not only have never experienced, but the contrary to which we have experienced all our lives, and experience still. Of this image therefore all we now possess are the mere terms, — " *the image of God!* " These naked words, are all we now hear, and all we know. . . .

Now the very intent of the Gospel is to restore this image of God. Man's intellect and will have indeed remained; but wholly corrupted. And the divine object of the Gospel is, that we might be restored to that original, and indeed to a better and higher, image; an image, in which we are born again unto eternal life, or rather, unto the hope of eternal life, by faith; in order that we might live in God, and with God, and might be " one " with Him, as Christ so beautifully and largely setteth it forth, in the seventeenth chapter of Saint John.

Nor are we born again unto *life* only, but unto *righteousness* also: because faith layeth hold of the merit of Christ, and sets us free, through the death of Christ. Hence arises another righteousness in us; namely, that " newness of life," in which we study to obey God as taught by the Word, and helped by the Holy Spirit. This righteousness however *begins* only, in this life, nor ever can be perfected in this flesh. Nevertheless, this newness of righteousness pleaseth God: not as being perfect in itself, nor as being any price for our sins: but because it proceedeth from the heart; and because it rests on a confidence in the mercy of God, through Christ. And farther; through the gospel there comes unto us this other blessing also; — through it, is conferred upon us the Holy Spirit; who resists in us unbelief, envy, and other sins and corruptions; to the intent that we may solemnly desire to adorn the name of the Lord and His holy Word.

In this manner does the image of God *begin* to be restored in us, through the Gospel, by this new creation, in this life. But in this life it is not perfected. When however it is perfected, in the kingdom of the Father, then will our will be truly free and good, our mind truly illuminated, and our memory constant and perfect. Then will it come to pass also that all creatures shall be more subject unto us, than ever they were unto Adam in paradise.

— Commentary on Genesis, *pp. 87–93.*

3. SIN AND ITS FORGIVENESS

We must confess, as Paul says in Rom. 5:11, that sin originated from one man Adam, by whose disobedience all men were made sinners, and subject to death and the devil. This is called original or capital sin. The fruits of this sin are afterwards the evil deeds which are forbidden in the Ten Commandments, such as unbelief, false faith, idolatry, to be without the fear of God, arrogance, blindness, and, to speak briefly, not to know or regard God; secondly, to lie, to swear by God's name, not to pray, not to call upon God, not to regard God's Word, to be disobedient to parents, to murder, to be unchaste, to steal, to deceive, etc. This hereditary sin is so deep a corruption of nature, that no reason can understand it, but it must be believed from the revelation of Scriptures, Ps. 51:5; Rom. 5:12 sqq.; Ex. 33:3; Gen. 3:7 sqq. Wherefore the dogmas of the scholastic doctors are pure errors and obscurations contrary to this article, for by them it is taught: That since the fall of Adam the natural powers of man have remained entire and incorrupt, and that man by nature has right reason and a good will, as the philosophers teach. And that man has a free will to do good and omit evil, and, again, to omit good and do evil. Also that man by his natural powers can observe and do all the commands of God. And that, by his natural powers, he can love God above all things, and his neighbor as himself. Also if a man do as much as is in him, God certainly grants to him his grace. And if he wish to come to the sacrament, there is no need of a good intention to do good, but it is sufficient if he have not a wicked purpose to commit sin; so entirely good is his nature and so efficacious the sacrament. Also that it is not founded upon Scripture that, for a good work, the Holy Ghost with his grace is necessary. Such and many similar things have arisen from want of understanding and learning concerning both sins and Christ our Saviour, and they are truly heathen dogmas which we cannot endure. For if these dogmas would be right, Christ has died in vain, since there is in man no sin and misery for which he should have died; or he would have died only for the body, not for the soul, inasmuch as the soul is entirely sound, and the body only is subject to death.

— "*Smalcald Articles,*" *Part Three, Sec. I,* Book of Concord, *Vol. I, pp. 321 f.*

Isaiah lxiv says, " We are all of us unclean, and all our righteousness is as a filthy stinking rag." Observe that the prophet ex-
cepts nobody, but says, " we are all of us unclean," and yet he was
a holy prophet. Again, if our righteousness is unclean and a stench
in God's nostrils, what will unrighteousness be? Moreover, he says
" all righteousness," none excepted. So, then, if there is such a
thing as a good work without sin, this prophet lies, which God forbid! Is not this passage of Isaiah clear enough?
— " *An Argument in Defense of All the Articles of Dr. Martin
Luther Wrongly Condemned in the Roman Bull,*" Works of Martin
Luther, *Vol. III, p. 99.*

What do we read in the lives of all the saints? What is it that
they confess and prove with all their works, prayers, fastings, labors and manifold exercises, except that by these things they are
striving against their own flesh, to chastise it, make it subject to
the spirit and quench its evil lusts and desires? So St. Paul writes
to the Colossians, " Slay your members which are on the earth,
unchastity, uncleanness, evil desire, covetousness "; and again in
Romans viii, " If ye through the spirit do slay the deeds of the
flesh, ye shall live before God; but if ye live after the flesh, ye shall
die," and to the Philippians, " I chastise my body and compel it to
service, that I may not preach to others and myself be cast away."
And so I might go on. Who of the saints does not sigh, groan, lament and cry out about his own flesh and his evil desires?

How often does St. Jerome lament that evil desire rages in his
flesh, not only after baptism, but even when he has fasted, watched
and labored unto weariness, and is most a saint! St. Cyprian, in
a sermon on the deadly pestilence, comforts himself by thinking of
his sins, and says: " Ceaselessly, and with care and sorrow, we
must fight against carnal desires, against the allurements of the
world. The spirit of man is compassed about and besieged by the
assaults of the devil and can hardly meet, hardly withstand them
all. If avarice is overthrown, lust rises; if lust is put down, ambition takes its place; if ambition is despised, then anger grows bitter, pride puffs itself up, drunkenness assails, hatred breaks the
bonds of concord, envy destroys friendship. You must curse, though
God has forbidden it; you must swear, though it is wrong. So
many persecutions must the spirit of man endure, so many perils

must the heart expect; and shall we still be glad to abide here long among the devil's swords? We should far rather long and pray that sudden death may help us haste to Christ." . . .

The lives and confessions of these and all the other saints prove the saying of St. Paul in Romans vii, " I delight in the law of God after my spirit, yet find in my members a contrary law of sin," so that no one can deny that sin is still present in all the baptised and holy men on earth, and that they must fight against it.

— " *An Argument in Defense of All the Articles of Dr. Martin Luther Wrongly Condemned in the Roman Bull*," Works of Martin Luther, *Vol. III, pp. 27–29.*

As to myself, I must confess, I am more than astonished, that, when Paul so often uses those universally applying words " all," " none," " not," " not one," " without," thus, " they are all gone out of the way, there is none that doeth good, no not one; " all are sinners and condemned by the one sin of Adam; we are justified by faith " without " the law; " without " the works of the law; so that, if any one wished to speak otherwise so as to be more intelligible, he could not speak in words more clear and more plain; — I am more than astonished, I say, how it is, that words and sentences, contrary and contradictory to these universally applying words and sentences, have gained so much ground; which say, — Some are not gone out of the way, are not unrighteous, are not evil, are not sinners, are not condemned: there is something in man which is good and which endeavours after good: as though that man, whoever he be, who endeavours after good, were not comprehended in this one word " all," or " none," or " not."

— Bondage of the Will, #*CLIII, pp. 361 f.*

God forgives sins merely out of grace for Christ's sake; but we must not abuse the grace of God. God has given signs and tokens enough, that our sins shall be forgiven; namely, the preaching of the gospel, baptism, the Lord's Supper, and the Holy Ghost in our hearts.

Now it is also needful we testify in our works that we have received the forgiveness of sins, by each forgiving the faults of his brother. There is no comparison between God's remitting of sins and ours. For what are one hundred pence, in comparison with ten thousand pounds? as Christ says, naught. And although we deserve nothing by our forgiving, yet we must forgive that thereby we may prove and give testimony that we from God have received forgiveness of our sins.

The forgiveness of sins is declared only in God's Word, and there we must seek it; for it is grounded on God's promises. God forgives thee thy sins, not because thou feelest them and art sorry, for this sin itself produces, without deserving, but he forgives thy sins because he is merciful, and because he has promised to forgive for Christ's sake.

— Table-Talk, *#CCLI.*

Original sin, after regeneration, is like a wound that begins to heal; though it be a wound, yet it is in course of healing, though it still runs and is sore.

So original sin remains in Christians until they die, yet itself is mortified and continually dying. Its head is crushed in pieces, so that it cannot condemn us.

— Table-Talk, *#CCLVI.*

We teach and comfort the afflicted sinner after this manner: Brother, it is not possible for thee to become so righteous in this life, that thou shouldest feel no sin at all, that thy body should be clear like the sun, without spot or blemish: but thou hast as yet wrinkles and spots, and yet art thou holy notwithstanding. But thou wilt say: How can I be holy, when I have and feel sin in me? I answer: In that thou dost feel and acknowledge thy sin, it is a good token: give thanks unto God, and despair not. It is one step of health, when the sick man doth acknowledge and confess his infirmity. But how shall I be delivered from sin? Run to Christ, the physician, which healeth them that are broken in heart, and saveth sinners. Follow not the judgment of reason, which telleth thee, that he is angry with sinners: but kill reason, and believe in Christ. If thou believe, thou art righteous, because thou givest glory unto God, that he is almighty, merciful, true, etc. thou justifiest and praisest God. To be brief, thou yieldest unto him his divinity, and whatsoever else belongeth unto him: and the sin which remaineth in thee, is not laid to thy charge, but is pardoned for Christ's sake, in whom thou believest, who is perfectly just: whose righteousness is thy righteousness, and thy sin is his sin.

— Commentary on Galatians, *pp. 174 f.*

4. THE BONDAGE OF THE WILL

Free-will is plainly a divine term, and can be applicable to none but the divine Majesty only: for He alone " doth, (as the Psalm sings) what He will in Heaven and earth." (Ps. cxxxv. 6.) Whereas, if it be ascribed unto men, it is not more properly ascribed, than the divinity of God Himself would be ascribed unto them: which would be the greatest of all sacrilege. Wherefore, it becomes Theologians to refrain from the use of this term altogether, whenever they wish to speak of human ability, and leave it to be applied to God only. And moreover, to take this same term out of the mouths and speech of men; and thus to assert, as it were, for their God, that which belongs to His own sacred and holy Name. . . .

But, if we do not like to leave out this term altogether, (which would be most safe, and also most religious) we may, nevertheless, with a good conscience teach, that it be used so far as to allow man a " Free-will," not in respect of those which are above him, but in respect only of those things which are below him: that is, he may be allowed to know, that he has, as to his goods and possessions, the right of using, acting, and omitting, according to his " Free-will; " although, at the same time, that same " Free-will " is overruled by the Free-will of God alone, just as He pleases: but that, God-ward, or in things which pertain unto salvation or damnation, he has no " Free-will," but is a captive, slave, and servant, either to the will of God, or to the will of Satan.

— Bondage of the Will, *#XXVI, pp. 76–79.*

A man void of the Spirit of God, does not evil against his will as by violence, or as if he were taken by the neck and forced to it, in the same way as a thief or cut-throat is dragged to punishment against his will; but he does it spontaneously, and with a desirous willingness. And this willingness and desire of doing evil he cannot, by his own power, leave off, restrain, or change; but it goes on still desiring and craving. And even if he should be compelled by force to do any thing *outwardly* to the contrary, yet the craving will *within* remains averse to, and rises in indignation against that which forces or resists it. But it would not rise in indignation, if it were changed, and made willing to yield to a constraining power. This is what we mean by the necessity of immutability: — that the will cannot change itself, nor give itself another bent; but rather the more it is resisted, the more it is irritated to crave; as is manifest from its indignation. This would not be the case if it were free, or had a " Free-will." Ask experience, how hardened against all persuasion they are, whose inclinations are fixed upon any one thing. For if they yield at all they yield through force, or through something attended with greater advantage; they never yield willingly. And if their inclinations be not thus fixed, they let all things pass and go on just as they will.

But again, on the other hand, when God works in us, the *will*, being changed and sweetly breathed on by the Spirit of God, desires and acts, not from *compulsion*, but *responsively*, from pure willingness, inclination, and accord; so that it cannot be turned another way by any thing contrary, nor be compelled or overcome even by the gates of hell; but it still goes on to desire, crave after, and love that which is good; even as before, it desired, craved after, and loved that which was evil. This, again, experience proves. How invincible and unshaken are holy men, when, by violence and other oppressions, they are only compelled and irritated the more to crave after good! Even as fire, is rather fanned into flames than extinguished, by the wind. So that neither is there here any willingness, or " Free-will," to turn itself into another direction, or to desire any thing else, while the influence of the Spirit and grace of God remain in the man.

In a word, if we be under the god of this world, without the operation and Spirit of God, we are led captives by him at his will, as Paul saith. (2 Tim. ii. 26.) So that, we cannot will any thing but that which he wills. For he is that " strong man armed," who so keepeth his palace, that those whom he holds captive are kept in peace, that they might not cause any motion or feeling against him; otherwise, the kingdom of Satan, being divided against it-

self, could not stand; whereas, Christ affirms it does stand. And all
this we do willingly and desiringly, according to the nature of
will: for if it were forced, it would be no longer *will.* For compulsion is (so to speak) *unwillingness.* But if the " stronger than he "
come and overcome him, and take us as His spoils, then, through
the Spirit, we are His servants and captives (which is the royal
liberty) that we may desire and do, willingly, what He wills.

Thus the human will is, as it were, a beast between the two. If
God sit thereon, it wills and goes where God will: as the Psalm
saith, " I am become as it were a beast before thee, and I am continually with thee." (Ps. lxxiii. 22–23.) If Satan sit thereon, it wills
and goes as Satan will. Nor is it in the power of its own will to
choose, to which rider it will run, nor which it will seek; but the
riders themselves contend, which shall have and hold it.

— Bondage of the Will, #*XXV, pp. 72–74.*

Paul says, in II Timothy ii, " Instruct those that oppose the
truth; peradventure God will give them repentance, that they acknowledge the truth, and return from the snares of the devil, by
whom they are taken captive at his will." Where is the free will
here when the captive is of the devil, not indeed unable to do anything, but able to do only what the devil wills? Is that freedom, to
be captive at the devil's will, so that there is no help unless God
grant repentance and improvement? So also says John viii, When
the Jews said they were free, Christ said, " Verily I say unto you,
all they who sin are servants or possessions of sin; if the son make
you free, ye shall be free indeed." So St. Augustine changes the
term " free will," in his work *Against Julian,* book ii, and calls it
servum arbitrium, " a will in bondage."

— " *An Argument in Defense of All the Articles of Dr. Martin
Luther Wrongly Condemned in the Roman Bull,"* Works of Martin
Luther, *Vol. III, pp. 108 f.*

This is my absolute opinion: he that will maintain that man's
free-will is able to do or work anything in spiritual cases be they
never so small, denies Christ. This I have always maintained in my
writings, especially in those against Erasmus, one of the learnedest
men in the whole world, and thereby will I remain, for I know it to

be the truth, though all the world should be against it; yea, the decree of Divine Majesty must stand fast against the gates of hell.
— Table-Talk, #CCLXII.

I wish that the word " free will " had never been invented. It is not in the Scriptures, and it were better to call it " self-will," which profiteth not. Or, if anyone wishes to retain it, he ought to apply it to the new-created man, so as to understand by it the man who is without sin. He is assuredly free, as was Adam in Paradise, and it is of him that the Scriptures speak when they touch upon our freedom; but they who lie in sins are unfree and prisoners of the devil; yet because they can become free through grace, you can call them men of free will, just as you might call a man rich, although he is a beggar, because he can become rich. But it is neither right nor good thus to juggle with words in matters of such great seriousness.
— " An Argument in Defense of All the Articles of Dr. Martin Luther Wrongly Condemned in the Roman Bull," Works of Martin Luther, Vol. III, pp. 110 f.

> Dear Christians, one and all rejoice,
>   With exultation springing,
> And with united heart and voice
>   And holy rapture singing,
> Proclaim the wonders God hath done,
> How his right arm the victory won;
>   Right dearly it hath cost him.
>
> Fast bound in Satan's chains I lay,
>   Death brooded darkly o'er me;
> Sin was my torment night and day,
>   Therein my mother bore me,
> Deeper and deeper still I fell,
> Life was become a living hell,
>   So firmly sin possessed me.
>
> My good works could avail me naught,
>   For they with sin were stained;
> Free-will against God's judgment fought,
>   And dead to good remained.

Grief drove me to despair, and I
Had nothing left me but to die,
      To hell I fast was sinking.

God saw, in his eternal grace,
      My sorrow out of measure;
He thought upon his tenderness —
      To save was his good pleasure.
He turned to me a Father's heart —
Not small the cost — to heal my smart
      He gave his best and dearest.

He spake to his beloved Son:
      'Tis time to take compassion;
Then go, bright jewel of my crown,
      And bring to man salvation;
From sin and sorrow set him free,
Slay bitter death for him, that he
      May live with thee forever.

— Luther's Hymns, *p. 75.*

VI

The Christian Life

❧

1. REPENTANCE AND CONFESSION
2. JUSTIFICATION BY FAITH
3. PRAYER
4. LIVING THE CHRISTIAN LIFE

The Christian Life

1. REPENTANCE AND CONFESSION

O̲UR Lord and Master Jesus Christ, when He said *Poenitentiam agite*,[1] willed that the whole life of believers should be repentance.

This word cannot be understood to mean sacramental penance, i.e., confession and satisfaction, which is administered by the priests.

Yet it means not inward repentance only; nay, there is no inward repentance which does not outwardly work divers mortifications of the flesh.

— "*Disputation on Indulgences*," Works of Martin Luther, *Vol. I, p. 29.*

I learned that this word is in Greek *metanoia* and is derived from *meta* and *noun*, i.e., *post* and *mentem*,[2] so that *poenitentia* or *metanoia* is a "coming to one's senses," and is a knowledge of one's own evil, gained after punishment has been accepted and error ac-

---

[1] Matt. 4:17. Greek, μετανοεῖτε; English, "repent"; German, *Busse tun.* The Latin and German versions may also be rendered, "Do penance"; the Greek, on the other hand, can only mean "Repent." [This explanatory note and the ones that follow are from the Philadelphia edition of the *Works of Martin Luther.* Ed.]

[2] Gr., μετὰ, Lat., *post*, Eng., "after"; Gr. νοῦς, Lat., *mens*, Eng., "mind."

knowledged; and this cannot possibly happen without a change in our heart and our love. All this answers so aptly to the theology of Paul, that nothing, at least in my judgment, can so aptly illustrate St. Paul.

Then I went on and saw that *metanoia* can be derived, though not without violence, not only from *post* and *mentem,* but also from *trans* and *mentem,*[3] so that *metanoia* signifies a changing [4] of the mind and heart, because it seemed to indicate not only a change of the heart, but also a manner of changing it, i.e., the grace of God.

— " *Disputation on Indulgences,*" Works of Martin Luther, *Vol. I, pp. 40 f.*

A contrite heart is a rare thing and a great grace, and is not attained by thinking of sin and hell, but only by receiving the inpoured Holy Spirit. Otherwise Judas would have had the very best contrition, for he thought of his sin with great sorrow. On the other hand, a forced and feigned contrition is a common thing, as experience shows, for many confessions are made in Lent and yet there is little improvement in men's lives.

— " *An Argument in Defense of All the Articles of Dr. Martin Luther Wrongly Condemned in the Roman Bull,*" Works of Martin Luther, *Vol. III, p. 44.*

To teach that repentance is to be reached by merely meditating upon sin and its consequences, is lying, stinking, seducing hypocrisy. We ought, first of all, to look into the wounds of Christ, and see in them His love toward us and our ingratitude toward Him, and thus, with heartfelt affection to Christ and detestation of self, to meditate upon our sin. That is a true contrition and a fruitful repentance. For contrition must precede meditation upon sin. Such meditation must flow out of contrition and be its work, not vice versâ. There must be contrition before there can be any meditation upon sin, just as there must be love and desire before there

---

[3] The Greek μετὰ can also be translated by the Latin *trans,* which, in compounds, denotes movement from one place, or thing, or condition to another.
[4] Lat. *transmutatio,* " the act or process of changing," not simply " a change " (*mutatio*).

can be any good works or any meditation upon them. Meditation is a fruit of contrition; contrition is the tree. In our country fruit grows on trees and out of trees, and meditation upon sin grows out of contrition; but in the holy land of pope and papists trees may grow on the fruits, contrition out of sins; the people walk on their ears, no doubt, and do everything upside down.

— " *An Argument in Defense of All the Articles of Dr. Martin Luther Wrongly Condemned in the Roman Bull,*" Works of Martin Luther, *Vol. III, p. 47.*

There is no doubt that confession is necessary and commanded by God. Thus we read in Matthew iii: " They were baptised of John in Jordan, confessing their sins." And in I John i: " If we confess our sins, he is faithful and just to forgive us our sins. If we say that we have not sinned, we make him a liar, and his word is not in us." If the saints may not deny their sin, how much more ought those who are guilty of open and great sins to make confession! But most effectively of all does Matthew xviii prove the institution of confession, in which passage Christ teaches that a sinning brother should be rebuked, haled before the Church, accused and, if he will not hear, excommunicated. But he hears when, heeding the rebuke, he acknowledges and confesses his sin.

Of private confession, which is now observed, I am heartily in favor, even though it cannot be proved from the Scriptures; it is useful and necessary, nor would I have it abolished — nay, I rejoice that it exists in the Church of Christ, for it is a cure without an equal for distressed consciences. For when we have laid bare our conscience to our brother and privately made known to him the evil that lurked within, we receive from our brother's lips the word of comfort spoken by God Himself; and, if we accept it in faith, we find peace in the mercy of God speaking to us through our brother.

— " *The Babylonian Captivity of the Church,*" Works of Martin Luther, *Vol. II, pp. 249 f.*

In this our age, the consciences of almost all have been led astray by human doctrines into a false trust in their own righteousness and their own works, and knowledge about faith and trust in God has almost ceased. Therefore, for him who is about to go to confession, it is before all things necessary that he should not place his trust in his confession — either the confession which he is about to make or the confession which he has made — but that, with complete fulness of faith, he put his trust only in the most gracious promise of God; to wit, he must be altogether certain that He, Who has promised pardon to the man who shall confess his sins, will most faithfully fulfil His promise. For we are to glory, not because we confess, but because He has promised pardon to those who do confess; that is, not because of the worthiness or sufficiency of our confession (for there is no such worthiness or sufficiency), but because of the truth and certitude of His promise, as says the xxiv. Psalm: "For Thy Name's sake, O Lord, pardon mine iniquity." It does not say, " for my sake," or " for my worthiness' sake," or " for my name's sake," but " for Thy Name's sake."

— " *Discussion of Confession,*" Works of Martin Luther, *Vol. I,* *p. 81.*

Whether the hidden sins of the heart, which are known only to God and the man who commits them, belong to sacramental confession or not, is more than I can say. I should prefer to say that they do not. For the need of confessing these sins can in no way be proved, either by reason or by Scripture, and I have often suspected that it was all an invention of avaricious or curious or tyrannical prelates, who took this way of bringing the people of Christ to fear them. This is, in my opinion, laying hands on the judgment of God and is a violation of the rights of God, especially if men are forced to it.

— " *Discussion of Confession,*" Works of Martin Luther, *Vol. I,* *p. 86.*

2. JUSTIFICATION BY FAITH

A contrite heart is a precious thing, but it is found only where there is a lively faith in the promises and the threats of God. Such faith, intent on the immutable truth of God, startles and terrifies the conscience and thus renders it contrite, and afterwards, when it is contrite, raises it up, consoles and preserves it; so that the truth of God's threatening is the cause of contrition, and the truth of His promise the cause of consolation, if it be believed. By such faith a man merits the forgiveness of sins. Therefore faith should be taught and aroused before all else; and when faith is obtained, contrition and consolation will follow inevitably and of themselves. . . .

Beware, then, of putting your trust in your own contrition and of ascribing the forgiveness of sins to your own sorrow. God does not have respect to you because of that, but because of the faith by which you have believed His threatenings and promises, and which wrought such sorrow within you. Thus we owe whatever of good there may be in our penance, not to our scrupulous enumeration of sins, but to the truth of God and to our faith. All other things are the works and fruits of this, which follow of their own accord, and do not make a man good, but are done by a man already made good through faith in the truth of God.

— " *The Babylonian Captivity of the Church*," Works of Martin Luther, *Vol. II, pp. 248 f.*

When we are dealing with words and promises, there must be faith, even between men here on earth. No business and no community could long exist if no one was willing to take another's word or signature on faith. Now, as we plainly see, God deals with us in no other way than by His holy Word and the sacraments, which are like signs or seals of His Word. The very first thing necessary, then, is faith in these words and signs; for when God speaks and gives signs man must firmly and whole-heartedly believe that what He says and signifies is true, so that we do not consider Him a liar or a trickster, but hold Him to be faithful and true. This faith pleases God above all things, and does Him the highest honor, because it believes Him to be true, and a righteous God. Therefore He, in turn, counts this faith to us as righteousness good and sufficient unto salvation.

— " *An Argument in Defense of All the Articles of Dr. Martin Luther Wrongly Condemned in the Roman Bull*," Works of Martin Luther, *Vol. III, pp. 20 f.*

All depends on faith. He who does not believe is like one who must cross the sea, but is so timid that he does not trust the ship;

and so he must remain and never be saved, because he does not embark and cross over.

— "*A Treatise Concerning the Blessed Sacrament and Concerning the Brotherhoods*," Works of Martin Luther, *Vol. II, p. 25.*

Nothing makes a man good except faith, nor evil except unbelief.

It is indeed true that in the sight of men a man is made good or evil by his works, but this being made good or evil is no more than that he who is good or evil is pointed out and known as such; as Christ says, in Matthew vii, " By their fruits ye shall know them." But all this remains on the surface, and very many have been deceived by this outward appearance and have presumed to write and teach concerning good works by which we may be justified, without even mentioning faith; they go their way, always being deceived and deceiving, advancing, indeed, but into a worse state, blind leaders of the blind, wearying themselves with many works, and yet never attaining to true righteousness. Of such Paul says, in II Timothy iii, " Having the form of godliness, but denying its power, always learning and never attaining to the knowledge of the truth."

He, therefore, who does not wish to go astray with those blind men, must look beyond works, and laws and doctrines about works; nay, turning his eyes from works, he must look upon the person, and ask how that is justified. For the person is justified and saved not by works nor by laws, but by the Word of God, that is, by the promise of His grace, and by faith, that the glory may remain God's, Who saved us not by works of righteousness which we have done, but according to His mercy by the word of His grace, when we believed.

— "*A Treatise on Christian Liberty*," Works of Martin Luther, *Vol. II, pp. 332 f.*

In Romans iii, I know right well that the word *solum* was not in the Greek or Latin text. . . . It is a fact that these four letters *s-o-l-a*[5] are not there. . . . At the same time . . . the sense of them is there and . . . the word belongs there if the translation is

---

[5] The point of the criticism is that Luther has inserted the word " only," which does not appear in the original text.

to be clear and strong. I wanted to speak German, not Latin or Greek, since I had undertaken to speak German in the translation. But it is the nature of our German language that in speaking of two things, one of which is admitted and the other denied, we use the word "only" along with the word "not" or "no." So we say, "The farmer brings *only* grain and no money"; "No, I have no money now, but *only* grain"; "I have *only* eaten and not drunk "; "Did you *only* write it, and not read it over? " There are innumerable cases of this kind in daily use.

In all these phrases it is the German usage, even though it is not the Latin or Greek usage, and it is the way of the German language to add the word "only," in order that the word "not" or "no" may be more complete and clearer. To be sure, I can also say, "The farmer brings grain and no money," but the words "no money" do not sound as full and clear as if I were to say, "The farmer brings *only* grain and no money." Here the word "only" helps the word "no" so much that it becomes a complete, clear, German phrase. . . .

I was not only relying on the nature of the languages and following that when, in Romans iii, I inserted the word *solum*, "only," but the text itself and the sense of St. Paul demanded it and forced it upon me. He is dealing, in that passage, with the main point of Christian doctrine, viz., that we are justified by faith in Christ, without any works of the law, and he cuts away all works so completely, as even to say that the works of the law, though it is God's law and His Word, do not help us to righteousness. He cites Abraham as an example and says that he was justified so entirely without works, that even the highest work, which had then been newly commanded by God, before and above all other works, namely circumcision, did not help him to righteousness, but he was justified by faith, without circumcision and without any works at all. So he says, in Chapter iv, "If Abraham was justified by works, he may glory, but not before God." But when works are so completely cut away, the meaning of it must be that faith alone justifies, and one who would speak plainly and clearly about this cutting away of all works, must say, "Faith alone justifies us, and not works." The matter itself, and not the nature of the language only, compels this translation. . . .

I am not the only one or the first to say that faith alone justifies. Ambrose said it before me, and Augustine and many others; and if a man is going to read St. Paul and understand him, he will have to say the same thing and can say nothing else. Paul's words are too strong; they endure no works, none at all; and if it is not a work, it must be faith alone. How could it be such a fine, improving inoffensive doctrine, if people were taught that they might become righteous by works, beside faith? That would be as much as to say that it was not Christ's death alone that takes away our sins, but that our works, too, did something toward it; and it would be a fine honoring of Christ's death to say that our works helped it and could do that which He does, and that we were good and strong like Him. This is of the devil, who cannot leave the blood of Christ without abuse!

— " *On Translating: An Open Letter,*" Works of Martin Luther, *Vol. V, pp. 15–22.*

What then mean all those Scriptures which promise a kingdom and threaten hell? Why is the word reward so often repeated in the Scriptures; as, " Thou hast thy reward," " I am thy exceeding great reward? " Again, " Who rendereth unto every man according to his work; " and Paul, Rom. ii. 6, " Who by patient continuance in well doing, seek for eternal life," and many of the same kind?

It is answered: By all these passages, the *consequence of reward* is proved and nothing else, but by no means the *worthiness of merit:* seeing that, those who do good, do it not from a servile and mercenary principle in order to obtain eternal life, but they seek eternal life, that is, they are in that way, in which they shall come unto and find eternal life. So that seeking, is striving with desire, and pursuing with ardent diligence, that, which always leads unto eternal life. And the reason why it is declared in the Scriptures, that those things shall follow and take place after a good or bad life, is, that men might be instructed, admonished, awakened, and terrified. For as " by the law is the knowledge of sin " (Rom. iii. 20,) and an admonition of our impotency, and as from that, it cannot be inferred that we can do any thing ourselves; so, by these promises and threats, there is conveyed an admonition, by which we are taught, what will follow sin and that impotency made known by the law; but there is not, by them, any thing of worthiness ascribed unto our merit.

Wherefore, as the words of the law are for instruction and illumination, to teach us what we ought to do, and also what we are not able to do; so the words of reward, while they signify what will be hereafter, are for exhortation and threatening, by which the just are animated, comforted, and raised up to go forward, to persevere, and to conquer; that they might not be wearied or disheartened either in doing good or in enduring evil; as Paul exhorts his Corinthians, saying, " Be ye steadfast, knowing that your labour is not in vain in the Lord." (1 Cor. xv. 58.) So also God supports Abraham, saying " I am thy exceeding great reward." (Gen. xv. 1.) Just in the same manner as you would console any one, by signifying to him, that his works certainly pleased God, which kind of consolation the Scripture frequently uses; nor is it a small consolation for any one to know, that he so pleases God, that nothing but a good consequence can follow, even though it seem to him impossible.

— Bondage of the Will, *#LXXI, pp. 191–193.*

Our faith in Christ does not free us from works, but from false opinions concerning works, that is, from the foolish presumption that justification is acquired by works. For faith redeems, corrects and preserves our consciences, so that we know that righteousness does not consist in works, although works neither can nor ought to be wanting; just as we cannot be without food and drink and all the works of this mortal body, yet our righteousness is not in them, but in faith; and yet those works of the body are not to be despised or neglected on that account. In this world we are bound by the needs of our bodily life, but we are not righteous because of them. " My kingdom is not of this world," says Christ, but He does not say, " My kingdom is not here, that is, in this world." And Paul says, " Though we walk in the flesh, we do not war after the flesh," and in Galatians ii, " The life which I now live in the flesh, I live in the faith of the Son of God." Thus what we do, live, and are in works and in ceremonies, we do because of the necessities of this life and of the effort to rule our body; nevertheless we are righteous not in these, but in the faith of the Son of God.

— *"A Treatise on Christian Liberty,"* Works of Martin Luther, *Vol. II, p. 344.*

We conclude therefore with Paul, " that we are justified by faith only in Christ, without the law." Now after that a man is once justified, and possesseth Christ by faith, and knoweth that he is his righteousness and life, doubtless he will not be idle, but as a good tree he will bring forth good fruits. For the believing man hath the Holy Ghost, and where the Holy Ghost dwelleth, he will not suffer a man to be idle, but stirreth him up to all exercises of piety and godliness, and of true religion, to the love of God, to the patient suffering of afflictions, to prayer, to thanksgiving, to the exercise of charity towards all men.

— Commentary on Galatians, *p. 114.*

The true way to Christianity is this, that a man do first acknowledge himself by the law, to be a sinner, and that it is impossible for him to do any good work. For the law saith, " thou art an evil tree, and therefore all that thou thinkest, speakest, or dost, is against God," (Matt. vii. 7). Thou canst not therefore deserve grace by thy works: which if thou go about to do, thou doublest thy offence: for since thou art an evil tree, thou canst not but bring forth evil fruits, that is to say, sins. " For whatsoever is not of faith, is sin," (Rom. xiv. 23). Wherefore he that would deserve grace by works going before faith, goeth about to please God with sins, which is nothing else but to heap sin upon sin, to mock God, and to provoke his wrath. When a man is thus taught and instructed by the law, then is he terrified and humbled, then he seeth indeed the greatness of his sin, and cannot find in himself one spark of the love of God: therefore he justifieth God in his word, and confesseth that he is guilty of death and eternal damnation. The first part then of Christianity is the preaching of repentance, and the knowledge of ourselves.

The second part is: if thou wilt be saved, thou mayest not seek salvation by works: " for God hath sent his only begotten Son into the world, that we might live through him. He was crucified and died for thee, and offered up thy sins in his own body." Here is no congruence or work done before grace, but wrath, sin, terror and death. Wherefore the law doth nothing else but utter sin, terrify and humble, and by this means prepareth us to justification, and driveth us to Christ. For God hath revealed unto us by his word, that he will be unto us a merciful father, and without our deserts (seeing we can deserve nothing) will freely give unto us remission of sins, righteousness, and life everlasting for Christ his Son's sake.

— Commentary on Galatians, *p. 92.*

You ask, how shall we begin to be godly and what shall we do that God may begin his work in us? Answer: Do you not understand, it is not for you to work or to begin to be godly, as little as it is to further and complete it. Everything that you begin is in and remains sin, though it shines ever so brightly; you cannot do anything but sin, do what you will. Hence, the teaching of all the schools and monasteries is misleading, when they teach man to begin to pray and do good works, to found something, to give, to sing, to become spiritual and thereby to seek God's grace.

You say, however: Then I must sin from necessity, if by my free will I work and live without God? and I could not avoid sin, no matter what I would do? Answer: Truly, it is so, that you must remain in sin, do what you will, and that everything is sin you do alone out of your own free will. For if out of your own free will you might avoid sin and do that which pleases God, what need would you have of Christ? He would be a fool to shed his blood for your sin, if you yourself were so free and able to do aught that is not sin. From this you learn how the universities and monasteries with their teachings of free will and good works, do nothing else but darken the truth of God so that we know not what Christ is, what we are and what our condition is. They lead the whole world with them into the abyss of hell, and it is indeed time that we eradicate from the earth all chapters and monasteries.

Learn then . . . what takes place when God begins to make us godly, and what the first step is in becoming godly. There is no other beginning than that your king comes to you and begins to work in you. . . . This is what is meant by " Thy king cometh," (Matt. 21:5). You do not seek him, but he seeks you. You do not find him, he finds you. For the preachers come from him, not from you; their sermons come from him, not from you; your faith comes from him, not from you; everything that faith works in you comes from him, not from you; and where he does not come, you remain outside; and where there is no Gospel there is no God, but only sin and damnation, free will may do, suffer, work and live as it may and can. Therefore you should not ask, where to begin to be godly; there is no beginning, except where the king enters and is proclaimed.

— *Gospel Sermon, First Sunday in Advent* (Lenker Edition, *Vol. X, #21–25*).

3. PRAYER

By " prayer " we understand simply formal words or expressions — as, for instance, the Lord's Prayer and the psalms — which sometimes express more than our request. In " supplication " we strengthen prayer and make it effective by a certain form of persuasion; for instance, we may entreat one to grant a request for the sake of a father, or of something dearly loved or highly prized. We entreat God by his Son, his saints, his promises, his name. Thus Solomon says (Ps. 132:1), " Jehovah, remember for David all his affliction." And Paul urges (Rom. 12:1), " I beseech you therefore, brethren, by the mercies of God "; and again (II Cor. 10:1), " I . . . entreat you by the meekness and gentleness of Christ." " Petitioning " is stating what we have at heart, naming the desire we express in prayer and supplication. In the Lord's Prayer are seven petitions, beside prayer proper. Christ says (Mt. 7:7–8) : " Ask, and it shall be given you; seek, and ye shall find; knock, and it shall be opened unto you: for every one that asketh receiveth; and he that seeketh findeth; and to him that knocketh it shall be opened." In " thanksgiving " we recount blessings received and thus strengthen our confidence and enable ourselves to wait trustingly for what we pray.

Prayer is made vigorous by petitioning; urgent by supplication; by thanksgiving, pleasing and acceptable. Strength and acceptability combine to prevail and secure the petition. This, we see, is the manner of prayer practiced by the Church; and the holy fathers in the Old Testament always offered supplication and thanks in their prayers. The Lord's Prayer opens with praise and thanksgiving and the acknowledgment of God as a Father; it earnestly presses toward him through filial love and a recognition of fatherly tenderness. For supplication, this prayer is unequaled. Hence it is the sublimest and the noblest prayer ever uttered.

— *Epistle Sermon, Fourth Sunday in Advent* (Lenker Edition, *Vol. VII, #31–32*).

We should pray, not as the custom is, counting many pages or beads, but fixing our mind upon some pressing need, desire it with all earnestness, and exercise faith and confidence toward God in the matter, in such wise that we do not doubt that we shall be heard. So St. Bernard instructs his brethren and says: " Dear brethren, you shall by no means despise your prayer, as if it were in vain, for I tell you of a truth that, before you have uttered the words, the prayer is already recorded in heaven; and you shall confidently expect from God one of two things: either that your prayer will be granted, or that, if it will not be granted, the granting of it would not be good for you."

Prayer is, therefore, a special exercise of faith, and faith makes the prayer so acceptable that either it will surely be granted, or something better than we ask will be given in its stead. So also says St. James: " Let him who asketh of God not waver in faith; for if he wavers, let not that man think that he shall receive any thing of the Lord." This is a clear statement, which says directly: he who does not trust, receives nothing, neither that which he asks, nor anything better.

And to call forth such faith, Christ Himself has said, Mark xi: " Therefore I say unto you, What things soever ye desire, when ye pray, believe that ye receive them, and ye shall surely have them." And Luke xi: " Ask, and it shall be given you; seek, and ye shall find; knock, and it shall be opened unto you; for every one that asketh receiveth; and he that seeketh findeth; and to him that knocketh it shall be opened. Or what father is there of you, who, if his son shall ask bread, will he give him a stone? or if he ask a fish, will he give him a serpent? or if he ask an egg, will he give him a scorpion? But if you know how to give good gifts to your children, and you yourselves are not naturally good, how much more shall your Father which is in heaven give a good spirit to all them that ask Him! "

Who is so hard and stone-like, that such mighty words ought not to move him to pray with all confidence joyfully and gladly? But how many prayers must be reformed, if we are to pray aright according to these words! Now, indeed, all churches and monastic houses are full of praying and singing, but how does it happen that so little improvement and benefit result from it, and things daily grow worse? The reason is none other than that which St. James indicates when he says: " You ask much and receive not, because ye ask amiss." For where this faith and confidence is not in the prayer, the prayer is dead, and nothing more than a grievous labor and work. If anything is given for it, it is none the less only temporal benefit without any blessing and help for the soul; nay, to the great injury and blinding of souls, so that they go their way, babbling much with their mouths, regardless of whether they receive, or desire, or trust; and in this unbelief, the state of mind most opposed to the exercise of faith and to the nature of prayer, they remain hardened.

From this it follows that one who prays aright never doubts that his prayer is surely acceptable and heard, although the very thing for which he prays be not given him. For we are to lay our need before God in prayer, but not prescribe to Him a measure, manner, time or place; but if He wills to give it to us better or in another way than we think, we are to leave it to Him; for frequently we do not know what we pray, as St. Paul says, Romans viii; and God works and gives above all that we understand, as he says, Ephesians iii, so that there be no doubt that the prayer is acceptable and heard, and we yet leave to God the time, place, measure and limit; He will surely do what is right. They are the true worshipers, who worship God in spirit and in truth. For they who believe not that they will be heard, sin upon the left hand against this Commandment, and go far astray with their unbelief. But they who set a limit for Him, sin upon the other side, and come too close with their tempting of God. So He has forbidden both, that we should err from His Commandment neither to the left nor to the right, that is, neither with unbelief nor with tempting, but with simple faith remain on the straight road, trusting Him, and yet setting Him no bounds. . . .

There is no Christian who does not have time to pray without ceasing. But I mean the spiritual praying, that is: no one is so heavily burdened with his labor, but that if he will he can, while working, speak with God in his heart, lay before Him his need and that of other men, ask for help, make petition, and in all this exercise and strengthen his faith.

This is what the Lord means, Luke xviii, when He says, " Men ought always to pray, and never cease," although in Matthew vi. He forbids the use of much speaking and long prayers, because of which he rebukes the hypocrites; not because the lengthy prayer of the lips is evil, but because it is not that true prayer which can be made at all times, and without the inner prayer of faith is nothing. . . .

But what are the things which we must bring before Almighty God in prayer and lamentation, to exercise faith thereby? Answer: First, every man's own besetting need and trouble, of which David says, Psalm xxxii: " Thou art my refuge in all trouble which compasseth me about; Thou art my comfort, to preserve me from all evil which surrounds me." Likewise, Psalm cxlii: " I cried unto the Lord with my voice; with my voice unto the Lord did I make my supplication. I poured out my complaint before Him; I showed before Him my trouble." In the mass a Christian shall keep in mind the short-comings or excesses he feels, and pour out all these freely before God with weeping and groaning, as woefully as he can, as to his faithful Father, who is ready to help him. And if you do not know or recognise your need, or have no trouble, then you shall know that you are in the worst possible plight. For this is the greatest trouble, that you find yourself so hardened, hard-hearted and insensible that no trouble moves you.

There is no better mirror in which to see your need than simply the Ten Commandments, in which you will find what you lack and what you should seek. If, therefore, you find in yourself a weak faith, small hope and little love toward God; and that you do not praise and honor God, but love your own honor and fame, think much of the favor of men, do not gladly hear mass and sermon, are indolent in prayer, in which things every one has faults, then you shall think more of these faults than of all bodily harm to goods, honor and life, and believe that they are worse than death and all mortal sickness. These you shall earnestly lay before God, lament and ask for help, and with all confidence expect help, and believe that you are heard and shall obtain help and mercy.

— *"Treatise on Good Works,"* Works of Martin Luther, *Vol. I*, *pp. 225–231.*

None can believe how powerful prayer is, and what it is able to effect, but those who have learned it by experience.

It is a great matter when in extreme need, to take hold on prayer. I know, whenever I have earnestly prayed, I have been amply heard, and have obtained more than I prayed for; God, indeed, sometimes delayed, but at last he came.

Ecclesiasticus says: "The prayer of a good and godly Christian availeth more to health, than the physician's physic."

O how great a thing, how marvellous, a godly Christian's prayer is! how powerful with God; that a poor human creature should speak with God's high Majesty in heaven, and not be affrighted, but, on the contrary, know that God smiles upon him for Christ's sake, his dearly beloved Son. The heart and conscience, in this act of praying, must not fly and recoil backwards by reason of our sins and unworthiness, or stand in doubt, or be scared away. We must not do as the Bavarian did, who, with great devotion, called upon St. Leonard, an idol set up in a church in Bavaria, behind which idol stood one who answered the Bavarian, and said: Fie on thee, Bavarian; and in that sort often repulsed and would not hear him, till at last, the Bavarian went away, and said: Fie on thee, Leonard.

When we pray, we must not let it come to: Fie upon thee; but certainly hold and believe, that we are already heard in that for which we pray, with faith in Christ. Therefore the ancients ably defined prayer an *Ascensus mentis ad Deum*, a climbing up of the heart unto God.

— Table-Talk, *#CCCXXVIII.*

Under the papacy it is taught that the saints in heaven do pray for us, though we cannot know this, since the Scriptures tell us no such thing. Not only so, but the saints have been made gods, so that they have to be our patrons, on whom we call, even though some of them have never existed. To each of these saints some special power and might have been ascribed. One has power over fire, another over water, another over pestilence, fever and all kinds of disease. Indeed it seems that God has to be idle and let the saints work and act in His stead. . . .

There is not a single word of God commanding us to call on either angels or saints to intercede for us, and we have no example of it in the Scriptures. There we find that the angels spoke with the fathers and the prophets but none of these angels was asked to intercede for them. So Jacob, the father of them all, did not ask the angel, with whom he fought, for any intercession, but only took a blessing from him. On the contrary, we find, in the Apocalypse, that the angel would not allow himself to be worshiped by John. Thus the worship of saints shows itself to be a mere trumpery of men and an invention of their own, outside the Word of God and the Scriptures.

It is not proper, however, for us to undertake anything in the way of worship without God's Word, and one who does so is tempting God. Therefore it is not to be advised or endured that one should call upon the departed saints to intercede for him or should teach others to do it; but it is rather to be condemned and others are to be taught to avoid it. For this reason I, too, shall not advise it and so burden my conscience with other peoples' iniquities. It was exceedingly bitter for me to tear myself away from the worship of the saints, for I was steeped and fairly drowned in it. But the light of the Gospel is now so clear that henceforth no one has any excuse to remain in darkness. We all know very well what we ought to do.

Moreover, this is, in itself, a dangerous and offense-giving service, because people are easily accustomed to turning from Christ and quickly learn to put more confidence in the saints than in Christ Himself. Our nature is, in any case, all too prone to flee from God and Christ, and to trust in men; nay, it is exceedingly hard for one to learn to trust in God and Christ, though we have vowed and are in duty bound to do so. Therefore this offense is not to be endured, so that weak and fleshly people may not begin an idolatry, against the First Commandment and against our baptism. Be satisfied to turn confidence and trust away from the saints, to Christ, both by teaching and practice. Even then there are difficulties and hindrances enough. There is no need to paint the devil on the door; he will be on hand.

— " *On Translating: An Open Letter,*" Works of Martin Luther, *Vol. V, pp. 23 f.*

4. LIVING THE CHRISTIAN LIFE

As man, before he is created man, does nothing and endeavours nothing towards his being made a creature; and as, after he is made and created, he does nothing and endeavours nothing towards his preservation, or towards his continuing in his creature-existence, but each takes place along by the will of the omnipotent power and goodness of God, creating us and preserving us, without ourselves; but as God, nevertheless, does not work *in* us *without* us, seeing we are for that purpose created and preserved, that He might work in us and that we might co-operate with Him, whether it be out of His kingdom under His general omnipotence, or in His kingdom under the peculiar power of His Spirit; — so, man, before he is regenerated into the new creation of the kingdom of the Spirit, does nothing and endeavours nothing towards his new creation into that kingdom, and after he is re-created does nothing and endeavours nothing towards his perseverance in that kingdom; but the Spirit alone effects both in us, regenerating us and preserving us when regenerated, without ourselves; as James saith, " Of His own will begat He us by the word of His power, that we should be a kind of first-fruits of His creatures," — (Jas. i. 18) (where he speaks of the renewed creation:) nevertheless, He does not work *in* us *without* us, seeing that He has for this purpose created and preserved us, that He might operate in us, and that we might co-operate with Him: thus, by us He preaches, shews mercy to the poor, and comforts the afflicted.

— Bondage of the Will, *#CXXXI, pp. 317 f.*

Christian holiness, or the holiness of universal Christendom is that which comes when the Holy Spirit gives people faith in Christ, according to Acts xv, that is, He makes heart, soul, body, works and manner of life new and writes God's commandments, not on tables of stone, but on hearts of flesh according to II Corinthians iii. To speak plainly, according to the first Table He gives knowledge of God, so that those whom He enlightens can resist all heresies, in true faith, and overcome all false ideas and errors, and thus remain pure in faith against the devil. He also gives strength and comfort to feeble, despondent, weak consciences against the accusations and attacks of sin, so that souls are not despondent and do not despair and are not terrified at torment, pain, death, and God's wrath and judgment, but strengthened and comforted in hope, are bold and joyful in overcoming the devil. Thus He also gives true fear and love of God, so that we do not despise God and murmur or grow angry at His marvellous judgments, but love, praise, thank, and honor Him for all that happens. This is a new, holy life in the soul according to the First Table of Moses. It is called *tres virtutes theologicas,* " the three chief virtues of Christians," faith, hope, and love; and the Holy Ghost, who gives them and does and works these things for Christians whom Christ has won, is therefore called *Sanctificator,* or *Vivificator.* For the old Adam is dead and can do nothing, and must learn from the law that he can do nothing and is dead; he would not know it of himself.

In the Second Table, and in the body, He also sanctifies Christians and it is of His gift that they willingly obey parents and overlords, conduct themselves peacefully and humbly, are not wrathful or revengeful or malicious, not lewd, adulterers, unchaste, but pure and chaste, whether they have wives and children or not; and so forth. They do not steal or take usury, are not avaricious, do not cheat, etc., but work honorably, support themselves honestly, lend gladly, give and help whenever they can. Therefore, they do not lie, deceive, back-bite, but are kind, truthful, faithful, and reliable, and whatever else God's commandments require. This is done by the Holy Ghost, who sanctifies and awakens even the body to this new life, until it is completed in the life beyond. That is Christian holiness.

—" *On the Councils and the Churches,*" Works of Martin Luther, *Vol. V, pp. 267 f.*

The Samaritan, who laid the half-dead man on his beast, poured wine and oil into his wounds and bade the host take care of him. He did not entirely cure him at once; so we too are not entirely cured by baptism or repentance, but a beginning is made in us and a bandage of the first grace is bound upon us, that our recovery may proceed from day to day until we are entirely cured. Therefore St. James says, in James i, " God hath borne us by His Word, out of pure, gracious will, without our merit, that we may be a beginning of His work, or His creatures "; as if to say, " We are a work that God has begun but not yet completed so long as we live here on earth in the faith of His Word; but after death we shall be perfect, a divine work without sin or fault."

— " *An Argument in Defense of All the Articles of Dr. Martin Luther Wrongly Condemned in the Roman Bull,*" Works of Martin Luther, *Vol. III, p. 30.*

You are to understand, if you are a Christian, that you must experience all kinds of opposition and wicked dispositions in the flesh. For wherever there is faith, there come a hundred evil thoughts, a hundred strugglings more than before; only see to it that you act the man, and not suffer yourself to be taken captive; and continue to resist, and say, I will not, I will not. For we must here confess, that the case is much like that of an ill-matched couple, who are continually complaining of one another, and what one will do the other will not.

That may yet be called a truly Christian life that is never at perfect rest, and has not so far attained as to feel no sin, provided that sin be felt, indeed, but not favored. Thus we are to fast, pray, labor, to subdue and suppress lust. . . . While flesh and blood continue, so long sin remains; wherefore it is ever to be struggled against. Whoever has not learned this by his own experience, must not boast that he is a Christian.

— Commentary on Peter and Jude, *pp. 119 f.*

We see, then, that all our sufferings are as nothing, when we consider the nails, dungeons, irons, faggots, wild beasts, and all the endless tortures of the saints; nay, when we ponder the afflictions of men now living, who endure in this life the most grievous persecutions of the devil. For there is no lack of men who are suffering more sharp and bitter pains than we, in soul as well as in body.

— *"The Fourteen of Consolation,"* Works of Martin Luther, *Vol. I, p. 135.*

Christians are to be exhorted that they be diligent in following Christ, their Head, through penalties, deaths, and hell;

And thus be confident of entering into heaven rather through many tribulations, than through the assurance of peace.

— *" Disputation on Indulgences,"* Works of Martin Luther, *Vol. I, p: 38.*

I set down first these two propositions concerning the liberty and the bondage of the spirit:

A Christian man is a perfectly free lord of all, subject to none.

A Christian man is a perfectly dutiful servant of all, subject to all.

— *"A Treatise on Christian Liberty,"* Works of Martin Luther, *Vol. II, p. 312.*

When Peter was with the Gentiles, he ate pork and sausage with them, but when the Jews came in, he would not touch this food and ate no more with them. Then the Gentiles who had become Christians, thought: Alas! we, too, must be like the Jews, eat no pork and live according to the law of Moses. But when Paul found that it would injure the liberty of the Gospel, he reproved Peter publicly and read him an apostolic lecture, saying: " If thou, being a Jew, livest after the manner of the Gentiles, why compellest thou the Gentiles to live as do the Jews? " Thus we, too, should order our lives and use our liberty at the proper time, so that Christian liberty may suffer no injury, and no offence be given to our weak brothers and sisters who are still without the knowledge of this liberty.

— *"The Eight Wittenberg Sermons,"* Works of Martin Luther, *Vol. II, p. 411.*

Hence, the Christian must take a middle course and face those two classes of men. He will meet first the unyielding, stubborn cer-

emonialists, who like deaf adders are not willing to hear the truth of liberty, but, having no faith, boast of, prescribe and insist upon their ceremonies as means of justification. Such were the Jews of old, who were unwilling to learn how to do good. These he must resist, do the very opposite and offend them boldly, lest by their impious views they drag many with them into error. In the presence of such men it is good to eat meat, to break the fasts and for the sake of the liberty of faith to do other things which they regard the greatest of sins. Of them we must say, "Let them alone, they are blind and leaders of the blind." For on this principle Paul would not circumcise Titus when the Jews insisted that he should, and Christ excused the Apostles when they plucked ears of corn on the sabbath; and there are many similar instances. The other class of men whom a Christian will meet, are the simple-minded, ignorant men, weak in the faith, as the Apostle calls them, who cannot yet grasp the liberty of faith, even if they were willing to do so. These he must take care not to offend; he must yield to their weakness until they are more fully instructed. For since these do and think as they do, not because they are stubbornly wicked, but only because their faith is weak, the fasts and other things which they think necessary must be observed to avoid giving them offence. For so love demands, which would harm no one, but would serve all men. It is not by their fault that they are weak, but their pastors have taken them captive with the snares of their traditions and have wickedly used these traditions as rods with which to beat them. From these pastors they should have been delivered by the teaching of faith and liberty. So the Apostle teaches us, Romans xiv, "If my meat cause my brother to offend, I will eat no flesh while the world standeth"; and again, "I know that through Christ nothing is unclean, except to him who esteemeth any thing to be unclean; but it is evil for the man who eats and is offended."
— "*A Treatise on Christian Liberty*," Works of Martin Luther, *Vol. II, pp. 344 f.*

From faith flow forth love and joy in the Lord, and from love a joyful, willing and free mind that serves one's neighbor willingly and takes no account of gratitude or ingratitude, of praise or blame, of gain or loss. For a man does not serve that he may put men under obligations, he does not distinguish between friends and enemies, nor does he anticipate their thankfulness or unthankfulness; but most freely and most willingly he spends himself and all that he has, whether he waste all on the thankless or whether he gain a reward. For as his Father does, distributing all things to all men richly and freely, causing His sun to rise upon the good and upon the evil, so also the son does all things and suffers all things with that freely bestowing joy which is his delight when through Christ he sees it in God, the dispenser of such great benefits.

— " *A Treatise on Christian Liberty*," Works of Martin Luther, *Vol. II, p. 338.*

God does not want hearers and repeaters of words, but doers and followers who exercise themselves in the faith that worketh by love. For a faith without love is not enough — rather it is not faith at all, but a counterfeit of faith, just as a face seen in a mirror is not a real face, but merely the reflection of a face.

— " *The Eight Wittenberg Sermons*," Works of Martin Luther, *Vol. II, p. 392.*

The Apostles Peter and Paul distinguish brotherly love, and love in general, from one another. Brotherhood is, that Christians should dwell altogether as brethren, and make no distinctions between themselves. For since we all have a common Christ, one baptism, one faith, one treasure, I am no better than thou; that which thou hast, I have also, and I am just as rich as thou. The treasure is the same, except that I may have it in a better shape than thou, since I may have it lying in gold, but thou in a poor garment. Therefore as we have the grace of Christ and all spiritual blessings in common, so should we also hold body and life, property and honor, in common, that one should be of service to another in all things. . . .

But love is greater than brotherhood, for it extends even to our enemies, and especially to those who are not worthy of love. For as faith performs its work where it sees nothing, so also should love see nothing, and there especially exercise its office where there appears nothing lovely, but only disaffection and hostility. Where there is nothing that pleases me I should the more seek to be pleased. And this spirit should go forth fervently, says St. Peter, from the whole heart, just as God loved us when we were not worthy of love.

— Commentary on Peter and Jude, *pp. 73–75.*

Christians should be aware of their citizenship in a better country, that they may rightly adapt themselves to this world. Let them not occupy the present life as if intending to remain in it; nor as do the monks, who flee responsibility, avoiding civil office and trying to run out of the world. For Peter says (I Pet. 2:11–20) rather that we are not to escape our fellows and live each for himself, but to remain in our several conditions in life, united with other mortals as God has bound us, and serving one another. At the same time, we are to regard this life as a journey through a country where we have no citizenship — where we are not at home; to think of ourselves as travelers or pilgrims occupying for a night the same inn, eating and drinking there and then leaving the place.

Let not the occupants of the humbler stations — servants and subjects — grumble: " Why should I vex myself with unpleasant household tasks, with farm work or heavy labor? This life is not my home anyway, and I may as well have it better. Therefore, I will abandon my station and enjoy myself. . . . No, this is not the right way. If you are unwilling to put up with your lot, as the guest in a tavern and among strangers must do, you also may not eat and drink.

Similarly, they who are favored with loftier positions in life may not, upon this authority, abandon themselves to the idea of living in the sheer idleness and lustful pleasure their more favored station permits, as if they were to be here always. . . .

Christians are subjects of two kingdoms — they have experience of two kinds of life. Here on earth where the world has its home and its heavenly kingdom, we surely are not citizens. According to Paul (Phil. 3:20), " our conversation " — our citizenship — " is with Christ in heaven "; that is, in yonder life, the life we await. As the Jews hoped to be released from Babylon, we hope to be released from this present life and to go where we shall be lordly citizens forever. But being obliged to continue in this wretched state — our Babylon — so long as God wills, we should do as the

Jews were commanded to do — mingle with other mortals, eat and drink, make homes, till the soil, fill civil offices and show good will toward our fellows, even praying for them, until the hour arrives for us to depart unto our home.

He who is guided by these facts, who comprehends the distinction between the kingdom of heaven and the kingdom of the world, will know how to resist successfully all classes of fanatics. For these latter paint this life in a terrible aspect. They want to run out of the world entirely, and are unwilling to associate with anyone; or they proceed to disturb civil regulations and to overthrow all order; or again, as with the Pope, they interfere in secular rule, desiring temporal authority, wholly under the name and color of Christianity.

Having as Christians forgiveness of sins, and being now people of God, children of his kingdom, citizens no longer of Babylon but of heaven, let us know that during the period of our sojourn here among strangers, it is ours to live righteously, honorably and chastely, to further civil and domestic peace and to lend counsel and aid to benefit even the wicked and ungrateful, meanwhile constantly striving after our inheritance and keeping in mind the kingdom whither we are bound.

— *Epistle Sermon, Third Sunday After Easter* (Lenker Edition, *Vol. VIII, #9–15*).

> A mighty Fortress is our God,
>   A Bulwark never failing;
> Our Helper He amid the flood
>   Of mortal ills prevailing:
> For still our ancient Foe
> Doth seek to work us woe;
> His craft and power are great,
> And, armed with cruel hate,
>   On earth is not his equal.
>
> Did we in our own strength confide,
>   Our striving would be losing;
> Were not the right Man on our side,
>   The Man of God's own choosing:

Dost ask who that may be?
Christ Jesus, it is He;
Lord Sabaoth His Name,
From age to age the same,
    And He must win the battle.

And though this world, with devils filled,
    Should threaten to undo us;
We will not fear, for God hath willed
    His truth to triumph through us:
The Prince of Darkness grim,
We tremble not for him;
His rage we can endure,
For lo! his doom is sure,
    One little word shall fell him.

That word above all earthly powers,
    No thanks to them, abideth;
The Spirit and the gifts are ours
    Through Him who with us sideth:
Let goods and kindred go,
This mortal life also:
The body they may kill:
God's truth abideth still,
    His Kingdom is forever.

— The Hymnal *of the Presbyterian Church in the U. S. A.* (1933), *Hymn 266, Tr. Frederick H. Hedge.*

VII

The Church

The Church

1. THE NATURE AND FUNCTION OF THE CHURCH

I BELIEVE in . . . a Holy Christian Church, a communion of saints, a forgiveness of sins."

This means —

I believe that there is on earth, through the whole wide world, no more than one holy, common, Christian Church, which is nothing else than the congregation, or assembly of the saints, i.e., the pious, believing men on earth, which is gathered, preserved, and ruled by the Holy Ghost, and daily increased by means of the sacraments and the Word of God.

I believe that no one can be saved who is not found in this congregation, holding with it to one faith, word, sacraments, hope and love, and that no Jew, heretic, heathen or sinner can be saved along with it, unless he become reconciled to it, united with it and conformed to it in all things.

I believe that in this congregation, or Church, all things are common, that everyone's possessions belong to the others and no one has anything of his own; therefore, all the prayers and good works of the whole congregation must help, assist and strengthen me and every believer at all times, in life and death, and thus each bear the other's burden, as St. Paul teaches.

I believe that in this congregation, and nowhere else, there is forgiveness of sins; that outside of it, good works, however great they be or many, are of no avail for the forgiveness of sins; but that within it, no matter how much, how greatly or how often men may sin, nothing can hinder forgiveness of sins, which abides wherever and as long as this one congregation abides. To this congregation Christ gives the keys, and says, in Matthew xviii, " Whatsoever ye shall bind on earth shall be bound in heaven." In like manner He says, in Matthew xvi, to the one man Peter, who stands as the representative of the one and only Church, " Whatsoever thou shalt loose on earth shall be loosed in heaven."

— " *A Brief Explanation of the Ten Commandments, the Creed, and the Lord's Prayer,*" Works of Martin Luther, *Vol. II, pp. 372– 374.*

" I believe one holy Christian Church, the Communion of Saints." There the Creed indicates clearly what the Church is, namely, " a communion of saints," that is, a group or assembly of such people as are Christians and holy. That is a Christian, holy group, or Church. But this word " church " is not German and does not convey the sense or idea that is to be taken from this article.

In Acts xix, the chancellor calls *ecclesia* the assembly or people who had run together in a crowd on the market-place, and says, " It can be settled in a regular assembly "; and again, " When he had thus spoken he dismissed the assembly." In this passage and others, *ecclesia,* or church, means nothing else than an assembled people, though they were heathen, and not Christians, just as the town-councilors summon the community to the town-hall. Now there are many peoples in the world, but the Christians are a peculiar people, a called people, and they are therefore called not simply *ecclesia,* " church," or " people," but *sancta, catholica, Christiana,* that is, " a Christian, holy people," which believes in Christ. Therefore, it is called a Christian people and has the Holy Ghost, who sanctifies it daily, not only through the forgiveness of sins, . . . but by the abolition, purging out, and slaying of sins, and because of this they are called a holy people. " Holy Christian Church," then, is the same thing as " a people that is Christian and holy," or as we are accustomed to say, " the holy Christendom," or

" the entire Christendom "; in the Old Testament it is called
" God's people."

If these words had been used in the Creed: " I believe that there
is a holy Christian people," it would have been easy to avoid all
the misery that has come in with this blind, obscure word
" church "; for the term " Christian, holy people " would have
brought along with it, clearly and powerfully, both understanding
and the judgment on the question " What is and what is not a
church? . . . But because we use this blind word " church " in
the Creed, the common man thinks of the stone house, which we
call a church, and so the painters depict it; or if things turn out
better, they paint the apostles, the disciples, and the Mother of
God, as on Pentecost, with the Holy Ghost hovering over them.
That will pass; but it is only the holy Christian Church of one
time, the beginning. *Ecclesia*, however, ought to mean the holy
Christian people, not only of the time of the apostles, who are long
since dead, but clear to the end of the world, so that there is always
living on earth a Christian, holy people in which Christ lives,
works, and reigns *per redemptionem*, through grace and forgiveness of sins, the Holy Ghost *per vivificationem et sanctificationem*,
through the daily purging out of sins and renewal of life, so that
we do not remain in sin, but can and should lead a new life in good
works of all kinds, such as the Ten Commandments, or Two Tables of Moses, require, and not in the old, wicked works: that is
St. Paul's teaching.

— " *On the Councils and the Churches*," Works of Martin Luther, *Vol. V, pp. 264–266.*

For the sake of brevity and a better understanding, we shall call
the two churches by different names. The first, which is the natural,
essential, real and true one, let us call a spiritual, inner Christendom. The other, which is man-made and external, let us call a
bodily, external Christendom: not as if we would part them asunder, but just as when I speak of a man, and call him, according to
the soul, a spiritual, according to the body, a physical, man; or as
the Apostle is wont to speak of the inner and of the outward man.
Thus also the Christian assembly, according to the soul, is a communion of one accord in one faith, although according to the body

it cannot be assembled at one place, and yet every group is assembled in its own place. This Christendom is ruled by Canon Law and the prelates of the Church. To this belong all the popes, cardinals, bishops, prelates, monks, nuns and all those who in these external things are taken to be Christians, whether they are truly Christians at heart or not. For though membership in this communion does not make true Christians, because all the orders mentioned may exist without faith; nevertheless this communion is never without some who at the same time are true Christians, just as the body does not give the soul its life, and yet the soul lives in the body and, indeed, can live without the body. Those who are without faith and are outside of the first community, but are included in this second community, are dead in the sight of God, hypocrites, and but like wooden images of true Christians.

— *"The Papacy at Rome,"* Works of Martin Luther, *Vol. I, pp. 355 f.*

The external marks, whereby one can perceive where this Church is on earth, are baptism, the Sacrament, and the Gospel.

— *"The Papacy at Rome,"* Works of Martin Luther, *Vol. I, p. 361.*

First. This Christian, holy people is to be known by this, that it has God's Word, though in quite unequal measure, as St. Paul says. Some have it altogether pure, others not entirely pure. Those who have it pure are called those who build on the foundation, gold, silver, precious stones; those who have it impure are they who build hay, straw, wood on the foundation, yet will be saved through fire. . . .

We speak, however, of the external Word orally preached by men like you and me. For Christ left this behind Him as an outward sign whereby His Church, His Christian, holy people in the world, was to be recognized. We speak, too, of this oral Word as it is earnestly believed and publicly confessed before the world, as He says, " He that confesseth me before men, him will I confess before my Father and His angels "; for there are many who know it secretly, but will not confess it. Many have it and do not believe in it or act by it, for those who believe in it and act by it are few, as the parable of the seed, in Matthew xiii, tells us: three parts of the field get it and have it, but only the fourth part, the fine, good field, " bringeth forth fruit with patience."

Wherever, therefore, you hear or see this Word preached, believed, confessed, and acted on, there do not doubt that there must be a true *ecclesia sancta catholica*, a Christian, holy people, even though it be small in numbers; for God's Word does not go away empty (Isaiah lv), but must have at least a fourth part, or a piece of the field. If there were no other mark than this one alone, it would still be enough to show that there must be a Christian church there; for God's Word cannot be present without God's people, and God's people cannot be without God's Word. Who would preach or listen to preaching, if no people of God were there? And what could or would God's people believe, if God's Word were not there? . . .

Second. God's people, or the Christian holy people, is known by the holy Sacrament of Baptism, when it is rightly taught and believed and used according to Christ's ordinance. That, too, is a public sign and precious, holy possession whereby God's people is made holy, for it is a holy bath of regeneration through the Holy Ghost, in which we bathe and are washed by the Holy Ghost from sin and death, as in the innocent, holy blood of the Lamb of God. Where you see this mark, know that the holy Christian people must be there, even though the pope does not baptize you or even if you know nothing about his holiness and power. The little children know nothing about that, though when they grow up they are, sad to say! led astray from their baptism, as St. Peter complains, in II Peter ii, " They entice through lasciviousness those who had escaped and who now walk in error." No, do not be confused by the question of who does the baptizing; for baptism does not belong to the baptizer and is not given to him, but it belongs to him who is baptized, for whom it was established by God and to whom it is given; just as the Word of God does not belong to the preacher (except in so far as he hears and believes it) but to him who hears and believes, and to him it is given.

Third. God's people, or a Christian, holy Church is known by the holy Sacrament of the Altar, when it is rightly administered according to Christ's institution and is believed and received. That, too, is a public mark and precious, holy possession, bequeathed by Christ, whereby His people is made holy. By means of this sacrament it exercises itself in faith, and openly confesses that it is a Christian people, as it does also by means of the Word of God and baptism. Here again you need not ask whether the pope says mass for you or not, consecrates you, confirms or anoints you, or puts a chasuble on you. You can receive the mass with no clothing at all, as one may who is sick in bed, except that outward decency compels the wearing of decent and honorable clothing. Nor do you need to ask whether you have a tonsure or have been anointed; nor need you argue about whether you are man or woman, young or old, any more than you would ask about all these things in connection with baptism or preaching. It is enough that you are consecrated and anointed with the high and holy oil of God, of the Word of God, of baptism, and of this sacrament; then you are anointed highly and gloriously enough and dressed in a sufficient priestly garb. Do not be led astray by the question whether the man who gives you the sacrament is holy. . . . For the sacrament does not belong to him who administers it, but to him to whom it is administered, unless he also takes it. In that case he is one of those who receive it, and it is given to him also.

Where you see this sacrament administered with a right usage, be sure that God's people is there. It was said above about the Word, where God's Word is, there must the Church be; so, also, where Baptism and the Sacrament are, there must God's people be, and vice versa. For these holy things no one has, gives, practices, uses, or confesses, except God's people only, even though some false and unbelieving Christians are secretly among them. These people do not deprive the people of God of its holiness, especially so long as they are present secretly, for open sinners the Church, or people of God, does not tolerate in its midst, but punishes them and makes them holy; or, if they will not suffer that, it casts them out of the holy place by means of the ban and holds them as heathen (Matthew xviii).

Fourth. The people of God, or holy Christians, are known by the keys, which they publicly use. Christ decrees, in Matthew xviii that if a Christian sins, he shall be rebuked, and if he does not amend his ways, he shall be bound and cast out; but if he amends, he shall be set free. This is the power of the keys. Now the use of the keys is two-fold, — public, and private. There are some whose consciences are so weak and timid, that even if they have received no public condemnation, they cannot be comforted unless they get a special absolution from the pastor. On the other hand, there are some who are so hard they will not have their sins individually forgiven and remitted even in their hearts and by the pastor. Therefore the use of the keys must be of both kinds, public and private. Now wherever you see the sins of some persons forgiven or rebuked, publicly or privately, know that God's people is there; for if God's people is not there, the keys are not there; and if the keys are not there, God's people is not there. Christ has bequeathed them as a public mark and holy possession, whereby the Holy Ghost, won through Christ's death, imparts holiness anew to fallen sinners and by them Christians confess that they are a holy people, under Christ, in this world; and those who will not be converted and made holy again are to be cast out of this holy people; that is, they are to be bound and excluded by means of the keys.

Fifth. The Church is known outwardly by the fact that it consecrates or calls ministers, or has offices which they occupy. For we must have bishops, pastors, or preachers, to give, administer and use, publicly and privately, the four things, or precious possessions, that have been mentioned, for the sake of and in the name of the Church, or rather because of their institution by Christ, as St. Paul says, in Ephesians iv, *Accepit dona in hominibus,* " and gave some to be apostles, prophets, evangelists, teachers and governors, etc." The whole group cannot do these things, but must commit them, or allow them to be committed, to someone. What would happen if everyone wanted to speak or administer the sacraments and no one would yield to another? This duty must be committed to one person, and he alone must be allowed to preach, baptize, absolve, and administer the sacraments; all the rest must be content with this and agree to it. Wherever you see this, be assured that God's people, the Christian, holy people, is present.

It is true, indeed, that the Holy Ghost has made exception, in this matter, of women, children, and incompetent folk, and, except in cases of necessity, chooses only qualified males. Thus we read here and there in St. Paul's epistles that a bishop must be apt to teach, pious, and the husband of one wife, and in I Corinthians xiv, that a woman shall not teach in the assembly. In a word, it shall be a well-prepared, selected man, and children, women, and other persons are not qualified for it, though they are qualified to hear God's Word and to receive baptism, the Sacrament, and absolution, and are true, holy fellow-Christians, as St. Peter says. . . .

Sixth. The holy, Christian people is known by prayer and public thanksgiving and praise to God. Where you see and hear that the Lord's Prayer is prayed and the use of it is taught; where Psalms, or spiritual songs, are sung, in accordance with the Word of God and the right faith; when the Creed, the Ten Commandments, and the Catechism are openly used; — there be sure that a holy Christian people is; for prayer, too, is one of the precious holy possessions, whereby everything is made holy, as St. Paul says. Thus the Psalms also are nothing but prayers, in which praise, thanks and honor are rendered to God, and the Creed and Ten Commandments, and God's Word, too, are all holy possessions, whereby the Holy Ghost makes holy the holy people of Christ. We speak, however, of prayers and songs that can be understood, from which it is possible to learn and whereby men may amend their lives. . . .

Seventh. The holy, Christian Church is outwardly known by the holy possession of the Holy Cross. It must endure all hardship and persecution, all kinds of temptation and evil (as the Lord's Prayer says) from devil, world, and flesh; it must be inwardly sad, timid, terrified; outwardly poor, despised, sick, weak; thus it becomes like its head, Christ. The reason must be only this, — that it holds fast to Christ and God's Word and thus suffers for Christ's sake, according to Matthew v, " Blessed are they that endure persecution for my sake." They must be righteous, quiet, obedient, ready to serve their rulers and everyone else with body and wealth, doing no one any harm. But no people on earth must endure such bitter hatred. They must be worse than Jews, heathen, Turks; they must be called heretics, knaves, devils, accursed and the worst people in the world, to the point where they are " doing God service " who hang them, drown them, slay them, torture them, hunt them down, plague them to death, and where no one has pity on them, but gives them myrrh and gall to drink, when they thirst, — not because they are adulterers, murderers, thieves or scoundrels, but because they will to have Christ alone, and no other God. Where you see or hear this, there know that the holy Christian Church is, as He says, in Matthew v, " Blessed are ye, when men curse you and reject your name as an evil, wicked thing for my sake. Be glad and rejoice, for your reward in heaven is great." With this holy possession the Holy Ghost makes this people, not only holy, but blessed. . . .

Beside these seven chief things there are other outward signs whereby the holy Christian Church is known, viz., those whereby the Holy Ghost makes us holy according to the Second Table of Moses, — as when he helps us to honor father and mother from the heart, and helps them to raise their children in a Christian way and to lead honorable lives; when we serve our princes and lords faithfully and obediently and are subject to them, and they, in turn, love their subjects and protect and guard them; when we are angry with no one, bear no wrath, hatred, envy, or vengefulness toward our neighbor, but gladly forgive him, gladly lend to him, help and counsel him; when we are not unchaste, immoderate in drinking, proud, haughty, boastful, but pure, self-controlled, sober, kindly, gentle, and humble; do not steal, rob, take usury, indulge in greed, cheat, but are mild, kind, satisfied, generous; are not false, lying and perjuring, but truthful, reliable, and whatever else is taught in these commandments, all of which St. Paul teaches abundantly in more than one place. For we need the Decalog not only because it tells us in legal fashion what we are bound to do, but also in order that we may see in it how far the Holy Ghost has brought us in His sanctifying work, and how much we still fall short, so that we may not become careless and think that we have now done all that is required. Thus we are constantly to grow in sanctification and ever to become more and more " a new creature " in Christ.

Beside these external marks and holy possessions the Church has still other external customs. It is not made holy by them or through them, either in body or soul; they are not instituted or commanded by God; and yet, as has been said of them at length above, they are of great necessity and usefulness, and are fine and proper. Such customs are the keeping of certain holidays and of certain hours, before or after noon, as times for preaching and prayer, and the use of church buildings, or houses, altars, pulpits, fonts, lights, candles, bells, vestments and the like. . . . Christians can become and remain holy without these things, if the preaching is done on the street, without a pulpit, if sins are forgiven, if the Sacrament is administered without an altar, baptism without a font; and indeed it is of daily occurrence that, because of peculiar circumstances, sermons are preached and baptism and the Sacrament administered in homes. But for the sake of the children and the simple folk, it is a fine thing and promotes good order to have a definite time, place, and hour for these things, so that people can adapt themselves and meet together, as St. Paul says, in I Corinthians xiv, "Let all be done in fine order." This order no one ought, and no Christian does, despise without cause, out of mere pride, and only for the sake of creating disorder; but for the sake of the multitude everyone ought to join in observing it, or at least not disturb or hinder it. That would be to act against love and kindness.

Nevertheless, these things ought to remain free. If from necessity, or for some other good reason, we cannot preach at six or seven or twelve or one o'clock, on Sunday or Monday, in the choir or at St. Peter's, then let the preaching be done at other hours, on other days, in other places, so long as the common people are not disturbed by such a change, but are carried along in it. For these things are entirely external and, so far as times and places and persons are concerned, they can be regulated altogether by reason and are completely subject to it. God, Christ, and the Holy Ghost ask no questions about these things, any more than they ask about what or where we eat, drink, dress, live, marry, go, or stay; except as has been said, that no one ought, without good reason, to take these matters into his own hands and disturb or hinder the common people. At a wedding or other social gathering no one ought to annoy the bride or the rest of the guests by peculiar or disturbing conduct, but rather behave as the rest do, and sit and walk and stand and dance and eat and drink with them. It is not possible to place a special table, kitchen, cellar, and servant at every individual's disposal. If one needs anything, let him get up from the table and leave the others to sit there in peace. So in these matters, too, everything should be done peacefully and in order and yet it should all be free and subject to change, if times and persons or other circumstances demand; then the crowd follows along harmoniously. For, as has been said, these things make no Christian either more holy or more unholy.

— " *On the Councils and the Churches*," Works of Martin Luther, *Vol. V, pp. 270–296.*

One of the wickedest offenses possible to commit against the Church is the stirring up of doctrinal discord and division, a thing the devil encourages to the utmost. This sin usually has its rise with certain haughty, conceited, self-seeking leaders who desire peculiar distinction for themselves and strive for personal honor and glory. They harmonize with none and would think themselves disgraced were they not honored as superior and more learned individuals than their fellows, a distinction they do not merit. They will give honor to no one, even when they have to recognize the superiority of his gifts over their own. In their envy, anger, hatred and vengefulness, they seek occasion to create factions and to draw people to themselves. Wherefore Paul exhorts first to the necessary virtue of love, having which men will be enabled to exercise humility, patience and forbearance toward one another. . . .

Unity of the Church does not consist in similarity of outward form of government, likeness of Law, tradition and ecclesiastical customs, as the Pope and his followers claim. They would exclude from the Church all not obedient to them in these outward things, though members of the one faith, one baptism, and so on. The Church is termed " one holy, catholic or Christian Church," because it represents one plain, pure Gospel doctrine, and an outward confession thereof, always and everywhere, regardless of dissimilarity of physical life, or of outward ordinances, customs and ceremonies.

But they are not members of the true Church of Christ who, instead of preserving unity of doctrine and oneness of Christian faith, cause divisions and offenses — as Paul says (Rom. 16:17) — by the human doctrines and self-appointed works for which they contend, imposing them upon all Christians as necessary. They are perverters and destroyers of the Church, as we have elsewhere frequently shown. The consolation of the true doctrine is ours, and we hold it in opposition to Popedom, which accuses us of having withdrawn from them, and so condemns us as apostates from the Church. They are, however, themselves the real apostates, persecuting the truth and destroying the unity of the Spirit under the name and title of the Church and of Christ. Therefore, according to the command of God, all men are under obligation to shun them and withdraw from them.

— *Epistle Sermon, Seventeenth Sunday After Trinity* (Lenker Edition, *Vol. IX, #18–24*).

The world at the present time is sagaciously discussing how to quell the controversy and strife over doctrine and faith, and how to effect a compromise between the Church and the Papacy. Let the learned, the wise, it is said, bishops, emperor and princes, arbitrate. Each side can easily yield something, and it is better to concede some things which can be construed according to individual interpretation, than that so much persecution, bloodshed, war, and terrible, endless dissension and destruction be permitted. Here is lack of understanding, for understanding proves by the Word that such patchwork is not according to God's will, but that doctrine, faith and worship must be preserved pure and unadulterated; there must be no mingling with human nonsense, human opinions or wisdom. The Scriptures give us this rule: " We must obey God rather than men." Acts 5:29.

We must not, then, regard nor follow the counsels of human wisdom, but must keep ever before us God's will as revealed by his Word; we are to abide by that for death or life, for evil or good. If war or other calamity results complain to him who wills and commands us to teach and believe our doctrine. The calamity is not of our effecting; we have not originated it. And we are not required to prove by argument whether or no God's will is right and to be obeyed. If he wills to permit persecution and other evils to arise in consequence of our teaching, for the trial and experience of true Christians and for the punishment of the ungrateful, let them come; and if not, his hand is doubtless strong enough to defend and preserve his cause from destruction, that man may know the events to be of his ordering. And so, praise his name, he has done in our case. He has supported us against the strong desires of our adversaries. Had we yielded and obeyed them, we would have been drawn into their falsehood and destruction. And God will still support us if we deal uprightly and faithfully in these requirements, if we further and honor the Word of God, and be not unthankful nor seek things that counterfeit God's Word.

— *Epistle Sermon, Twenty-fourth Sunday After Trinity* (Lenker Edition, *Vol. IX, #26–27*).

I ask that men make no reference to my name, and call themselves not Lutherans, but Christians. What is Luther? My doctrine, I am sure, is not mine, nor have I been crucified for any one. St. Paul, in I Corinthians iii, would not allow Christians to call themselves Pauline or Petrine, but Christian. How then should I, poor, foul carcase that I am, come to have men give to the children of Christ a name derived from my worthless name? No, no, my dear friends; let us abolish all party names, and call ourselves Christians after Him Whose doctrine we have.

— *" An Earnest Exhortation for All Christians, Warning Them Against Insurrection and Rebellion,"* Works of Martin Luther, *Vol. III, p. 218.*

2. THE MINISTRY OF THE CHURCH

Where God's word is purely taught, there is also the upright and true church; for the true church is supported by the Holy Ghost, not by succession of inheritance. It does not follow, though St. Peter had been bishop at Rome, and at the same time Christian communion had been at Rome, that, therefore, the pope and the Romish church are true; for if that should be of value or conclusive, then they must needs confess that Caiaphas, Annas, and the Sadducees were also the true church; for they boasted that they were descended from Aaron.

— Table-Talk, *#CCCLXIX.*

Christ says to St. Peter, Matthew xvi: " Thou art, or art called, Peter; and on the *Petram* (i.e., on the rock) I will build My Church. And I will give unto thee the keys of the kingdom of heaven, and whatsoever thou shalt bind on earth, shall be bound in heaven, and

whatsoever thou shalt loose on earth, shall be loosed in heaven."
From these words they [i.e., the papists] have claimed the keys for
St. Peter alone; but the same Matthew has barred such erroneous
interpretation in the xviii. chapter, where Christ says to all in common, " Verily, I say unto you, whatsoever ye shall bind on earth,
shall be bound in heaven, and whatsoever ye shall loose on earth,
shall be loosed in heaven." It is clear that Christ here interprets
His own words, and in this xviii. chapter explains the former xvi.;
namely, that the keys are given to St. Peter in the stead of the whole
Church, and not for his own person. Thus also John, in the last
chapter, " He breathed on them and said, Receive ye the Holy
Ghost; whosesoever sins you remit, they are remitted unto them,
and whosesoever sins ye retain, they are retained." To maintain
the sole authority of St. Peter, when there are two texts against one,
many men have labored in vain. But the Gospel is too clear, and
they have had to admit until now that in the first passage nothing
special was given to St. Peter for his own person.

Thus it was also understood by many of the ancient Church fathers. It is likewise proved by the words of Christ just before He
gave the keys to St. Peter, where He asks not Peter only, but all of
them: " What think ye of Me? " Then Peter answers for them all,
" Thou art Christ, the Son of the living God." Therefore the words
in Matthew xvi. must be understood in accordance with the words
in chapter xviii. and in John xx, and one passage must not be explained in a manner contrary to two strong ones, but the one be
properly explained by the two. The proof is all the stronger where
there are two instead of only one, and it is but fair that one should
follow the two, and not two the one.

— " *The Papacy at Rome*," Works of Martin Luther, *Vol. I, pp.
373 f.*

The chief cause that I fell out with the pope was this: the pope
boasted that he was the head of the church, and condemned all that
would not be under his power and authority; for he said, although
Christ be the Head of the church, yet, notwithstanding, there must
be a corporal head of the church upon earth. With this I could have
been content, had he but taught the Gospel pure and clear, and not
introduced human inventions and lies in its stead. Further, he took

upon him power, rule, and authority over the Christian church, and over the Holy Scriptures, the Word of God; no man must presume to expound the Scriptures, but only he, and according to his ridiculous conceits; so that he made himself lord over the church, proclaiming her at the same time a powerful mother, and empress over the Scriptures, to which we must yield and be obedient; this was not to be endured. They who, against God's Word, boast of the church's authority, are mere idiots. The pope attributes more power to the church, which is begotten and born, than to the Word, which has begotten, conceived, and borne the church.

We, through God's grace, are not heretics, but schismatics, causing, indeed, separation and division, wherein we are not to blame, but our adversaries, who gave occasion thereto, because they remain not by God's Word alone, which we have, hear, and follow.
— Table-Talk, *#CCCCLIII.*

As many of us as have been baptised are all priests without distinction. . . . For thus it is written in I Peter ii, " Ye are a chosen generation, a royal priesthood, and a priestly kingdom." Therefore we are all priests, as many of us as are Christians. But the priests, as we call them, are ministers chosen from among us, who do all that they do in our name. And the priesthood is nothing but a ministry, as we learn from I Corinthians iv, " Let a man so account of us as of the ministers of Christ, and the dispensers of the mysteries of God."
— *" The Babylonian Captivity of the Church,"* Works of Martin Luther, *Vol. II, p. 279.*

Priests, bishops or popes — are neither different from other Christians nor superior to them, except that they are charged with the administration of the Word of God and the sacraments, which is their work and office.
— *" An Open Letter to the Christian Nobility,"* Works of Martin Luther, *Vol. II, p. 69.*

Let every one, therefore, who knows himself to be a Christian be assured of this, and apply it to himself, — that we are all priests, and there is no difference between us; that is to say, we have the same power in respect to the Word and all the sacraments. However, no one may make use of this power except by the consent of the community or by the call of a superior. For what is the common property of all, no individual may arrogate to himself, unless he be called. . . . The priesthood is properly nothing but the ministry of the Word, mark you, of the Word — not of the law, but of the Gospel. And the diaconate is not the ministry of reading the Gospel or the Epistle, as is the present practice, but the ministry of distributing the Church's alms to the poor, so that the priests may be relieved of the burden of temporal matters and may give themselves more freely to prayer and the Word. For this was the purpose of the institution of the diaconate, as we read in Acts vi. Whoever, therefore, does not know or preach the Gospel, is not only not a priest or bishop, but he is a plague of the Church, who under the false title of priest or bishop — in sheep's clothing, forsooth — oppresses the Gospel and plays the wolf in the Church.

— "*The Babylonian Captivity of the Church,*" Works of Martin Luther, *Vol. II, pp. 282 f.*

The Scriptures make us all priests alike, as I have said, but the churchy priesthood which is now universally distinguished from the laity and alone called a priesthood, in the Scriptures is called *ministerium, servitus, dispensatio, episcopatus, presbyterium,* and at no place *sacerdotium* or *spiritualis.* I must translate that. The Scriptures, I say, call the spiritual estate and priestly office a ministry, a service, an office, an eldership, a fostering, a guardianship, a preaching office, shepherds. We shall proceed to prove this thoroughly. St. Paul says to Timothy: " The servant of the Lord must not strive." He calls Timothy a servant of God whose special duty it is to preach and be a spiritual leader of the people. Again, II Corinthians xii: " Are they ministers of Christ? So am I." And I Corinthians iv: " Let a man so account of us, as of ministers of Christ and stewards of the mysteries of God." Christ also, in Matthew xxiv, speaks at length about these stewards.

The word " priest " has come from the Greek, in which *presbyteros* means what *senior* means in Latin and *elder* in our own tongue, because in olden times the spiritual authority was always vested in the elder persons, just as a city's councilors derive their

Latin name *Senatus* from their age. Young people never made good rulers. So " priest " is a title indicating age and not rank, it does not make a man spiritual or a minister. St. Peter says, I Peter v: " I who am an elder, exhort you, my fellow-elders, to feed the flock of Christ which is among you." Again, where he says, " Ye younger, submit yourselves unto the elder," we, on account of our perverted use of words, would be compelled to say, " unto priests or spirituals."

Bishop is also derived from the Greek, where he is called *episcopus*, corresponding to the Latin *speculator*, and our own " watchman on his look-out," just as we speak of a towerman in the watchtower, who keeps watch over the city to guard against harm by fire or foe. This means that every minister or spiritual ruler should be a bishop, i.e., an overseer, one who keeps watch and sees to it that in his city and among his people the Gospel and faith in Christ may be established and may be defended against all foes, be they devil or heresy. Thus St. Luke says in Acts xx: " Paul called the priests of the church," that is, the elders of the Christians in Ephesus, " and said unto them, Take heed unto yourselves and to all the flock, the sheep of Christ, over which the Holy Ghost hath made you bishops, to feed the church of God, which he hath purchased with his own blood." Here it is clear that the elders were called bishops, that is to say, overseers of the church of God, that is to say, of the Christians, who are God's people. . . . " Priest " and " bishop " are used interchangeably in the Scriptures, as, for instance, by St. Paul in Titus i: " Thou shouldest appoint priests in every city " (that is, an elder over them), and soon after he speaks of this priest in this wise: " A bishop must be blameless," and clearly calls the same man priest, bishop, elder, and watchman. That we now have bishops, rectors, priests, chaplains, canons, monks, and other similar titles signifying a difference in office, should not surprise us; it has all come from our habit of so interpreting Scripture that not a word of it retains its true meaning. Therefore God and His Scriptures know nothing of bishops as we now have them. These things are all a result of man-made laws and ordinances, and through long usage have taken such hold on us that we imagine the spiritual estate is founded on the Scriptures, although it is twice as worldly as the world itself, because it calls itself and pretends to be spiritual, but there is no truth in its claim.

I called this priesthood churchy because it grew out of the church's organization and is not founded in the Scriptures. For it was the custom years ago, and ought to be yet, that in every Christian community, since all were spiritual priests, one, the oldest or most learned and most pious, was elected to be their servant, officer, guardian, watchman, in the Gospel and the sacraments, even as the mayor of a city is elected from the whole body of its citizens. If tonsures, consecrations, ointments, vestments made priests and bishops, then Christ and His apostles were never priests or bishops.

— " *Answer to the Superchristian, Superspiritual, and Superlearned Book of Goat Emser*," Works of Martin Luther, *Vol. III, pp. 321–324.*

A true pastor . . . serves men in body and soul, in property and honor. See now how he serves God and what a glorious sacrifice, or service, he renders; for by his work and his word the kingdom of God is maintained in the world; so, too, are kept the Name and the honor and the glory of God, the true knowledge of God, the right faith and understanding of Christ, the fruits of the suffering and blood and death of Christ, the gifts and works and power of the Holy Spirit, the true and saving use of baptism and the Sacrament, the right and pure doctrine of the Gospel, the right way of disciplining and crucifying the body. Who could ever give high enough praise to any one of these things? What more can be said about them? The more one does with these things, the more he carries on the battle against the devil, the world's wisdom, and the imaginations of the flesh; the more victories he wins; the more he puts down error and prevents heresy. For he must strive and fight against the gates of hell and overcome the devil. He does it, too; and yet not he, but his work and his word. These are the innumerable and unspeakable works and miracles of the preaching-office. In a word, if one would praise God to the uttermost, one must praise His Word and the preaching of it; for it is God's Word, and the preaching of it is His.

— " *A Sermon on Keeping Children in School*," Works of Martin Luther, *Vol. IV, pp. 149 f.*

In all ages of the Church two things have done and are doing great harm, namely, poverty and riches. For in the first place, we see the apostles and true bishops and preachers in such straitened circumstances, that no one gave them anything and they themselves were not able to acquire anything; hence everybody felt shy of such an office and no one wished to enter it. In the second place, when the church became extremely wealthy through great endowments and stipends and sat in all luxury, the ministers themselves neglected the office of preaching and the care of souls, and themselves became lords.

Just so it is also at present: Where true pastors and preachers are so poorly supported that no one donates anything to them, and moreover what they have is snatched out of their mouths by a shameless and unthankful world, by princes, noblemen, townsmen and farmers, so that they with their poor wives and children must suffer need, and when they die leave behind them pitiable, rejected widows and orphans. By this very many good-hearted and very clever people are more and more discouraged from becoming pastors and preachers. For all arts, trades and callings in life serve to the end that we may through them fortify ourselves against hunger and poverty; but with the office of the ministry the contrary is the case, whoever will perform its duties faithfully, must expose himself to danger and poverty.

From this then will follow the ruin of the Church, in that the parishes will stand vacant, the pulpits be neglected and again preachers arrive who seek not faithfully God's Word nor the kingdom of Christ; but who think, as they preach, what the people will gladly hear, so that they may continue in that direction and again become rich; and in this manner things will again go to ruin.

— *Gospel Sermon, Seventh Sunday After Trinity* (Lenker Edition, *Vol. XIII, #4–6*).

Young people must be brought up to learn the Holy Scriptures; when such of them as know they are designed for the ministry present themselves and offer their service, upon a parish falling void, they do not intrude themselves, but are as a maid who, being arrived at woman's estate, when one makes suit to marry her, may do it, with a good and safe conscience towards God and the world. To thrust out another is to intrude; but when in the church a place is void, and thou sayest: I will willingly supply it, if ye please to make use of me; then thou art received, it is a true vocation and calling. Such was the manner of Isaiah, who said: " Here I am; send me." He came of himself when he heard they stood in need of a preacher; and so it ought to be; we must look whether people have need of us or no, and then whether we be desired or called.

— Table-Talk, #CCCXCI.

3. THE WORSHIP OF THE CHURCH

The word, to worship, means to stoop and bow down the body with external gestures; to serve in the work. But to worship God in spirit is the service and honor of the heart; it comprehends faith and fear in God. The worshipping of God is two-fold, outward and inward — that is, to acknowledge God's benefits, and to be thankful unto him.

— Table-Talk, #DCCVIII.

To praise the Lord with gladness is not a work of man; it is rather a joyful suffering, and the work of God alone. It cannot be taught in words, but must be learned in one's own experience. Even as David says, in Psalm xxxiv, " O taste and see that the Lord is sweet: blessed is the man that trusteth in Him." He puts tasting before seeing, because this sweetness cannot be known unless one has experienced and felt it for oneself; and no one can attain to such experience unless he trusts in God with his whole heart, when he is in the depths and in sore straits. Therefore David makes haste to add, " Blessed is the man that trusteth in God." Such a one will experience the work of God within himself, and will thus come to feel His sweetness, and thereby attain to all knowledge and understanding.

— " *The Magnificat,*" Works of Martin Luther, *Vol. III, pp. 131 f.*

Even if different people make use of different rites, let no one either judge or despise the other; but let each one abound in his own opinion, and let them understand and know even if they do differently; and let each one's rite be agreeable to the other, lest diverse opinions and sects yield diverse uses, just as happened in the Roman Church. For external rites, even if we are not able to do without them, — just as we cannot do without food and drink, — nevertheless, do not commend us to God, just as food does not commend us to God. But faith and love commend us to God. Wherefore let this word of Paul govern here: The kingdom of God is not food and drink, but righteousness, peace and joy in the Holy Spirit. Thus no rite is the Kingdom of God, but faith within you, etc.

— " *Formula of Mass and Communion for the Church at Wittenberg*," Works of Martin Luther, *Vol. VI, pp. 92 f.*

It would also be a good thing if there were fewer saint's days, since in our times the works done on them are for the greater part worse than those of the work days, what with loafing, gluttony, and drunkenness, gambling and other evil deeds; and then, the mass and the sermon are listened to without edification, the prayer is spoken without faith. It almost happens that men think it is sufficient that we look on at the mass with our eyes, hear the preaching with our ears, and say the prayers with our mouths. It is all so formal and superficial! We do not think that we might receive something out of the mass into our hearts, learn and remember something out of the preaching, seek, desire and expect something in our prayer.

— " *Treatise on Good Works*," Works of Martin Luther, *Vol. I,* p. 222.

Ceremonies are to be given the same place in the life of a Christian as models and plans have among builders and artisans. They are prepared not as permanent structures, but because without them nothing could be built or made. When the structure is completed they are laid aside. You see, they are not despised, rather, they are greatly sought after; but what we despise is the false estimate of them, since no one holds them to be the real and permanent structure. If any man were so egregiously foolish as to care for nothing all his life long except the most costly, careful and persistent preparation of plans and models, and never to think of the structure itself, and were satisfied with his work in producing such plans and mere aids to work, and boasted of it, would not all men pity his insanity, and estimate that with what he has wasted something great might have been built?

— " *A Treatise on Christian Liberty*," Works of Martin Luther, *Vol. II, p. 347.*

It is not now, nor has it ever been, in our mind to abolish entirely the whole formal cultus of God, but to cleanse that which is in use, which has been vitiated by most abominable additions, and to point out a pious use. For this cannot be denied, that masses and the communion of bread and wine are a rite divinely instituted by Christ, which was observed, first under Christ Himself, then under the apostles, most simply and piously and without any additions. But so many human inventions have been added to it in course of time, that nothing of the mass and communion has come down to our age except the name.

— " *Formula of Mass and Communion for the Church at Wittenberg*," Works of Martin Luther, *Vol. VI, pp. 84 f.*

Christ . . . teaches us, in Matthew vi, not to speak much when we pray, as the Gentiles do, for they think that they shall be heard for their much speaking. Even so there is to-day in the churches a great ringing of bells, blowing of trumpets, singing, shouting, and intoning, yet I fear precious little worship of God, Who would be worshiped in spirit and in truth, as He says in John iv.

Solomon says, in Proverbs xxvii, " He that blesseth his friend with a loud voice, rising early in the morning, it shall be counted a curse to him." For such a one awakens the suspicion that he is endeavoring to adorn an evil cause; he protests too much and only defeats his own end. On the other hand, he that curses his neighbor with a loud voice, rising up early in the morning (that is, not indifferently, but with great zeal and urgency), is to be regarded as a praiser of him. For men do not believe him, but deem him impelled by hatred and a wicked heart; he hurts his own cause and helps his neighbor's. In the same way, to think to worship God with many words and a great noise, is to count Him either deaf or ignorant, and to suppose we must waken or instruct Him. Such an

opinion of God tends to His shame and dishonor rather than to
His worship.

— " *The Magnificat*," Works of Martin Luther, *Vol. III, p. 160.*

Common prayer is precious and the most powerful, and it is for
its sake that we come together. For this reason also the Church is
called a House of Prayer, because in it we are as a congregation
with one accord to consider our need and the needs of all men,
present them before God, and call upon Him for mercy. But this
must be done with heart-felt emotion and sincerity, so that we feel
in our hearts the need of all men, and that we pray with true sympathy for them, in true faith and confidence. Where such prayers
are not made in the mass, it were better to omit the mass. For
what sense is there in our coming together into a House of Prayer,
which coming together shows that we should make common prayer
and petition for the entire congregation, if we scatter these prayers,
and so distribute them that everyone prays only for himself, and
no one has regard for the other, nor concerns himself for another's
need? How can that prayer be of help, good, acceptable and a
common prayer, or a work of the Holy Day and of the assembled
congregation, which they make who make their own petty prayers,
one for this, the other for that, and have nothing but self-seeking,
selfish prayers, which God hates? . . .

The Christian Church on earth has no greater power or work
than such common prayer against everything that may oppose it.
This the evil spirit knows well, and therefore he does all that he
can to prevent such prayer. Gleefully he lets us go on building
churches, endowing many monastic houses, making music, reading,
singing, observing many masses, and multiplying ceremonies beyond all measure. This does not grieve him, nay, he helps us do
it, that we may consider such things the very best, and think that
thereby we have done our whole duty. But in that meanwhile this
common, effectual and fruitful prayer perishes and its omission is
unnoticed because of such display, in this he has what he seeks. For
when prayer languishes, no one will take anything from him, and
no one will withstand him. But if he noticed that we wished to prac-
tise this prayer, even if it were under a straw roof or in a pig-sty,

he would indeed not endure it, but would fear such a pig-sty far more than all the high, big and beautiful churches, towers and bells in existence, if such prayer be not in them. It is indeed not a question of the places and buildings in which we assemble, but only of this unconquerable prayer, that we pray it and bring it before God as a truly common prayer. . . .

We should do as they do who wish to ask a favor of great princes. These do not plan merely to babble a certain number of words, for the prince would think they mocked him, or were insane; but they put their request very plainly, and present their need earnestly, and then leave it to his mercy, in good confidence that he will grant it. So we must deal with God of definite things, namely, mention some present need, commend it to His mercy and goodwill, and not doubt that it is heard; for He has promised to hear such prayer, which no earthly lord has done.

— "*Treatise on Good Works*," Works of Martin Luther, *Vol. I, pp. 233–237.*

I am not of the opinion that all arts are to be cast down and destroyed on account of the Gospel, as some fanatics protest; on the other hand I would gladly see all arts, especially music, in the service of Him who has given and created them.

— "*Spiritual Hymn Booklet*," Works of Martin Luther, *Vol. VI, p. 284.*

That the singing of spiritual hymns is a goodly thing and pleasing to God, I do not think is hidden from any Christian, since everyone is aware not only of the example of the kings and prophets in the Old Testament, (who praised God with singing and playing, with poesy and all manner of string music), but also of the universality of this custom in Christendom from the beginning, especially psalm singing. Indeed, St. Paul also instituted this in I Corinthians 14:15, and exhorted the Colossians (3:16) to sing spiritual songs and psalms heartily unto the Lord in order that God's Word and Christian teaching might be propagated by this means and practiced in every way.

— "*Spiritual Hymn Booklet*," Works of Martin Luther, *Vol. VI, p. 283.*

I always loved music; whoso has skill in this art, is of a good temperament, fitted for all things. We must teach music in schools; a schoolmaster ought to have skill in music, or I would not regard him; neither should we ordain young men as preachers, unless they have been well exercised in music.
— Table-Talk, #DCCXCIV.

Music is a noble gift of God, next to theology. I would not change my little knowledge of music for a great deal.
— Conversations with Luther, p. 99.

4. THE PREACHING OF THE CHURCH

A minister of Christ is a steward in the mysteries of God. He should regard himself and insist that others regard him as one who administers to the household of God nothing but Christ and the things of Christ. In other words, he should preach the pure Gospel, the true faith, that Christ alone is our life, our way, our wisdom, power, glory, salvation; and that all we can accomplish of ourselves is but death, error, foolishness, weakness, shame and condemnation. Whosoever preaches otherwise should be regarded by none as a servant of Christ or a steward of the divine treasurer; he should be avoided as a messenger of the devil.
— *Epistle Sermon, Third Sunday in Advent* (Lenker Edition, *Vol. VII, #23*).

To speak deliberately and slowly best becomes a preacher; for thereby he may the more effectually and impressively deliver his sermon. Seneca writes of Cicero, that he spake deliberately from the heart.
— Table-Talk, #CCCCV.

Let him take care to keep to the text and attend to what is before him and make people understand that. Those preachers who say whatever comes into their mouths remind me of a maid going to market. When she meets another maid she stops and chats a while, then she meets another and talks with her, too, and then a third and a fourth, and so gets to market very slowly. So with preachers who wander off the text; they would like to say every-thing at one time, but they can't.

— Conversations with Luther, *p. 189.*

We ought to direct ourselves in preaching according to the con-dition of the hearers, but most preachers commonly fail herein; they preach that which little edifies the poor simple people. To preach plain and simply is a great art: Christ himself talks of till-ing ground, of mustard-seed, &c.; he used altogether homely and simple similitudes.

— Table-Talk, *#CCCCVII.*

Young divines ought to study Hebrew, to the end they may be able to compare Greek and Hebrew words together, and discern their properties, nature and strength.

— Table-Talk, *#CCCCXXV.*

Though the faith and the Gospel may be proclaimed by simple preachers without the languages, such preaching is flat and tame, men grow at last wearied and disgusted and it falls to the ground. But when the preacher is versed in the languages, his discourse has freshness and force, the whole of Scripture is treated, and faith finds itself constantly renewed by a continual variety of words and works.

— *"To the Councilmen of All Cities in Germany That They Es-tablish and Maintain Christian Schools,"* Works of Martin Luther, *Vol. IV, p. 119.*

I would not have preachers in their sermons use Hebrew, Greek, or foreign languages, for in the church we ought to speak as we use to do at home, the plain mother tongue, which every one is acquainted with. It may be allowed in courtiers, lawyers, advo-cates, &c., to use quaint, curious words. Doctor Staupitz is a very learned man, yet he is a very irksome preacher; and the people had rather hear a plain brother preach, that delivers his words simply to their understanding, than he. In churches no praising or extolling should be sought after. St. Paul never used such high and stately words as Demosthenes and Cicero did, but he spake, properly and plainly, words which signified and showed high and stately matters, and he did well.

— Table-Talk, #*CCCCIX*.

Preaching is twofold in character: it may teach or it may incite and exhort.

— *Epistle Sermon, First Sunday in Advent* (Lenker Edition, *Vol. VII*, #22).

A bee is a small animal which makes sweet honey, but which nevertheless can sting. So a preacher has the sweetest consolations, yet when aroused to anger he can say biting and stinging things.

— Conversations with Luther, *p. 196.*

A preacher should be a logician and a rhetorician, that is, he must be able to teach, and to admonish; when he preaches touching an article, he must, first, distinguish it. Secondly, he must define, describe, and show what it is. Thirdly, he must produce sentences out of the Scriptures, therewith to prove and strengthen it. Fourthly, he must, with examples, explain and declare it. Fifthly, he must adorn it with similitudes; and, lastly, he must admonish and rouse up the lazy, earnestly reprove all the disobedient, all false doctrine, and the authors thereof; yet, not out of malice and envy, but only to God's honor, and the profit and saving health of the people.

— Table-Talk, #*CCCCXIX*.

A good preacher should have these properties and virtues: first, to teach systematically; secondly, he should have a ready wit; thirdly, he should be eloquent; fourthly, he should have a good voice; fifthly, a good memory; sixthly, he should know when to make an end; seventhly, he should be sure of his doctrine; eighthly, he should venture and engage body and blood, wealth and honor, in the Word; ninthly, he should suffer himself to be mocked and jeered of every one.

— Table-Talk, #*CCCXCVII*.

To me a long sermon is an abomination, for the desire of the audience to listen is destroyed, and the preacher only defeats himself.
— Conversations with Luther, *p. 188.*

It is best not to preach long sermons, and to speak simply and like a child. . . . Preaching is meant for the children! In the school one may be learned. Christ had an extremely simple way of talking, and still he was eloquence itself. The prophets, to be sure, are not very rhetorical, but they are much more difficult. Therefore simple speech is the best and truest eloquence. When Mörlin, Medler or Jacob preaches, it is just as when the plug is drawn from a full cask; the liquid runs out as long as there is any left within. But such volubility of tongue doesn't really lay hold of the audience, though it delights some, nor is it even instructive. It is better to speak distinctly, so that what is said may be comprehended.
— Conversations with Luther, *pp. 195 f.*

These are the three things, it is commonly said, that mark a good preacher; first, that he take his place; secondly, that he open his mouth and say something; thirdly, that he know when to stop.
— Commentary on Sermon on the Mount, *p. 13.*

Preaching is often a trial to me, for I think: " Suppose you turn some creature the wrong way, then you are really guilty of his damnation." Such a fear has often kept me in hell itself until God brought me back.
— Conversations with Luther, *p. 158.*

It is not in my power to fashion the hearts of men as the potter moulds the clay, and to do with them as I please. I can get no farther than to men's ears; their hearts I cannot reach. And since I cannot pour faith into their hearts, I cannot, nor should I, force any one to have faith. That is God's work alone, who causes faith to live in the heart. Therefore we should give free course to the Word, and not add our works to it. We have the *jus verbi,*[1] but not

---

[1] Right to speak.

the *executio;* [2] we should preach the Word, but the consequences must be left to God's own good pleasure.
— "*The Eight Wittenberg Sermons,*" Works of Martin Luther, *Vol. II, pp. 397 f.*

When you are going to preach, first pray and say: " Dear Lord, I would preach for thy honor; though I can do nothing good of myself, do thou make it good." Don't think about Melanchthon or Bugenhagen or me or any learned man, and don't try to be learned in the pulpit. I have never been troubled because I could not preach well, but I am overawed to think that I have to preach before God's face and speak of his infinite majesty and divine being. Therefore be strong and pray.
— Conversations with Luther, *p. 191.*

Truth is mightier than eloquence; the Spirit stronger than genius; faith greater than learning; and, as Paul says (I Cor. 1:25), " The foolishness of God is wiser than men." The eloquent Cicero was often beaten in the courts by less eloquent men; Julian (of Eclanum) was more eloquent than Augustine. In a word, truth conquers lying eloquence even though it only stammers, as it is written (Psalm 8:2), " Out of the mouths of babes and sucklings hast thou perfected strength, to destroy the enemy and the avenger."
— Luther's Correspondence, *Vol. II, #549, p. 124.*

It is not enough nor is it Christian, to preach the works, life and words of Christ as historical facts, as if the knowledge of these would suffice for the conduct of life, although this is the fashion of those who must to-day be regarded as our best preachers; and far less is it enough or Christian to say nothing at all about Christ and to teach instead the laws of men and the decrees of the Fathers. And now there are not a few who preach Christ and read about Him that they may move men's affections to sympathy with Christ, to anger against the Jews and such like childish and womanish nonsense. Rather ought Christ to be preached to the end that faith in Him may be established, that He may not only be Christ, but

---

[2] Power to do.

be Christ for thee and for me, and that what is said of Him and what His Name denotes may be effectual in us. And such faith is produced and preserved in us by preaching why Christ came, what He brought and bestowed, what benefit it is to us to accept Him.

— "*A Treatise on Christian Liberty*," Works of Martin Luther, *Vol. II, pp. 326 f.*

5. THE COUNCILS OF THE CHURCH

The Church has no power to make new divine promises, as some prate, who hold that what is decreed by the Church is of no less authority than what is decreed by God, since the Church is under the guidance of the Holy Spirit. But the Church owes its life to the word of promise through faith, and is nourished and preserved by this same word. That is to say, the promises of God make the Church, not the Church the promise of God. For the Word of God is incomparably superior to the Church, and in this Word the Church, being a creature, has nothing to decree, ordain or make, but only to be decreed, ordained and made. For who begets his own parent? Who first brings forth his own maker? This one thing indeed the Church can do — it can distinguish the Word of God from the words of men; as Augustine confesses that he believed the Gospel, moved thereto by the authority of the Church, which proclaimed, this is the Gospel. Not that the Church is, therefore, above the Gospel; if that were true, she would also be above God, in Whom we believe because she proclaims that He is God. But, as Augustine elsewhere says, the truth itself lays hold on the soul and thus renders it able to judge most certainly of all things; but the truth it cannot judge, but is forced to say with unerring certainty that it is the truth. For example, our reason declares with unerring certainty that three and seven are ten, and yet it cannot give a reason why this is true, although it cannot deny that it is true; it is taken captive by the truth and does not so much judge the truth as it is judged by the truth. Thus it is also with the mind of the Church, when under the enlightenment of the Spirit she judges and approves doctrines; she is unable to prove it, and yet is most certain of having it. For as in philosophy no one judges general conceptions, but all are judged by them, so it is in the Church with the mind of the Spirit, that judgeth all things and is judged by none, as the Apostle says.

Who knows which is the Church that has the Spirit? since when such decisions are made there are usually only a few bishops or scholars present; it is possible that these may not be really of the Church, and that all may err, as councils have repeatedly erred, particularly the Council of Constance,[3] which fell into the most wicked error of all. Only that which has the approval of the Church universal, and not of the Roman church alone, rests on a trustworthy foundation.

— "*The Babylonian Captivity of the Church*," Works of Martin Luther, *Vol. II, pp. 273–275.*

Councils ought not to appoint or establish any thing new, for they should know that they are not assembled for that purpose, but to defend the old faith against new teachers; though, to be sure, they may put new persons in old offices (but then persons cannot be called articles of faith or good works, since they are uncertain, mortal men), and this has to be done outside the councils, in the churches, more than in the councils; nay, it must be done every day.

— "*On the Councils and the Churches*," Works of Martin Luther, *Vol. V, p. 212.*

What is a council, or what is its work? If it is not to set up new articles of faith, then all the world has heretofore been wretchedly deceived, for it knows nothing else and holds nothing else except that what a council decides is an article of faith, or at least a work necessary to salvation, so that he who does not keep the council's decree can never be saved, because he is disobedient to the Holy Ghost, the council's Master. Ah, well! I think that my conscience is clear, and no council, as I said above, has power to establish new articles of faith, because the four chief councils did not do so. Therefore I shall here speak my opinion and answer the main question as follows.

First. A council has no power to establish new articles of faith, despite the fact that the Holy Ghost is in it; for even the Apostolic

---

[3] The council that condemned and burned John Hus (1414–1418).

Council at Jerusalem (Acts xvi) established nothing new in the way of faith, but only St. Peter's conclusion, viz., that all their ancestors had believed this article. A man must be saved without the law, only through the grace of Christ.

Second. A council has the power, and is bound, to suppress and condemn new articles of faith according to Holy Scripture and the ancient faith as the Council of Nicæa condemned the new article of Arius, that of Constantinople the new article of Macedonius, that of Ephesus the new article of Nestorius, that of Chalcedon the new article of Eutyches.

Third. A council has no power to command new good works. Nor can it do so, for all good works are already abundantly commanded in Holy Scripture. What more good works can one imagine than those which the Holy Ghost has taught in the Scriptures, such as humility, patience, gentleness, mercy, faithfulness, faith, kindness, peace, obedience, self-control, chastity, giving, serving, etc., in a word, love? What good work can one imagine that is not included in the command of love? If it is outside of love, what kind of a good work is it? For love, according to St. Paul's teaching, is the fulfillment of all commandments, as Christ Himself also says in Matthew v.

Fourth. A council has the power, and is bound, to condemn wicked works that are contrary to love, according to the Scriptures and the ancient way of the Church, and to rebuke the individuals who are guilty of them, as the decree of the Nicene Council rebukes the ambition of other vices of the bishops and deacons. . . .

Fifth. A council has no power to impose upon Christians new ceremonies, — such as feast-days, festivals, food, drink, garb, — that are to be observed on pain of mortal sin or at peril of conscience. If they do this, there stands St. Augustine to Januarius, and says, *Hoc genus liberas habet observationes*,[4] and Christ appointed few ceremonies. Since a council has no power to impose them, we have power to omit them; nay, St. Paul forbids us to keep them, in Colossians ii saying, " Let not your conscience be troubled over a part of days and fasts, food or drink, etc."

Sixth. A council has the power, and is bound, to condemn such

---

4 " Observance of things of this kind is free."

ceremonies according to the Scriptures, for they are unchristian and set up a new idolatry, or service of God that God has not commanded, but forbidden.

Seventh. A council has no power to interfere in worldly law and government, for St. Paul says, " He who will serve God in spiritual strife must cast off worldly affairs."

Eighth. A council has the power, and is bound, to condemn attempts of this kind and new laws, according to the Scriptures, that is, to cast the pope's decretals into the fire.

Ninth. A council has no power to make statutes or decrees that seek nothing else than tyranny, that is, statutes which give the bishops authority and power to command what they will and make everybody tremble and obey. On the contrary, it has the power, and is bound, to condemn such things according to Holy Scripture, I Peter v, " Ye shall not lord it over the people "; and Christ says *Vos non sic*,[5] " He that would be highest, let him be your servant."

Tenth. A council has power to appoint some ceremonies, provided, first, that they do not strengthen the bishops' tyranny! second, that they are needful and profitable to the people and provide a fine and orderly discipline and way of life. Thus it is needful to have some days and also some places for people to assemble; likewise definite hours for preaching, distributing the sacraments, and for praying, singing, and praising and thanking God. So St. Paul says, in I Corinthians xiv, " Let all things be done in order and decently." With such measures the bishops' tyranny is not sought, but the need, the profit, and the order of the people. In short, we must have such things, and cannot do without them, if the Church is to abide. . . .

A council, then, is nothing else than a consistory or court in which the judges, after hearing the parties, give their verdict, but with proper humility, saying, " According to the law our office is *anathematizare*, ' to condemn '; not, however, according to our own idea or will, or to newly invented law, but according to the old law, which is recognized as law throughout the empire." Thus a council condemns even a heretic, not according to its own opinion, but according to the imperial law, i.e., according to the Holy

---

[5] " Ye shall not be so."

Scriptures, which they confess to be the law of the holy Church. This law, empire, and judge is verily to be feared on peril of eternal damnation, for the law is God's Word, the empire is God's Church, and the judge is the officer, or servant, of both. . . .

Finally. A council should have to do only with matters of faith, and that only when the faith is in special need. Openly evil works can be condemned, and good works administered at home by temporal government, pastors, and parents. But false good works belong to matters of faith, because they corrupt the true faith. Therefore they, too, belong in the council if the pastors are too weak, though the councils, as I have said, did not trouble themselves about them.

— *"On the Councils and the Churches,"* Works of Martin Luther, *Vol. V, pp. 243–257.*

Heresy can never be prevented by force. That must be taken hold of in a different way, and must be opposed and dealt with otherwise than with the sword. Here God's Word must strive; if that does not accomplish the end it will remain unaccomplished through secular power, though it fill the world with blood. Heresy is a spiritual matter, which no iron can strike, no fire burn, no water drown. God's Word alone avails here, as Paul says, II Corinthians x, " Our weapons are not carnal, but mighty through God to destroy every counsel and high thing that exalteth itself against the knowledge of God, and to bring into captivity every thought to the obedience of Christ."

— *" Secular Authority: To What Extent It Should Be Obeyed,"* Works of Martin Luther, *Vol. III, p. 259.*

Whenever and wherever it has been the law to put false prophets and heretics to death, in the course of time it has come to pass that none but the most holy prophets and most innocent men were slain by this law, for wicked rulers made it a pretext and judged whom they wished as false prophets and heretics. I fear the same will happen with us, if we ever allow ourselves to put men to death for opinions even in one just instance, as now we see the papists shed innocent blood instead of guilty by this law. Wherefore, I am not able to admit in any case that false teachers be put to death; it is sufficient to banish them, and if our posterity abuse this penalty at least their sin will be less and will hurt only themselves.

— Luther's Correspondence, *Vol. II, #800, p. 447.*

6. THE MISSIONARY MESSAGE OF THE CHURCH

We should so preach Christ as one who will reject nobody, however weak he may be, but will gladly receive and comfort and strengthen everybody; that we may always picture him to ourselves as a good shepherd. Then hearts will turn to him of their own accord, and need not be forced and driven. The Gospel graciously invites and makes men willing, so that they desire to go, and do go, to him with all confidence. And it begets a love for Christ in their hearts, so that they willingly do what they should, whereas formerly they had to be driven and forced. When we are driven, we do a thing with displeasure and against our will. That is not what God desires; therefore it is done in vain. But when I see that God deals with me graciously, he wins my heart, so that I am constrained to fly to him; consequently, my heart is filled with happiness and joy.

— *Gospel Sermon, Second Sunday After Easter* (Lenker Edition, *Vol. XII, #20*).

We have often said heretofore that the Gospel, properly speaking, is not something written in books, but an oral proclamation, which shall be heard in all the world and shall be cried out freely before all creatures, so that all would have to hear it if they had ears; that is to say, it shall be preached so publicly that to preach it more publicly would be impossible. For the Law, which was of old, and what the prophets preached, was not cried out in all the world before all creatures, but it was preached by the Jews in their synagogues. But the Gospel shall not be thus confined; it shall be preached freely unto all the world.

— *Gospel Sermon, Ascension Day* (Lenker Edition, *Vol. XII, #3*).

The command of a temporal ruler goes no farther than to the confines of his own kingdom; likewise that of a father to his own household: but this commission of Christ, (Mark 16:14–20), concerns all kings, princes, countries and people, great and small, young and old, simple and wise, sinners and saints. With this one message he claims all dominion and power, all wisdom, holiness, majesty and the right to rule on earth with unlimited authority. What else can the world think and say about it than this: What! this one man and his eleven poor beggars dare to assume authority over Moses and all the prophets, yes, even over all people? Even Moses was sent only to Pharaoh and his people in Egypt. Is this man, then, to have the whole world for his field? He is in relation to it no more than a common laborer!

It must be a master of no mean authority who dares to exercise the right to send forth messengers not only to one or several crowned heads, but to all rulers throughout the world. Christ does all this as though he possessed full power and authority over them as his subjects, charging his disciples that they should fear no one, no matter how great and powerful he might be, but should cheerfully go forth, continuing to the remotest parts of the world, and preach the Gospel, with the assurance that they could not fail to be heard and that no one was able to hinder them.

Thus was it fulfilled. " Beginning at Jerusalem," the kingdom touched the whole world. No other kingdom ever had such power. There never yet lived a ruler who achieved supremacy over even one-half of the world. How is it then, that from Jerusalem to the remotest corners of the earth all men know of this king who is called Christ? And all this was accomplished without a single sword-thrust and without military power; simply through these poor beggars, whom Christ sent forth into so many kingdoms and principalities that resisted them with the sword, with fire and water and with their whole might. If the apostles had been dependent upon their own power, they would have miserably failed before crossing their own thresholds. They had been afraid of their own people, the Jews, and had hidden themselves behind bolted doors. But later on, upon the strength of this commission, they boldly went forth, not only among their own people, but in all kingdoms, through all principalities, and in the face of all powers and resistance of the world and the devil.

Whence did they obtain such courage and strength? Surely not from any king of Persia nor emperor of Rome, Turkey or Tartary.

No, it was from the Lord alone, who ascended into heaven and commanded them to go and preach to the whole creation. And as Christ began to set up his kingdom, so it will continue till the end of the world. Certainly he is not Lord in any temporal sense. He is the one to whom all authority in heaven and on earth is given, as he himself declares in Matt. 28:18. To him must be subjected both angels and men, and all creatures, as God also saith to him in Psalm 2:8: " Ask of me, and I will give thee the nations for thine inheritance, and the uttermost parts of the earth for thy possession." This is the reason why we know and believe in him. Only Christ could have brought the world everywhere to believe in one who was apparently a simple Jew.

These words of his command are marvelously powerful. Therein he shows that he is greater than all emperors, kings and rulers on earth, by his own power subjecting unto himself all creatures. He does not commission his disciples to convey his greetings or to ask favors of certain rulers on earth, but in full authority he issues to all rulers a command that they shall accept his message and obey his orders. It is evident, too, that this commander is mightier than any angel. Angels are, indeed, mighty and powerful beings, sent by God to do his bidding with reference to certain of his servants; as, for instance, we see Moses leading his people out of Egypt by an angel. But Christ issues his own command, that shall reach all the world, yea, even all creatures, intimating that all belongs to him. Such authority is given to none else but this son born of the Virgin. He must, therefore, be the one Lord over all things, over angels and men, the only God and Maker of all creatures.

— *Gospel Sermon, Ascension Day* (Lenker Edition, *Vol. XII, #11–15*).

> Dear is to me the holy Maid, —
> I never can forget her;
> For glorious things of her are said;
> Than life I love her better:
> So dear and good,
> That if I should
> Afflicted be,
> It moves not me;

For she my soul will ravish
  With constancy and love's pure fire,
And with her bounty lavish
  Fulfil my heart's desire.

She wears a crown of purest gold,
  Twelve shining stars attend her;
Her raiment, glorious to behold,
  Surpasses far in splendor
    The sun at noon;
    Upon the moon
    She stands, the Bride
    Of him who died:
Sore travail is upon her;
  She bringeth forth a noble Son
Whom all the world doth honor;
  She bows before his throne.

Thereat the Dragon raged, and stood
  With open mouth before her;
But vain was his attempt, for God
  His buckler broad threw o'er her.
    Up to his throne
    He caught his Son,
    But left the foe
    To rage below.
The mother, sore afflicted,
  Alone into the desert fled,
There by her God protected,
  By her true Father fed.

— Luther's Hymns, *p. 126.*

VIII

The Sacraments

1. BAPTISM
2. THE LORD'S SUPPER

The Sacraments

Nowhere in Holy Scriptures is this word *sacrament* employed in the meaning to which we are accustomed; it has an entirely different meaning. For wherever it occurs it signifies not the sign of a sacred thing, but a sacred, secret, hidden thing. Thus Paul writes in I Corinthians iv, " Let a man so account of us as the ministers of Christ, and dispensers of the mysteries — i.e., sacraments — of God." Where we have the word *sacrament* the Greek text reads *mystery*, which word our version sometimes translates and sometimes retains in its Greek form. . . .

Therefore, *sacrament,* or *mystery,* in Paul's writings, is that wisdom of the Spirit, hidden in a mystery, as he says in I Corinthians ii, which is Christ, Who is for this very reason not known to the princes of this world, wherefore they also crucified Him, and Who still is to them foolishness, an offense, a stone of stumbling, and a sign which is spoken against. The preachers he calls dispensers of these mysteries because they preach Christ, the power and the wisdom of God, yet so that one cannot receive this unless one believe. Therefore, a sacrament is a mystery, or secret thing, which is set forth in words and is received by the faith of the heart.

— " *The Babylonian Captivity of the Church,*" Works of Martin Luther, *Vol. II, pp. 258 f.*

There are, strictly speaking, but two sacraments in the Church of God — baptism and bread; for only in these two do we find both the divinely instituted sign and the promise of forgiveness of sins.

— " *The Babylonian Captivity of the Church,*" Works of Martin Luther, *Vol. II, pp. 291 f.*

1. BAPTISM

What is baptism? Baptism is not simply water, but it is the water comprehended in God's command, and connected with God's Word. What is that Word of God? That which Christ, our Lord, says in the last chapter of Matthew: " Go ye into all the world and teach all the nations, and baptize them into the name of the Father and of the Son and of the Holy Spirit." What benefits does baptism confer? It works forgiveness of sins, delivers from death and the devil, and gives everlasting salvation to all who believe this, as the words and promises of God declare. Which are those words and promises of God?   Those which Christ, our Lord, says in the last chapter of Mark: " He that believeth and is baptized shall be saved; but he that believeth not shall be damned." How can water do such great things? It is not water indeed that does it, but the Word of God, which is in and with the water, and faith which trusts this Word of God in the water. For without the Word of God the water is simply water, and no baptism. But with the Word of God, it is a baptism, that is a gracious water of life and a washing of regeneration in the Holy Spirit; as St. Paul says, Tit. 3:5–8: " According to his mercy he saved us, by the washing of regeneration and renewing of the Holy Spirit; which he poured out upon us richly through Jesus Christ, our Saviour; that, being justified by his grace, we might be made heirs according to the hope of eternal life. This is a faithful saying." What does such baptizing with water signify? It signifies that the old Adam in us would, by daily sorrow and repentance, be drowned and die, with all sins and evil lusts; and again a new man daily come forth and arise, who shall live before God in righteousness and purity forever. Where is this written? St. Paul says, Rom. 6:4: " We were buried therefore with Christ through baptism into death; that like as he was raised from the dead through the glory of the Father, so we also might walk in newness of life."

— " *Small Catechism* " (Lenker Edition, *Vol. XXIV, pp. 27 f*).

In this Holy Sacrament we must have regard to three things — the sign, the significance thereof, and the faith. The sign consists in this, that we are thrust into the water in the Name of the Father and of the Son and of the Holy Ghost; but we are not left there, for we are drawn out again. . . .

The significance of baptism is a blessed dying unto sin and resurrection in the grace of God, so that the old man, which is conceived and born in sin, is there drowned, and a new man, born in grace, comes forth and rises. Thus St. Paul, in Titus iii, calls baptism a " washing of regeneration," since in this washing man is born again and made new. As Christ also says, in John iii, " Except ye be born again of water and the Spirit of grace, ye shall not enter into the Kingdom of Heaven." . . .

The sacrament, or sign, of baptism is quickly over, as we plainly see. But the thing it signifies, viz., the spiritual baptism, the drowning of sin, lasts so long as we live, and is completed only in death. Then it is that man is completely sunk in baptism, and that thing comes to pass which baptism signifies. Therefore this life is nothing else than a spiritual baptism which does not cease till death. . . .

The life of a Christian, from baptism to the grave, is nothing else than the beginning of a blessed death, for at the Last Day God will make him altogether new.

In like manner the lifting up out of baptism is quickly done, but the thing it signifies, the spiritual birth, the increase of grace and righteousness, though it begins indeed in baptism, lasts until death, nay, even until the Last Day. Only then will that be finished which the lifting up out of baptism signifies. Then shall we arise from death, from sins and from all evil, pure in body and in soul, and then shall we live forever. Then shall we be truly lifted up out of baptism and completely born, and we shall put on the true baptismal garment of immortal life in heaven. . . .

Here, then, is the place to discuss the third thing in the sacrament, i.e., faith, to wit, that a man should firmly believe all this; viz., that this sacrament not only signifies death and the resurrection at the Last Day, by which man is made new for an everlasting, sinless life; but also that it assuredly begins and effects this, and unites us with God, so that we have the will to slay sin, even till the time of our death, and to fight against it; on the other hand, that it is His will to be merciful to us, to deal graciously with us, and not to judge us with severity, because we are not sinless in this life until purified through death. . . .

This faith is of all things the most necessary, for it is the ground of all comfort. He who has not this faith must despair in his sins. For the sin which remains after baptism makes it impossible for any good works to be pure before God. For this reason we must hold boldly and fearlessly to our baptism, and hold it up against all sins and terrors of conscience, and humbly say, " I know full well that I have not a single work which is pure, but I am baptised, and through my baptism God, Who cannot lie, has bound Himself in a covenant with me, not to count my sin against me, but to slay it and blot it out."

— "*Treatise on Baptism,*" Works of Martin Luther, *Vol. I, pp. 56–63.*

The first thing in baptism to be considered is the divine promise, which says: " He that believeth and is baptised shall be saved." This promise must be set far above all the glitter of works, vows, religious orders, and whatever man has added thereto; for on it all our salvation depends. But we must so consider it as to exercise our faith therein and in nowise doubt that we are saved when we are baptised. For unless this faith be present or be conferred in baptism, baptism will profit us nothing, nay, it becomes a hindrance to us, not only in the moment of its reception, but all the days of our life; for such unbelief accuses God's promise of being a lie, and this is the blackest of all sins. If we set ourselves to this exercise of faith, we shall at once perceive how difficult it is to believe this promise of God. For our human weakness, conscious of its sins, finds nothing more difficult to believe than that it is saved or will be saved; and yet unless it does believe this, it cannot be saved, because it does not believe the truth of God that promiseth salvation.

— " *The Babylonian Captivity of the Church,*" Works of Martin Luther, *Vol. II, p. 220.*

Man baptises and does not baptise: he baptises, for he performs the work, immersing the person to be baptised; he does not baptise, for in that act he officiates not by his own authority, but in the stead of God. Hence, we ought to receive baptism at the hands of a man just as if Christ Himself, nay, God Himself, were baptising us with His own hands. For it is not man's baptism, but Christ's and God's baptism, which we receive by the hand of a man; just as every other created thing that we make use of by the hand of another, is God's alone. Therefore beware of dividing baptism in such a way as to ascribe the outward part to man and the inward part to God. Ascribe both to God alone, and look upon the person administering it as the instrument in God's hands, by which the Lord sitting in heaven thrusts you under the water with His own hands, and speaking by the mouth of His minister promises you, on earth with a human voice, the forgiveness of your sins.

This the words themselves indicate, when the priest says: " I baptise thee in the Name of the Father, and of the Son, and of the Holy Ghost. Amen " — and not: " I baptise thee in my own name." It is as though he said: " What I do, I do not by my own authority, but in the name and stead of God, so that you should regard it just as if our Lord Himself had done it in a visible manner. The Doer and the minister are different persons, but the work of both is the same work, or, rather, it is the work of the Doer alone, through my ministry."

— " *The Babylonian Captivity of the Church,*" Works of Martin Luther, *Vol. II, pp. 224 f.*

Baptism is called in the Greek language *baptismos,* in Latin *mersio,* which means to plunge something entirely into the water, so that the water closes over it. And although in many places it is the custom no longer to thrust and plunge children into the font of baptism, but only to pour the baptismal water upon them out of the font, nevertheless the former is what should be done. . . .

This usage is also demanded by the significance of baptism, for baptism signifies that the old man and the sinful birth of flesh and blood are to be wholly drowned by the grace of God.

— " *Treatise on Baptism,*" Works of Martin Luther, *Vol. I, p. 56.*

Some will perhaps point to the baptism of infants, who do not grasp the promise of God and cannot have the faith of baptism; so that either faith is not necessary or else infant baptism is without effect. Here I say what all say: Infants are aided by the faith of others, namely, those who bring them to baptism. For the Word of God is powerful, when it is uttered, to change even a godless heart, which is no less deaf and helpless than any infant. Even so the infant is changed, cleansed and renewed by inpoured faith, through the prayer of the Church that presents it for baptism and believes, to which prayer all things are possible. Nor should I doubt that even a godless adult might be changed, in any of the sacraments, if the same Church prayed and presented him; as we read in the Gospel of the man sick of the palsy, who was healed through the faith of others.

— " *The Babylonian Captivity of the Church*," Works of Martin Luther, *Vol. II, pp. 236 f.*

Tell me, why do you baptize a man when he has come to the age of reason? You answer: He hears God's Word and believes. I ask: How do you know that? You answer: He professes it with his mouth. What shall I say? How, if he lies and deceives? You cannot see his heart. Very well, then you baptize for no other reason than for what the man shows himself to be externally, and you are uncertain of his faith, and must believe that if he has not more within in his heart than you perceive without, neither his hearing, nor his profession, nor his faith will help him; for it may all be a delusion and no true faith. Who then are you, that you say external hearing and profession are necessary to baptism; where these are wanting one must not baptize? You yourself must confess that such hearing and profession are uncertain, and not enough for one to receive baptism. Now upon what do you baptize? How will you justify your actions when you thus bungle baptism and bring it into doubt? Is it not the fact that you must come and say that it is not becoming for you to know or do more than that he whom you are to baptize be brought to you and ask baptism from you; and you must believe or commit the matter to God, whether he inwardly truly believes or not? In this way you are excused and baptize aright. Why then will you not do the same for the children, whom Christ commands to be brought to him and promises to bless? But you wish first to have the outward hearing and profession, which

you yourself acknowledge is uncertain and not sufficient for baptism on the part of the one to be baptized. And you let go the sure word of Christ in which he bids the little children to be brought unto him, on account of your uncertain external hearing.
— *Gospel Sermon, Third Sunday After Epiphany* (Lenker Edition, *Vol. XI, #38*).

That the baptism of infants is pleasing to Christ his own work demonstrates. He has sanctified many of those who had received this baptism, and today not a few can be found whose doctrine and life attest the indwelling of the Holy Spirit. We also, by the grace of God, have received the power of interpreting the Scriptures and of knowing Christ, which is not possible without the Holy Spirit. Now if God did not approve infant baptism he would not have given to any of these the Holy Spirit, not even in the smallest measure. In short, from time immemorial to this day, no one on earth could have been a Christian. Now, since God has confirmed baptism through the gift of his Holy Spirit, as is plainly evident in some of the fathers — St. Bernard, Gerson, John Huss and others — and the Christian church will abide to the end of the world, it must be confessed that infant baptism is pleasing to God. For God can never be his own opponent, nor support lies and knavery, nor bestow his grace and Spirit to that end. This is perhaps the best and strongest proof for the simple and unlearned people. For no one can take from us, or overthrow, the article of faith, " I believe in the holy Christian Church, the communion of saints."
— *" Large Catechism "* (Lenker Edition, *Vol. XXIV, p. 166*).

To view and use baptism aright we must let it become to us a source of strength and comfort when sin and conscience oppress us. Then you may say: It is a fact that I am baptized, but, being baptized, I have the promise that I shall be saved and obtain eternal life for both soul and body. For this reason, two things take place in baptism: water is poured upon our bodies, which can perceive nothing but the water; and the Word is spoken to the soul, that the soul may have its share also. Now, as water and Word constitute one baptism, so shall both body and soul be saved and live forever: the soul through the Word, in which it believes; but the body because it is united with the soul and grasps baptism in such a manner as it may. Hence, no greater jewel can adorn our body or soul than baptism; for through it perfect holiness and salvation become accessible to us, which are otherwise beyond the reach of man's life and energy.

— "*Large Catechism*" (Lenker Edition, *Vol. XXIV, p. 165*).

If, then, the holy sacrament of baptism is a thing so great, so gracious and full of comfort, we should pay earnest heed to thank God for it ceaselessly, joyfully, and from the heart, and to give Him praise and honor.

— "*Treatise on Baptism,*" Works of Martin Luther, *Vol. I, p. 70.*

2. THE LORD'S SUPPER

What is the sacrament of the Altar? It is the true body and blood of our Lord Jesus Christ, under the bread and wine, instituted by Christ himself for us Christians to eat and drink. Where is this written? The holy Evangelists, Matthew, Mark and Luke, together with St. Paul, write thus: " Our Lord Jesus Christ, in the night in which he was betrayed, took bread; and when he had given thanks, he brake it, and gave it to his disciples, saying, Take, eat; this is my body, which is given for you; this do in remembrance of me. After the same manner, when he had supped, he took also the cup, and when he had given thanks, he gave it to them, saying, Drink ye all of it; this cup is the New Testament in my blood, which is shed for you, for the remission of sins; this do, as oft as ye drink it, in remembrance of me." What benefit is such eating and drinking? It is shown us by these words: " Given and shed for you, for the re- mission of sins; " namely, that in the Sacrament, forgiveness of sins, life and salvation are given us through these words. For where there is forgiveness of sins, there is also life and salvation. How can bodily eating and drinking do such great things? It is not the eating and drinking indeed that does it, but the words which stand here: " Given and shed for you, for the remission of sins." These words, together with the bodily eating and drinking, are the chief thing in the Sacrament; and he that believes these words, has what they say and mean, namely the forgiveness of sins. Who then re-

ceives this Sacrament worthily? Fasting and bodily preparation
are indeed a good outward discipline; but he is truly worthy and
well prepared who has faith in these words: " Given and shed for
you, for the remission of sins." But he who believes not these words,
or doubts, is unworthy and unprepared; for the words, " For you,"
require only believing hearts.

— " *Small Catechism* " (Lenker Edition, *Vol. XXIV, pp. 28 f*).

Like the sacrament of holy baptism, the holy sacrament of the
altar, or of the holy and true body of Christ, has three parts which
it is necessary for us to know. The first is the sacrament, or sign,
the second is the significance of this sacrament, the third is the
faith required by both of these; the three parts which must be
found in every sacrament. The sacrament must be external and visible, and have some material form; the significance must be internal and spiritual, within the spirit of man; faith must apply and
use both these. . . .

The sacrament, or outward sign, is in the form of bread and
wine, just as baptism has as its sign water; although the sign is not
simply the form of bread and wine, but the use of the bread
and wine in eating and drinking, just as the water of baptism is
used by immersion or by pouring. For the sacrament, or sign,
must be received, or must at least be desired, if it is to work a
blessing. . . .

The significance or purpose of this sacrament is the fellowship
of all saints, whence it derives its common name *synaxis* or *com-
munio*, that is, fellowship; and *communicare* means to take part
in this fellowship, or as we say, to go to the sacrament, because
Christ and all saints are one spiritual body, just as the inhabitants
of a city are one community and body, each citizen being a member of the other and a member of the entire city. All the saints,
therefore, are members of Christ and of the Church, which is a spiritual and eternal city of God, and whoever is taken into this city
is said to be received into the community of saints, and to be in-
corporated into Christ's spiritual body and made a member of
Him.

— " *A Treatise Concerning the Blessed Sacrament and Concerning the Brotherhoods*," Works of Martin Luther, *Vol. II, pp. 9 f*.

There follows the third part of the sacrament, that is faith, on which all depends. For it is not enough to know what the sacrament is and signifies. It is not enough that you know it is a fellowship and a gracious exchange or blending of our sin and suffering with the righteousness of Christ and His saints; you must also desire it and firmly believe that you have received it.

— *"A Treatise Concerning the Blessed Sacrament and Concerning the Brotherhoods,"* Works of Martin Luther, *Vol. II, pp. 19 f.*

There are two passages that do clearly bear upon this matter — the Gospel narratives of the institution of the Lord's Supper, and Paul in I Corinthians xi.

— *"The Babylonian Captivity of the Church,"* Works of Martin Luther, *Vol. II, p. 179.*

" This is the cup of a new eternal testament in My blood, that is shed for you and for many for the remission of sin." As though He said: " Behold, man, in these words I promise and bequeath thee forgiveness of all thy sin and eternal life. And in order that thou mayest be certain and know that such promise remains irrevocably thine, I will die for it, and will give My body and blood for it, and will leave them both to thee as sign and seal, that by them thou mayest remember Me." So He says: " As oft as ye do this, remember Me." Even as a man who bequeathes something includes therein what shall be done for him afterward, as is the custom at present in the requiems and masses for the dead, so also Christ has ordained a requiem for Himself in this testament; not that He needs it, but because it is necessary and profitable for us to remember Him; whereby we are strengthened in faith, confirmed in hope and made ardent in love. For as long as we live on earth our lot is such that the evil spirit and all the world assail us with joy and sorrow, to extinguish our love for Christ, to blot out our faith, and to weaken our hope. Wherefore we sorely need this sacrament, in which we may gain new strength when we have grown weak, and may daily exercise ourselves unto the strengthening and uplifting of the spirit. . . .

Now we see how many parts there are in this testament, or the mass. There is, first, the testator who makes the testament, Christ. Second, the heirs to whom the testament is bequeathed, we Christians. Third, the testament in itself, the words of Christ when He says: " This is My body which is given for you. This is My blood which is shed for you, a new eternal testament, etc." Fourth, the seal or token, the sacrament, bread and wine, and under them His true body and blood.

— " *Treatise on the New Testament*," Works of Martin Luther, *Vol. I, pp. 300–302.*

The testament is far more important than the sacrament, so the words are much more important than the signs. For the signs might be lacking, if only one have the words, and thus one might be saved without sacrament, yet not without testament. For I can daily enjoy the sacrament in the mass, if I only keep before my eyes the testament, that is, the words and covenant of Christ, and feed and strengthen my faith thereby.

We see, then, that the best and greatest part of all sacraments and of the mass is the words and covenant of God, without which the sacraments are dead and are nothing at all; like a body without a soul, a cask without wine, a purse without gold. . . .

I fear that many have made out of the mass a good work, whereby they thought to do a great service to Almighty God. Now, if we have rightly understood what has been said above, namely, that the mass is nothing else than a testament and sacrament, in which God pledges Himself to us and gives us grace and mercy, I think it is not fitting that we should make a good work or merit out of it. For a testament is not *beneficium acceptum, sed datum;* [1] it does not derive benefit from us, but brings us benefit. Who has ever heard that he who receives an inheritance does a good work? He does derive benefit. Likewise in the mass we give Christ nothing, but only take from Him.

— " *Treatise on the New Testament*," Works of Martin Luther, *Vol. I, pp. 306–308.*

Let this stand at the outset as our infallibly certain proposition, — the mass, or sacrament of the altar, is Christ's testament which He left behind Him at His death, to be distributed among His believers. For that is the meaning of His word, — " This is the chalice, the new testament in my blood." . . .

[1] " Not a benefit received, but a benefit conferred."

Let us enquire, therefore, what a testament is, and we shall learn at the same time what the mass is, what its use and blessing, and what its abuse. A testament, as every one knows, is a promise made by one about to die, in which he designates his bequest and appoints his heirs. Therefore a testament involves, first, the death of the testator, and secondly, the promise of the bequest and the naming of the heir. Thus St. Paul discusses at length the nature of a testament in Romans iv, Galatians iii and iv, and Hebrews ix. The same thing is also clearly seen in these words of Christ. Christ testifies concerning His death when He says: " This is my body, which shall be given; this is my blood, which shall be shed." He designates the bequest when He says: " Unto remission of sins." And He appoints the heirs when He says: " For you, and for many " — i.e., for such as accept and believe the promise of the testator; for here it is faith that makes men heirs, as we shall see.

You see, therefore, that what we call the mass is the promise of remission of sins made to us by God; and such a promise as has been confirmed by the death of the Son of God. For the one difference between a promise and a testament is that a testament is a promise which implies the death of him who makes it. A testator is a man making a promise who is about to die; whilst he that makes a promise is, if I may so put it, a testator who is not about to die. This testament of Christ was foreshadowed in all the promises of God from the beginning of the world; nay, whatever value those olden promises possessed was altogether derived from this new promise that was to come in Christ. Hence the words " covenant " and " testament of the Lord " occur so frequently in the Scriptures, which words signified that God would one day die. For where there is a testament, the death of the testator must needs follow (Hebrews ix). Now God made a testament: therefore it was necessary that He should die. But God could not die unless He became man. Thus both the incarnation and the death of Christ are briefly comprehended in this one word " testament."

— " *The Babylonian Captivity of the Church,*" Works of Martin Luther, *Vol. II, pp. 196 f.*

There are those who practice their arts and subtleties to such an extent that they ask where the bread remains when it is changed into Christ's flesh, and the wine when it is changed into His blood; also in what manner the whole Christ, His flesh and His blood, can be comprehended in so small a portion of bread and wine. What does it matter? It is enough to know that it is a divine sign, in which Christ's flesh and blood are truly present — how and where, we leave to Him.

— " *A Treatise Concerning the Blessed Sacrament and Concerning the Brotherhoods,*" Works of Martin Luther, *Vol. II, p. 20.*

There are many who . . . rely upon the fact that the mass or the sacrament is, as they say, *opus gratum opere operato,* that is, a work which of itself pleases God, even though they who perform it do not please Him. From this they conclude that, however unworthily masses are said, it is none the less a good thing to have many masses, since the harm comes to those who say or use them unworthily. I grant every one his opinion, but such fables please me not. For, if you desire to speak thus, there is no creature nor work that does not of itself please God, as is written, " God saw all His works and they pleased Him." What good can result therefrom, if one misuse bread, wine, gold, and every good creature, though of themselves they are pleasing to God? Nay, condemnation is the result. So too, here: the more precious the sacrament, the greater the harm which comes upon the whole congregation from its misuse. For it was not instituted for its own sake, that it might please God, but for our sake, that we might use it rightly, exercise our faith by it, and by it become pleasing to God.

— " *A Treatise Concerning the Blessed Sacrament and Concerning the Brotherhoods,*" Works of Martin Luther, *Vol. II, pp. 22 f.*

Every one will readily understand what there is in that oft quoted saying of Gregory's: " A mass celebrated by a wicked priest is not to be considered of less effect than one celebrated by any godly priest, and St. Peter's mass would not have been better than Judas the traitor's, if they had offered the sacrifice of the mass." Which saying has served many as a cloak to cover their godless doings, and because of it they have invented the distinction between *opus operati* and *opus operantis,* so as to be free to lead wicked lives themselves and yet to benefit other men. But Gregory speaks truth; only they misunderstand and pervert his words. For it is true beyond a question, that the testament or sacrament is given and received through the ministration of wicked priests no less completely than through the ministration of the most saintly. For who has any doubt that the Gospel is preached by the ungodly? Now the mass is part of the Gospel, nay, its sum and substance; for what is the whole Gospel but the good tidings of the forgiveness of sins? But whatever can be said of the forgiveness of sins and mercy of God, is all briefly comprehended in the word of this testament. Wherefore the popular sermons ought to be naught else than expositions of the mass, that is, a setting forth of the divine promise of this testament; that would be to teach faith and truly to edify the Church.

— "*The Babylonian Captivity of the Church*," Works of Martin Luther, *Vol. II, pp. 216 f.*

We have, therefore, two principal sacraments in the church, baptism and the bread. Baptism leads us into a new life on earth; the bread guides us through death into eternal life. And the two are typified by the Red Sea and the Jordan, and by the two lands, one beyond and one on this side the Jordan. Therefore our Lord said at the Last Supper: "I will not drink henceforth of this fruit of the vine, until that day when I drink it new with you in My Father's kingdom." So entirely is this sacrament intended and ordained to strengthen us against death, and to give us entrance into eternal life.

Finally, the blessing of this sacrament is fellowship and love, by which we are strengthened against death and all evil. This fellowship is twofold: on the one hand we partake of Christ and all saints, on the other hand we permit all Christians to be partakers of us, in whatever way they and we are able; so that by this sacrament all self-seeking love is uprooted and gives place to love which seeks the common good of all, and through this mutual love there is one bread, one drink, one body, one community, — that is the true union of Christian brethren.

— "*A Treatise Concerning the Blessed Sacrament and Concerning the Brotherhoods*," Works of Martin Luther, *Vol. II, p. 26.*

Christ, who freed our souls from danger,
And hath turned away God's anger,
Suffered pains no tongue can tell,
To redeem us from pains of hell.

That we never might forget it,
Take my flesh, he said, and eat it,
Hidden in this piece of bread,
Drink my blood in this wine, he said.

Whoso to this board repaireth,
Take good heed how he prepareth;
Death instead of life shall he
Find, who cometh unworthily.

Couldst thou earn thine own salvation,
Useless were my death and passion;
Wilt thou thine own helper be?
No meet table is this for thee.

If thou this believest truly,
And confession makest duly,
Thou a welcome guest art here,
This rich banquet thy soul shall cheer.

Sweet henceforth shall be thy labor,
Thou shalt truly love thy neighbor.
So shall he both taste and see
What thy Saviour hath done in thee.
— Luther's Hymns, *p. 103.*

IX

Christian Ethics

1. ECONOMICS AND SOCIETY
2. YOUTH AND EDUCATION
3. MARRIAGE AND DIVORCE
4. WAR AND PEACE
5. THE KINGDOM OF GOD

Christian Ethics

1. ECONOMICS AND SOCIETY

Christ Himself says, " Whatsoever ye would that men should do unto you, do ye even so to them; this is the whole law and all the prophets." Now no one wishes to receive ingratitude for benefits conferred or to let another take away his good name. No one wishes to have pride shown toward him. No one wishes to endure disobedience, wrath, a wife's impurity, robbery, lying, deceit, slander; but every one wishes to find in his neighbor kindliness, thankfulness, helpfulness, truth and fidelity. All this the Ten Commandments require.

— " A Brief Explanation of the Ten Commandments, the Creed, and the Lord's Prayer," Works of Martin Luther, *Vol. II, p. 358.*

The bare goodness of God is what ought rather to be preached and known above all else, and we ought to learn that, even as God saves us out of pure goodness, without any merit of works, so we in our turn should do the works without reward or selfseeking, for the sake of the bare goodness of God. We should desire nothing in them but His good pleasure, and not be anxious about a reward. That will come of itself, without our seeking. For though it is impossible that the reward should not follow, if we do well in a pure and right spirit, without thought of reward or enjoyment; nevertheless God will not have such a selfseeking and impure spirit, nor will it ever obtain a reward. A son serves his father willingly and without reward, as his heir, solely for the father's sake. But a son who served his father merely for the sake of the inheritance would indeed be an unnatural child and deserve to be cast off by his father.

— *"The Magnificat,"* Works of Martin Luther, *Vol. III, pp. 143 f.*

A man does not live for himself alone in this mortal body, so as to work for it alone, but he lives also for all men on earth, nay, rather, he lives only for others and not for himself. And to this end he brings his body into subjection, that he may the more sincerely and freely serve others, as Paul says in Romans xiv, " No one lives to himself, and no man dies to himself. For he that liveth, liveth unto the Lord, and he that dieth, dieth unto the Lord." Therefore, it is impossible that he should ever in this life be idle and without works toward his neighbors. For of necessity he will speak, deal with and converse with men, as Christ also, being made in the likeness of men, was found in form as a man, and conversed with men, as Baruch iii says.

— *" A Treatise on Christian Liberty,"* Works of Martin Luther, *Vol. II, p. 335.*

One who lives in a community must do his share in bearing and suffering the community's burdens, dangers, and injuries, even though, not he, but his neighbor has caused them: He must do this in the same way that he enjoys the peace, profit, protection, wealth, freedom, and convenience of the community, even though he has not won them or brought them into being.

— *" An Open Letter Concerning the Hard Book Against the Peasants,"* Works of Martin Luther, *Vol. IV, pp. 274 f.*

Christians are to serve one another by ministering temporal blessings. Especially are the poor and the wretched to be remembered, they who are strangers or pilgrims among us, or come to us houseless and homeless. These should receive the willing ministrations of Christians, and none be allowed to suffer want.

In the apostles' time, the primitive days of the Church, Christians were everywhere persecuted, driven from their possessions and forced to wander hither and thither in poverty and exile. It was necessary then to admonish Christians in general, and particularly those who had something of their own, not to permit these destitute ones to suffer want, but to provide for them. So, too, is it today incumbent upon Christians to provide for the really poor — not lazy beggars, or vagabonds — the outdoor pensioners, so called; and to maintain those who, because of old age or other infirmity, are unable to support themselves. The churches should establish common treasuries for the purpose of providing alms for cases of this kind. It was so ordained of the apostles in Acts 6:3. Paul, also, in many places admonishes to such works of love; for instance (Rom. 12:13) : " Communicating to the necessities of the saints."

— *Epistle Sermon, Sunday After Ascension Day* (Lenker Edition, *Vol. VIII*, #41–42).

There is no better service of God than Christian love, which helps and serves the needy, as Christ Himself will testify in the judgment of the last day (Matthew xxv). For this reason, too, the possessions of the Church were formerly called *bona ecclesiae*, that is, common possessions, as it were, a common chest, for all the needy among Christians.

— *" Preface to an Ordinance of a Common Chest,"* Works of Martin Luther, *Vol. IV, p. 95.*

Among Christians no one ought to go begging! . . . Every city could support its own poor, and if it were too small, the people in the surrounding villages also should be exhorted to contribute.

— *" An Open Letter to the Christian Nobility,"* Works of Martin Luther, *Vol. II, p. 134.*

The Holy Gospel, since it has come to light, rebukes and reveals all " the works of darkness," as St. Paul calls them, in Romans xiii. For it is a brilliant light, which lightens all the world and teaches

how evil are the world's works and shows the true works we ought
to do for God and our neighbor. Therefore some of the merchants,
too, have been awakened, and have become aware that in their
trading many a wicked trick and hurtful financial practice is in
use, and it must be feared that the word of Ecclesiasticus applies
here, and that " merchants can hardly be without sin." Nay, I
think St. Paul's saying in the last chapter of I Timothy, fits the
case, " Avarice is a root of all evil," and " Those that are minded
to be rich fall into the devil's snare and into many profitless and
hurtful lusts, which sink men in destruction and perdition." . . .

I have been urged and begged to touch upon these financial mis-
doings and to expose some of them, so that even though the majority may not want to do right, some, if only a few, may yet be delivered from the gaping jaws of avarice. For it must be that among
the merchants, as among other people, there are some who belong
to Christ and would rather be poor with God than rich with the
devil, as says Psalm xxxvii, " Better is the little that the righteous
hath than the great possessions of the godless." For their sake,
then, we must speak out. . . .

The merchants have among themselves one common rule, which
is their chief maxim and the basis of all their sharp practices. They
say: I may sell my goods as dear as I can. This they think their
right. Lo, that is giving place to avarice and opening every door
and window to hell. What does it mean? Only this: " I care nothing about my neighbor; so long as I have my profit and satisfy my
greed, what affair is it of mine if it does my neighbor ten injuries
at once? " There you see how shamelessly this maxim flies squarely
in the face not only of Christian love, but of natural law. Now
what good is there in trade? How can it be without sin when such
injustice is the chief maxim and the rule of the whole business?
On this basis trade can be nothing else than robbing and stealing
other people's property. . . .

The rule ought to be, not: I may sell my wares as dear as I can
or will, but: I may sell my wares as dear as I ought, or as is right
and proper. For your selling ought not to be a work that is entirely
within your own power and will, without law or limit, as though
you were a god and beholden to no one; but because this selling
of yours is a work that you perform toward your neighbor, it must
be so governed by law and conscience, that you do it without harm

and injury to your neighbor, and that you be much more concerned to do him no injury than to make large profits. But where are such merchants? How few merchants there would be and how trade would fall off, if they were to amend this evil rule and put things on a Christian basis! . . .

In deciding how much profit you ought to take on your business and your labor, there is no better way to reckon it than by estimating the amount of time and labor you have put on it and comparing it with that of a day laborer, who works at another occupation, and seeing how much he earns in a day. On that basis reckon how many days you have spent in getting your wares and bringing them to your place of business, how great the labor has been and how much risk you have run, for great labor and much time ought to have so much the greater returns. That is the most accurate, the best and the most definite advice that can be given in this matter; if anyone mislikes it, let him better it. My ground is, as I have said, in the Gospel, "A laborer is worthy of his hire," and Paul also says, " He that feedeth the flock shall eat of the milk; who goeth to war at his own cost and expense? " If you have a better ground than that, you are welcome to it. . . .

There are some who buy up the entire supply of certain goods or wares in a country or a city, so that they may have those goods solely in their own power and can then fix and raise the price and sell them as dear as they like or can. . . . The imperial and temporal laws forbid this and call it " monopoly," i.e., purchase for self-interest, which is not to be tolerated in city or country, and princes and lords would stop it and punish it if they did their duty. Merchants who do this act just as though God's creatures and God's goods were made for them alone and given to them alone, and as though they could take them from other people and set on them whatever price they chose.

— " *On Trading and Usury,*" Works of Martin Luther, *Vol. IV*, *pp. 12–27.*

We must put a bit in the mouth of the Fuggers and similar corporations.[1] How is it possible that in the lifetime of a single man

---

[1] The XVI Century was the hey-day of the great trading-companies, among which the Fuggers of Augsburg . . . easily took first place. The effort of these companies was directed toward securing monopolies in the staple arti-

such great possessions, worthy of a king, can be piled up, and yet everything be done legally and according to God's will? I am not a mathematician, but I do not understand how a man with a hundred gulden can make a profit of twenty gulden in one year, nay, how with one gulden he can make another [2] and that, too, by another way than agriculture or cattle-raising, in which increase of wealth depends not on human wits, but on God's blessing. I commend this to the men of affairs. I am a theologian, and find nothing to blame in it except its evil and offending appearance, of which St. Paul says, " Avoid every appearance or show of evil." This I know well, that it would be much more pleasing to God if we increased agriculture and diminished commerce, and that they do much better who, according to the Scriptures, till the soil and seek their living from it, as was said to us and to all men in Adam, " Accursed be the earth when thou laborest therein, it shall bear thee thistles and thorns, and in the sweat of thy face shalt thou eat thy bread." There is still much land lying untilled.

— " *An Open Letter to the Christian Nobility*," Works of Martin Luther, *Vol. II, pp. 160–162.*

The Psalmist did not venture, in Psalm lxxii, to condemn all those who amass riches in this world, but said, " If I say, I will speak thus; behold, I should offend against the generation of Thy children." That is to say, If I should call all men wicked who possess riches, health, and honor, I should be condemning even Thy saints, of whom there are many such. Paul also instructs Timothy to charge them that are rich in this world, that they be not high minded; but he does not forbid them to be rich. And Abraham, Isaac, and Jacob were rich men, as the Scriptures record. Daniel,

cles of commerce, and their ability to finance large enterprises made it possible for them to gain practical control of the home markets. The sharp rise in the cost of living which took place on the first half of the XVI Century was laid at their door. . . .

[2] The profits of the trading-companies were enormous. The 9 per cent. annually of the Welser (EHRENBERG, *Zeitalter der Fugger*, I, 195) pales into insignificance beside the 1634 per cent. by which the fortune of the Fuggers grew in twenty-one years (SCHULTE, *Die Fugger in Rom*, I, 3). In 1511 a certain Bartholomew Rem invested 900 gulden in the Hochstetter company of Augsburg; by 1517 he claimed 33,000 gulden profit. The company was willing to settle at 26,000, and the resulting litigation caused the figures to become public.

also, and his companions were raised to honor even in Babylon. Moreover many of the kings of Judah were saintly men. It is with regard to such persons that the Psalmist says, " If I say, I will speak thus; behold, I should offend against the generation of Thy children." God gives, even to His people, an abundance of these blessings, for their own comfort, and the comfort of others. Still, these things are not their proper blessings, but only shadows and emblems of their true blessings, which consist in faith, hope, love, and other gifts and graces, which love communicates to all.

— " *The Fourteen of Consolation,*" Works of Martin Luther, *Vol. I, pp. 164 f.*

What hindrance was their riches to the holy fathers Abraham, Isaac and Jacob? What hindrance was his royal throne to David, or his authority in Babylon to Daniel? or their high station or great riches to those who had them or who have them to-day, provided they do not set their hearts on them nor seek their own in them? Solomon says, in Proverbs xvi, " The Lord weigheth the spirits " — that is, He judgeth not according to the outward appearance, whether one be rich or poor, high or low, but according to the spirit, and how it behaves itself within. There must needs be such differences and distinctions of persons and stations in our life here on earth, yet the heart should neither cling to them nor fly from them — not cling to the high and rich, nor fly from the poor and lowly.

— " *The Magnificat,*" Works of Martin Luther, *Vol. III, p. 186.*

Let him take heed to himself, and see to it that he run not after gold, nor set his trust on money, but let the gold run after him, and money wait on his favor, and let him love none of these things nor set his heart on them; then he is the true, generous, wonder-working, happy man, as Job xxxi says: " I have never yet relied upon gold, and never yet made gold my hope and confidence." And Psalm lxii: " If riches increase, set not your heart upon them." So Christ also teaches, Matthew vi, that we shall take no thought, what we shall eat and drink and wherewithal we shall be clothed, since God cares for this, and knows that we have need of all these things.

But some say: " Yes, rely upon that, take no thought, and see whether a roasted chicken will fly into your mouth! " I do not say that a man shall not labor and seek a living; but he shall not worry, not be greedy, not despair, thinking that he will not have enough; for in Adam we are all condemned to labor, when God says to him, Genesis iii, " In the sweat of thy face shalt thou eat bread." And Job v, " As the birds to flying, so is man born unto labor." Now the birds fly without worry and greed; and so we also should labor without worry and greed; but if you do worry and are greedy, wishing that the roasted chicken fly into your mouth: worry and be greedy, and see whether you will thereby fulfil God's Commandment and be saved!

— " *Treatise on Good Works,*" Works of Martin Luther, *Vol. I*, *p. 279.*

The business man will not be a business man long, if preaching and law shall fail; this I know for sure. We theologians and jurists must continue, or all the rest will go to ruin with us; this will not fail. When the theologians disappear, God's Word also disappears, and there remain nothing but heathen, nay, nothing but devils; when the jurists disappear, then the law disappears, and peace with it, and there remains nothing but robbery, murder, crime, and violence, nay, nothing but wild beasts. But what earnings and profits the business man will have when peace is gone, I shall let his ledger tell him; and what good all his property will do him when preaching goes down, I shall let his conscience show him.

— " *A Sermon on Keeping Children in School,*" Works of Martin Luther, *Vol. IV, p. 173.*

2. YOUTH AND EDUCATION

It is a serious and important matter that we help and assist our youth, and one in which Christ and all the world are mightily concerned. By helping them we shall be helping ourselves and all men. . . . If it is necessary, dear sirs, to expend annually such great sums for firearms, roads, bridges, dams and countless similar items, in order that a city may enjoy temporal peace and prosperity, why should not at least as much be devoted to the poor, needy youth, so that we might engage one or two competent men to teach school?

For what other purpose do we older folk exist than to care for, instruct and bring up the young? The foolish youths cannot possibly instruct nor protect themselves; God has therefore entrusted them to us who are old and know by experience what is good for them, and He will compel us to render a strict account. Hence Moses also commands, " Ask thy father, and he will shew thee; thy elders, and they will tell thee."

But it is a sin and a disgrace that we must needs urge and be urged to train our children and youths and seek their best interests, when nature itself should drive us to do this and the examples even of the heathen afford us manifold instruction. There is not an irrational animal but looks after its young and teaches them what they need to know, except the ostrich, of which God says that she is hardened against her young ones, as though they were not hers, and leaves her eggs in the earth. And what would it profit us if we possessed and performed all else and became utter saints, and yet neglected the chief purpose of our life, namely, the care of the young? I believe also that among outward sins none so heavily burdens the world in the sight of God nor deserves such severe punishment as the sin we commit against our children by not giving them an education. . . .

There are various reasons why parents neglect their duty.

In the first place, there are those who lack the piety and decency, even if they had the ability, to do it. Like the ostrich, they are hardened against their young, and are content to have cast the eggs from them and to have brought children into the world; they will do nothing more. But these children must live among us and with us in the same city. How then can reason and above all Christian love suffer them to grow up untrained and to poison and pollute other children, until at last the whole city perish, as it happened in Sodom and Gomorrah, Geba, and other cities. Secondly, the great majority of parents are, alas! unfitted for this work and do not know how children are to be trained and taught, for they themselves have learned nothing but how to provide for the belly; whereas it takes persons of exceptional ability to teach and train children aright. Thirdly, even if parents were able and willing to do it themselves, they have neither the time nor the opportunity for it, what with their other duties and housework. Necessity compels us, therefore, to engage public schoolteachers for the children, unless everyone were willing to engage an instructor of his own. But that would be too heavy a burden upon the common man, and many a promising boy would be neglected on account of poverty. Besides, many parents die and leave orphans, and if we do not know by experience how these are cared for by their guardians, God Himself tells us by calling Himself the Father of the orphans, as of those who are neglected by everyone else. Moreover, there are some who have no children of their own, and who for that reason take no interest in the training of children.

It therefore becomes the business of councilmen and magistrates to devote the greatest care and attention to the young. For since the property, honor and life of the whole city are committed to their faithful keeping, they would fail in their duty toward God and man if they did not seek its welfare and improvement with all their powers day and night. Now the welfare of a city consists not alone in gathering great treasures and providing solid walls, beautiful buildings, and a goodly supply of guns and armor. Nay, where these abound and reckless fools get control of them, the city suffers only the greater loss. But a city's best and highest welfare, safety and strength consist in its having many able, learned, wise, honorable and well-bred citizens; such men can readily gather treasures and all goods, protect them and put them to a good use. . . .

" But," you say, " everyone may instruct his sons and daughters himself, or at least train them by means of discipline." I reply: We know indeed what such teaching and training amount to. Even when the severest discipline is applied and has turned out well, the net result is a certain enforced outward respectability; underneath are the same old blockheads, unable to converse on any subject or to be of assistance to anyone. But if children were instructed and trained in schools or elsewhere where there were learned and well-trained schoolmasters and schoolmistresses to teach the languages, the other arts, and history, they would hear the happenings and the sayings of all the world and learn how it fared with various cities, estates, kingdoms, princes, men, and women; thus they could in a short time set before themselves, as in a mirror, the character, life, counsels and purposes, success and failure of the whole world from the beginning. As a result of this knowledge, they could form their own opinions and adapt themselves to the course of this outward life in the fear of God, draw from history the knowledge and understanding of what should be sought and what avoided in this outward life, and become able also by this standard to assist and direct others. But the training which is undertaken at home, apart from such schools, attempts to make us wise through our own experience. Before that comes to pass we shall be dead a hundred times over, and shall have acted inconsiderately all our life; for much time is needed to acquire one's own experience.

Now since the young must romp and leap or at least have something to do that gives them pleasure, and since this should not be forbidden (nor would it be well to forbid them everything), why should we not furnish them such schools and lay before them such studies? By the grace of God it has now become possible for children to study with pleasure and in play languages, the other arts, or history. The kind of schools we attended are a thing of the past — that hell and purgatory in which we were tormented with cases and tenses, and yet learned less than nothing with all the flogging, trembling, anguish and misery. If we take so much time and trouble to teach children card-playing, singing and dancing, why do we not take as much time and trouble to teach them reading and other branches, while they are young and have the time, and are apt and eager to learn? For my part, if I had children and could accomplish it, they should study not only the languages and history, but singing, instrumental music, and all of mathematics. For what is all this but mere child's play? In these branches the Greeks in former times trained their children, who grew up into men and women of wondrous ability, skilled in every pursuit. How I regret now that I did not read more poets and historians, and that no one taught me them! I was obliged instead to read, with great cost, labor and injury, that devil's filth, the philosophers and sophists, from which I have all I can do to get myself clean.

Now you say, "But who can spare his children for so long a time, and train them all to be young gentlemen? There is work for them to do at home, etc." I reply: It is not in the least my intention to have such schools established as we had heretofore, in which a boy sat over his Donatus and Alexander [3] for twenty or thirty years and yet learned nothing. We are living in a new world today and things are being done differently. My idea is to let boys go to such a school for one or two hours a day, and spend the remainder of the time working at home, learning a trade or doing whatever their parents desired; so that both study and work might go hand in hand while they were young and able to do both. They spend at least ten times as much time with their pea-shooters or playing ball or racing and tussling. In like manner, a girl can surely find time enough to go to school one hour a day and still attend to all her duties at home; she sleeps, dances and plays away more time than that. There is only one thing lacking, and that is the earnest desire to train the young people and to benefit and serve the world with well-bred men and women. The devil very much prefers coarse blockheads and ne'er-do-wells, lest men live too comfortably on earth.

But the exceptional pupils, who give promise of becoming skilled teachers, preachers and holders of other spiritual positions, should be kept longer at school or altogether dedicated to a life of study.

— " *To the Councilmen of All Cities in Germany That They Establish and Maintain Christian Schools*," Works of Martin Luther, *Vol. IV, pp. 106–124.*

The school must be the next thing to the Church, for it is the place where young pastors and preachers are trained and out of which they are drawn to put in the places of those who die.

— " *On the Councils and the Churches*," Works of Martin Luther, *Vol. V, p. 298.*

When schools flourish, then things go well and the church is secure. Let us have more learned men and teachers! The youth furnish recruits for the church, they are the source of its well-being. If there were no schools, who would there be to take our places

[3] Aelius Donatus, *Ars Grammatica* and *Ars minor*; and Alexander de Villa Dei, *Doctrinale puerorum*, two widely used mediæval grammars, the latter in verse form.

when we die? In the church we are forced to have schools. God has preserved the church through schools, they are its conservatories. They have no fine exterior, but within they are most useful. In schools the children have learned the Lord's prayer and the creed; in the little schools the church has been wonderfully preserved.

— Conversations with Luther, *p. 96.*

In my admonitions I have often enough urged those who have influence, to use all diligence in drawing the young to school, where they may receive proper instruction to become pastors and preachers; and I have earnestly advised that in cases of necessity ample financial provision be made for students. But, alas, few communities, few States, are interested in the matter. . . . They presume to think there is no need for action; the matter will adjust itself; there will always be pastors and preachers. But assuredly they deceive themselves. . . . They will seek preachers and find none; they will have to hear rude, illiterate dolts.

— *Epistle Sermon, Twentieth Sunday After Trinity* (Lenker Edition, *Vol. IX, #5*).

I myself, if I could leave the preaching office and other things, or had to do so, would not be so glad to have any other work as that of schoolmaster, or teacher of boys, for I know that this is the most useful, the greatest, and the best, next to the work of preaching. Indeed, I scarcely know which of the two is the better; for it is hard to make old dogs obedient and old rascals pious; and that is the work at which the preacher must labor, often in vain. But young trees can be better bent and trained, though some of them break in the process. Let it be one of the greatest virtues on earth faithfully to train other people's children; very few people, almost none, in fact, do this for their own.

— *"A Sermon on Keeping Children in School,"* Works of Martin Luther, *Vol. IV, p. 174.*

One should not whip children too hard. My father once whipped me so severely that I fled from him and it was difficult for him to win me back again to himself. . . . One ought to educate a child, where there is hope of success; but if one sees that there is no hope, and that he can learn nothing, one ought not to whip him to death

on that account, but train him for something else. Some teachers
are as cruel as hangmen. For instance I was once whipped fifteen
times before noon, for no fault of mine, for I was expected to de-
cline and conjugate what I had not yet learned.

— Conversations with Luther, *pp. 1–3*.

3. MARRIAGE AND DIVORCE

God has done marriage the honor of putting it into the Fourth
Commandment, immediately after the honor due to Him, and commands, " Thou shalt honor father and mother." Show me an honor
in heaven or on earth, apart from the honor of God, that can equal
this honor! Neither the secular nor the spiritual estate has been so
highly honored. And if God had given utterance to nothing more
than this Fourth Commandment with reference to married life,
men ought to have learned quite well from this Commandment that
in God's sight there is no higher office, estate, condition and work
(next to the Gospel which concerns God Himself) than the estate
of marriage.

— *" To the Knights of the Teutonic Order,"* Works of Martin
Luther, *Vol. III, pp. 423 f.*

To get a wife is easy enough, but to love her with constancy is
difficult, and he who can do that may well be grateful to our Lord
God. Therefore if any one wants to marry a wife, let him take the
matter seriously and pray to our Lord God: " O Lord, if it is thy
divine will that I should live without a wife, then help me to do
so! If not, bestow upon me a good, pious maid, with whom I can
live my whole life long, one whom I love and who loves me." For
the mere union of the flesh is not sufficient. There must be con-
geniality of tastes and character.

— Conversations with Luther, *p. 63*.

When a man and a woman love and are pleased with each other,
and thoroughly believe in their love, who teaches them how they
are to behave, what they are to do, leave undone, say, not say,
think? Confidence alone teaches them all this, and more. They
make no difference in works: they do the great, the long, the much,

as gladly as the small, the short, the little, and vice versa; and that too with joyful, peaceful, confident hearts, and each is a free companion of the other. But where there is a doubt, search is made for what is best; then a distinction of works is imagined whereby a man may win favor; and yet he goes about it with a heavy heart, and great disrelish; he is, as it were, taken captive, more than half in despair, and often makes a fool of himself.

— "*Treatise on Good Works*," Works of Martin Luther, *Vol. I, p. 191.*

As to divorce, it is still a moot question whether it be allowable. For my part I so greatly detest divorce that I should prefer bigamy to it,[4] but whether it be allowable, I do not venture to decide.

— "*The Babylonian Captivity of the Church*," Works of Martin Luther, *Vol. II, p. 271.*

Those who want to be Christians are not to be divorced, but each to retain his or her spouse, and bear and experience good and evil with the same, although he or she may be strange, peculiar and faulty; or, if there be a divorce, that the parties remain unmarried; and that it will not do to make a free thing out of marriage, as if it were in our power to do with it, changing and exchanging, as we please; but it is just as Jesus says: " What God has joined together let not man put asunder."

For trouble here is owing solely to the fact that men do not regard marriage according to God's word as his work and ordinance, do not pay regard to his will, that he has given to every one his spouse, to keep her, and to endure for his sake the discomforts that married life brings with it; they regard it as nothing else than a mere human, secular affair, with which God has nothing to do. Therefore one soon becomes tired of it, and if it does not go as we wish, we soon begin to separate and change. Then God nevertheless so orders it, that we thereby make it no better; as it then generally happens, if one wants to change and improve matters, and no one wants to carry his cross, but have everything perfectly convenient and without discomfort, that he gets an exchange in which he finds

---

⁴ As he actually did in the case of Henry VIII and Philip of Hesse.

twice or ten times more discomfort, not alone in this matter but in all others. . . .

But you ask: Is there then no reason for which there may be separation and divorce between man and wife? Answer: Christ states here (Matt. v. 31–32) and in Matthew xix. 9, only this one, which is called adultery, and he quotes it from the law of Moses, which punishes adultery with death. Since now death alone dissolves marriages and releases from the obligation, an adulterer is already divorced not by man but by God himself, and not only cut loose from his spouse, but from this life. For by adultery he has divorced himself from his wife, and has dissolved the marriage, which he has no right to do; and he has thereby made himself worthy of death, in such a way that he is already dead before God, although the judge does not take his life. Because now God here divorces, the other party is fully released, so that he or she is not bound to keep the spouse that has proved unfaithful, however much he or she may desire it.

For we do not order or forbid this divorcing, but we ask the government to act in this matter, and we submit to what the secular authorities ordain in regard to it. Yet, our advice would be to such as claim to be Christians, that it would be much better to exhort and urge both parties to remain together, and that the innocent party should become reconciled to the guilty (if humbled and reformed) and exercise forgiveness in Christian love; unless no improvement could be hoped for, or the guilty person who had been pardoned and restored to favor persisted in abusing this kindness, and still continued in leading a public, loose life, and took it for granted that one must continue to spare and forgive him. . . .

In addition to this cause of divorce there is still another: if one of a married couple forsakes the other, as when through sheer petulance deserts the other. So, if a heathen woman were married to a Christian, or, as now sometimes happens, that one of the parties is evangelical and the other not (concerning which Paul speaks in I Cor. vii. 13), whether in such a case divorce would be right? There Paul concludes: If the one party is willing to remain, the other should not break the engagement; although they are not of one faith, the faith should not dissolve the marriage tie. But if it happens that the other party absolutely will not remain, then let him or her depart; and thou art not under any obligation to follow. But if a fellow deserts his wife without her knowledge or consent, forsakes house, home, wife and child, stays away two or three years, or as long as he pleases (as now often happens), and when he has run his riotous course and squandered his substance and wants to come home again and take his old place, that the other party must be under obligation to wait for him as long as he chooses, and then take up with him again: such a fellow ought not only to be forbidden house and home, but should be banished from the country, and the other party, if the renegade has been summoned and long enough waited for, should be heartily pronounced free.

— Commentary on Sermon on the Mount, *pp. 169–174.*

In these matters I decide nothing, as I have said, although there is nothing I would rather see decided, since nothing at present more grievously perplexes me and many more with me.

— "*The Babylonian Captivity of the Church,*" Works of Martin Luther, *Vol. II, pp. 272 f.*

4. WAR AND PEACE

War is one of the greatest plagues that can afflict humanity; it destroys religion, it destroys states, it destroys families. Any scourge, in fact, is preferable to it. Famine and pestilence become as nothing in comparison with it.

— Table-Talk, *#DCCLXXVII.*

The headstrong and the unyielding, they who excuse none but are determined to control all things by their own wisdom, lead the whole world into error. They are the cause of all the wars and calamities known on earth. Yet they claim justice as their sole motive. Well has it been said by a certain heathen: "*Summum jus, summa injustitia*" — the most extreme justice is the greatest injustice. Ecclesiastes 7:16 also warns: "Be not righteous overmuch; neither make thyself overwise." As the most extreme justice is the greatest injustice, so the most extreme wisdom is the

greatest folly. The old adage is, " When the wise act the fool, they are grossly foolish."
— *Epistle Sermon, Fourth Sunday in Advent* (Lenker Edition, *Vol. VII, #20*).

When men write about war, then, and say that it is a great plague, that is all true; but they should also see how great the plague is that it prevents. If people were good, and glad to keep peace, war would be the greatest plague on earth; but what are you going to do with the fact that people will not keep peace, but rob, steal, kill, outrage women and children, and take away property and honor? The small lack of peace, called war, or the sword, must set a check upon this universal, world-wide lack of peace, before which no one could stand. Therefore God honors the sword so highly that He calls it His own ordinance, and will not have men say or imagine that they have invented it or instituted it. For the hand that wields this sword and slays with it is then no more man's hand, but God's, and it is not man, but God, who hangs, tortures, beheads, slays and fights. All these are His works and His judgments. In a word, in thinking of the soldier's office, we must not have regard to the slaying, burning, smiting, seizing, etc. That is what the narrow, simple eyes of children do, when they see in the physician only a man who cuts off hands or saws off legs, but do not see that he does it to save the whole body. So, too, we must look at the office of the soldier, or the sword, with grown-up eyes, and see why it slays and acts so cruelly. Then it will prove itself to be an office that, in itself, is godly, as needful and useful to the world as eating and drinking or any other work. . . .

It is not right to begin war whenever any crazy lord takes it into his head. For at the very outset, I want to say, above all else, that he who starts war is wrong, and it is just that he who first draws sword shall be defeated, or even punished, in the end. This is what has usually happened in history; those who have started wars have lost them, and it has been seldom that they have been beaten who have had to defend themselves. Worldly government has not been instituted by God to break peace and start war, but to maintain peace and repress the fighters. So Paul says, in Romans xiii, that the duty of the sword is to protect and punish, to protect the good in peace and punish the wicked with war; and God, who tolerates no wrong, so disposes things that the fighters must be fought down, and as the proverb says, " No one has ever been so bad, that some-one is not worse." So, too, God has it sung of Him, in Psalm lxvii, *Dissipat gentes, quae bella volunt,* " The Lord scattereth the peoples who have desire for war." . . .

All this God confirms with fine examples in the Scriptures. He had His people first offer peace to the kingdoms of the Amorites and Canaanites and would not have His people begin the fight with them, so that this precept of His might be confirmed. On the other hand, when these kingdoms began the war and forced God's people to defend themselves, they had to go to pieces. Self-protection is a proper cause of war and therefore all laws agree that self-defense shall go unpunished, and he who kills another in self-defense is innocent in everyone's eyes. Again, when the people of Israel willed to smite the Canaanites without necessity, they were beaten (Numbers xiv) ; and when Joseph and Azarias wanted to fight in order to win honor, they were beaten; and Amaziah, king of Judah, also desired to war against the king of Israel, but read, in II Kings xiv, what happened to him; also King Ahab began to fight against the Syrians at Ramath, but lost and was destroyed (II Kings xxii) ; and the men of Ephraim would have devoured Jephthah and lost 42,000 men (Judges xii) ; and so on. You find that the losers were almost always those who started the war. The good king Josiah had to be slain because he began to fight against the king of Egypt, and had to make good the saying, " The Lord scattereth those who desire to war." Therefore my people in the Harz have a proverb, " I have verily heard that he who smites is smitten." Why so? Because God rules the world powerfully and leaves no wrong unpunished. He who does wrong has his punishment from God, as sure as he lives, unless he repents and gives compensation to his neighbor. . . . War is not right, even between equal and equal, unless it is fought with such a good conscience that one can say, " My neighbor compels and forces me to fight, though I would rather avoid it." In that case, it can be called not only war, but due protection and self-defense. For a distinction must be made among wars; some are begun out of a desire and will to fight and before one is attacked, others are forced by necessity and compulsion after the attack has been made by the other party. The first kind can be called wars of desire, the second wars of necessity. The first kind are of the devil; God give him no good fortune! The second kind are human misfortunes; God help in them! . . .

"Suppose my lord were wrong in going to war." I reply: If you know for sure that he is wrong, then you should fear God rather than men (Acts iv), and not fight or serve, for you cannot have a good conscience before God. "Nay," you say, "my lord compels me, takes my fief, does not give me my money, pay, and wages; and besides, I am despised and put to shame as a coward, nay, as a faith-breaker in the eyes of the world, as one who has deserted his lord in need." I answer: You must take that risk and, with God's help, let go what goes; He can restore it to you a hundred-fold, as He promises in the Gospel, "He that leaveth house, home, wife, goods, for my sake, shall get it back a hundredfold." In all other works, too, we must expect the danger that the rulers will compel us to do wrong; but since God will have us leave even father and mother for His sake, we must certainly leave lords for His sake. But if you do not know, or cannot find out whether your lord is wrong, you ought not to weaken an uncertain obedience with an uncertainty of right, but should think the best of your lord, as is the way of love, for "Love believeth all things; thinketh no evil" (I Corinthians xiii). Thus you are secure, and walk well before God. If they put you to shame, or call you faithless, it is better that God call you faithful and honorable than that the world call you faithful and honorable. What good would it do you, if the world held you for a Solomon or a Moses, and before God you were counted as bad as Saul or Ahab?

— "*Whether Soldiers, Too, Can Be Saved,*" Works of Martin Luther, *Vol. V, pp. 36–67.*

Pope Leo the Tenth, in the bull in which he put me under the ban, condemned, among other statements, the following one. I had said that "to fight against the Turk is the same thing as resisting God, who visits our sin upon us with this rod." From this article they may get it, who say that I prevent and dissuade from war against the Turk. . . . They undertook to fight against the Turk under the name of Christ, and taught men and stirred them up to do this, as though our people were an army of Christians against the Turks, who were enemies of Christ; and this is straight against Christ's doctrine and name. It is against His doctrine, because He says that Christians shall not resist evil, shall not fight or quarrel, not take revenge or insist on rights. It is against His name, because in such an army there are scarcely five Christians, and perhaps worse people in the eyes of God than are the Turks; and yet they would all bear the name of Christ. This is the greatest of all sins and one that no Turk commits, for Christ's name is used for sin and shame and thus dishonored. This would be especially so if the pope and the bishops were in the war, for they would put the greatest shame and dishonor on Christ's name, since they are called to fight against the devil with the Word of God and with prayer, and would be deserting their calling and office and fighting with the sword against flesh and blood. This they are not commanded, but forbidden to do.

O how gladly would Christ receive me at the Last Judgment, if when summoned to the spiritual office, to preach and care for souls, I had left it and busied myself with fighting and with the temporal sword! And how should Christ come to it that He or His have anything to do with the sword and go to war, and kill men's bodies, when He glories in it that He has come to save the world, not to kill people? For His work is to deal with the Gospel and by His Spirit to redeem men from sin and death, nay, to help them from this world to everlasting life. According to John vi, He fled and would not let Himself be made king; before Pilate He confessed, " My kingdom is not of this world "; and He bade Peter, in the garden, put up his sword, and said, " He that taketh the sword shall perish by the sword."

I say this not because I would teach that worldly rulers ought not be Christians, or that a Christian cannot bear the sword and serve God in temporal government. Would God they were all Christians, or that no one could be a prince unless he were a Christian! Things would be better than they now are and the Turk would not be so powerful. But what I would do is keep the callings and offices distinct and apart, so that everyone can see to what he is called, and fulfill the duties of his office faithfully and with the heart, in the service of God. . . .

If I were emperor, king, or prince in a campaign against the

Turk, I would exhort my bishops and priests to stay at home and mind the duties of their office, praying, fasting, saying mass, preaching, and caring for the poor, as not only Holy Scripture, but their own canon law teaches and requires. If, however, they were to be disobedient to God and their own law and desire to go along to war, I would teach them by force to attend to their office and not, by their disobedience, put me and my army under God's wrath and into danger. It would be less harmful to have three devils in the army than one disobedient, apostate bishop, who had forgotten his office and assumed that of another. For there can be no good fortune with such people around, who go against God and their own law. . . . For the Church ought not strive or fight with the sword; it has other enemies than flesh and blood, their name is the wicked devils in the air; therefore it has other weapons and swords and other wars, so that it has enough to do, and cannot mix in the wars of the emperor or princes, for the Scriptures say that there shall be no good fortune where men are disobedient to God. . . .

In the first place, it is certain that the Turk has no right or command to begin war and to attack lands that are not his. Therefore, his war is nothing else than outrage and robbery, with which God is punishing the world, as He often does through wicked knaves, and sometimes through godly people. For he does not fight from necessity or to protect his land in peace, as the right kind of a ruler does, but like a pirate or highwayman, he seeks to rob and damage other lands, who are doing and have done nothing to him. He is God's rod and the devil's servant; there is no doubt about that.

In the second place, it must be known that the man, whoever he is, who is going to make war against the Turk, must be sure that he has a commission from God and is doing right. He must not plunge in for the sake of revenge or have some other mad notion or reason. He must be sure of this, so that, win or lose, he may be in a state of salvation and in a godly occupation. There are two of these men, and there ought to be only two: the one is named Christian, the other Emperor Charles.

Christian should be first, with his army. For since the Turk is the rod of the wrath of the Lord our God and the servant of the raging devil, the first thing to be done is to smite the devil, his lord, and take the rod out of God's hand, so that the Turk may be found in his own strength only, all by himself, without the devil's help and without God's hand. This should be done by Sir Christian, that is, the pious, holy, dear body of Christians. They are the people who have the arms for this war and know what to do with them. If the Turk's god, the devil, is not first beaten, there is reason to fear that the Turk will not be so easy to beat. Now the devil is a spirit, who cannot be beaten with armor, guns, horses, and men, and God's wrath cannot be allayed by them, as it is written in Psalm xxxiii, " The Lord hath no pleasure in the strength of the horse, neither delighteth he in any man's legs; the Lord delighteth in them that fear him and wait for his goodness." Christian weapons and power must do it. . . .

The second man whose place it is to fight against the Turk is Emperor Charles, or whoever is emperor; for the Turk attacks his subjects and his empire, and it is his duty, as a regular ruler appointed by God, to defend his own. I repeat it here, that I would not urge anyone or tell anyone to fight against the Turk unless the first method, mentioned above, had been followed, and men had first repented and been reconciled to God, etc. If anyone will go to war besides, let him take his risk. It is not proper for me to say anything more about it beyond telling everyone his duty and instructing his conscience.

I see clearly that kings and princes are taking such a silly and careless attitude toward the Turk that I fear they are despising God and the Turk too greatly, or do not know, perhaps, that the Turk is such a mighty lord that no kingdom or land, whatever it is, is strong enough to resist him alone, unless God will do a miracle. Now I cannot expect any miracle or special grace of God for Germany, unless men amend their ways and honor the Word of God differently than has hitherto been done.

But enough has been said about that for those who will listen. We would now speak of the emperor.

In the first place, if there is to be war against the Turk, it should be fought at the emperor's command, under his banner, and in his name. Then everyone can assure his own conscience that he is obeying the ordinance of God, since we know that the emperor is our true overlord and head, and he who obeys him, in such a case, obeys God also, while he who disobeys him disobeys God also. If he dies in this obedience, he dies in a good state, and if he has previously repented and believes on Christ, he is saved. These things, I suppose, everyone knows better than I can teach him, and would to God they knew them as well as they think they do. Yet we will say something more about them.

In the second place, this banner and obedience of the emperor ought to be true and simple. The emperor should seek nothing else than simply to perform the work and duty of his office, which is to protect his subjects; and those under his banner should seek simply the work and duty of obedience. By this simplicity you should understand that there is to be no fighting of the Turk for the reasons for which the emperors and princes have heretofore been urged to war, such as the winning of great honor, glory, and wealth, the increasing of lands, or wrath and revengefulness and other things of the kind; for by these things men seek only their own self-interest, and therefore we have had no good fortune heretofore, either in fighting or planning to fight against the Turk.

— " *On War Against the Turk*," Works of Martin Luther, *Vol. V, pp. 81–103.*

It is indeed a splendid and a needful thing to build strong cities and castles against one's enemies; but that is nothing when compared with the work of a prince who builds a stronghold of peace, that is, who loves peace and administers it. Even the Romans, the greatest warriors on earth, had a saying that to make war without necessity was to go fishing with a golden net; if it was lost, the fishing could not pay for it; if it caught anything, the cost was too much greater than the profit. One must not begin a war, or work for it; it comes unbidden, all too soon. One must keep peace as long as ever one can, even though one must buy it with all the money that would be spent on the war, or won by the war. Victory never makes up for what is lost by war.

— " *An Exposition of the Eighty-second Psalm*," Works of Martin Luther, *Vol. IV, p. 304.*

5. THE KINGDOM OF GOD

" Thy kingdom come." What does this mean? The kingdom of God comes indeed of itself, without our prayer; but we pray in this petition that it may come also to us. How is this done? When our heavenly Father gives us his Holy Spirit, so that by his grace we believe his Holy Word and live godly, here in time, and in heaven forever. " Thy will be done on earth, as it is in heaven." What does this mean? The good and gracious will of God is done indeed without our prayer; but we pray in this petition that it may be done also among us. How is this done? When God defeats and hinders every evil counsel and purpose, which would not let us hallow God's name nor let his kingdom come, such as the will of the devil, the world, and our own flesh; but strengthens and keeps us steadfast in his Word and in faith unto our end. This is his gracious and good will.

— " *Small Catechism* " (Lenker Edition, *Vol. XXIV, pp. 25 f*).

What is the kingdom of God? The answer is: Simply what we learned in the Creed — that God sent his Son, Jesus Christ our Lord, into the world to redeem and deliver us from the devil's power and to bring us to himself and reign over us a king of righteousness, of life and salvation, defending us from sin, death and an evil conscience. And, further, that God gave us his Holy Spirit to teach us, through his holy Word, and by his power to enlighten and strengthen us in faith. We pray here (" Thy kingdom come "), then, that all this may be realized by us, and that we may so honor his name through his holy Word and our Christian life that we who have accepted it may abide and daily grow therein; that it may be accepted and followed among others and advance in power throughout the world; and that thus, led by the Holy Spirit, many may enter the kingdom of grace and become partakers of the blessings of redemption, and thus we may all remain together in this one kingdom which has now made its appearance among us.

The kingdom of God comes to us in two different ways: first, in time, through the Word and faith; secondly, it shall be revealed in eternity. We pray that it may come to those who are not yet therein, and also that in us who have received the same it may daily increase and remain ours in life eternal. All this is simply saying: Dear Father, we pray give us first thy Word, that the Gospel be sincerely preached throughout the world; and we pray, that it be accepted in faith, to work and live in us; so that through the Word and the power of the Holy Spirit, thy kingdom may prevail among us to the defeat of the devil's kingdom; so he shall have no claim and power over us and at last shall be utterly overthrown and sin and death and hell be destroyed, that we may live forever in perfect righteousness and blessedness.

You see that we do not here pray for a mere crust of bread, or for a temporal, perishable blessing; we pray for an eternal, priceless treasure and all that God himself can give. It would be far too great for any human heart to presume to ask, if God had not himself commanded us to pray for it. Because he is God, he claims the honor of giving far more richly and abundantly than any can comprehend — like an eternal and unfailing fountain, which, the more it pours forth and overflows, the more it has to give. He desires of us nothing more ardently than that we ask many and great things of him, and he is displeased if we do not confidently ask and entreat.

— *" Large Catechism "* (Lenker Edition, *Vol. XXIV, pp. 141–142*).

God builds up his Christendom in a way that he calls it, and what pertains to its government, the kingdom of heaven; to signify, that he has called and separated out of the world a people for himself here upon the earth through the Word of his Gospel; not to the end that it should be fitted and organized, like the outer and civil government, with temporal rule, power, possessions, government and maintenance of outward worldly righteousness, discipline, defence, peace, etc. For all this has already before been richly ordered, and it was commanded and put into man to rule in this life as well as he can; although this is also through sin weakened and spoiled so that it is not as it should be, and is a poor, miserable, weak government, as weak and transient as the human body, and is able to go no farther, where it is at its best, than the stomach, as long as the stomach performs its functions. But above that God has arranged and instituted his own divine government, after he revealed his fathomless grace and gave his Word to prepare and gather a people, whom he redeemed from his wrath, eternal death and sin, through which they fell into such misery, and from which they could not help themselves by any human wisdom, counsel or power, and taught them to know him aright and to praise and laud him forever.

Christ here, (Matt. 22:1–14), calls his kingdom the kingdom of heaven, where he does not rule in a temporal way nor deals with the things of this life; but he founded and developed an eternal, imperishable kingdom, which begins on the earth through faith, and in which we receive and possess those eternal riches, forgiveness of sins, comfort, strength, renewal of the Holy Spirit, victory and triumph over the power of satan, death and hell, and finally eternal life of body and soul, that is, eternal fellowship and blessedness with God.

Such a divine kingdom can be governed, built up, protected, extended and maintained only by means of the external office of the Word and of the Sacraments, through which the Holy Spirit is powerful and works in the hearts etc., as I have often said in speaking on this theme.

— *Gospel Sermon, Twentieth Sunday After Trinity* (Lenker Edition, *Vol. XIV, #2–4*).

We have often said that the Gospel or kingdom of God is nothing else than a state or government, in which there is nothing but forgiveness of sins. And wherever there is a state or government in which sins are not forgiven, no Gospel or kingdom of God is found there. Therefore we must clearly distinguish these two kingdoms from each other, in which sins are rebuked, and sins are forgiven, or in which our right is demanded, and our right is pardoned. In the kingdom of God, where God rules with the Gospel, there is no demand for right and dues, but all is pure forgiveness, pardon and giving, no anger, no punishment, but all is pure brotherly service and kindness.

By this, however, our civil rights are not abolished. For this parable, (Matt. 18:23–35), teaches nothing of the kingdom of this world, but only of the kingdom of God. Therefore, whoever is only under the civil government of the world, is far from the kingdom of heaven, for all this still belongs to perdition. As when a prince so rules his people as not to permit anyone to be wronged, and punishes the evil doer, does well and is praised. For thus it is in this government: Pay what thou owest, if not, you will be cast into prison. Such government we must have, but no one will thereby get to heaven, nor will the world be saved by it. But it is necessary for the reason that the world may not become worse, it is only a protection against and a prevention of wickedness. For if it were not for this government one would devour the other, and no person could protect his life, goods, wife and child. So in order that everything may not go to ruin, God has instituted functions of the sword, by which wickedness may in part be prevented, so that the civil government may secure and maintain peace, and no one may wrong another. Therefore it must be tolerated. And yet as we have said, it has not been established for citizens of heaven, but simply in order that the people may not fall deeper into hell, and make matters worse.

Therefore no one dare boast, who is under the civil government, that he therefore does right before God. Before him, all is yet wrong. For you must come to the point, that you also avoid what the world claims to be right.

— *Gospel Sermon, Twenty-second Sunday After Trinity* (Lenker Edition, *Vol. XIV*, #4–5).

> Wilt thou, O man, live happily,
> And dwell with God eternally,
> The ten commandments keep, for thus
> Our God himself biddeth us.
> > Kyri' Eleison!

> I am the Lord and God! take heed
> No other god doth thee mislead;
> Thy heart shall trust alone in me,
> My kingdom then thou shalt be.
> > Kyri' Eleison!

> Honor my name in word and deed,
> And call on me in time of need:

Hallow the Sabbath, that I may
Work in thy heart on that day.
Kyri' Eleison!

Obedient always, next to me,
To father and to mother be;
Kill no man; even anger dread;
Keep sacred thy marriage-bed.
Kyri' Eleison!

Steal not, nor do thy neighbor wrong
By bearing witness with false tongue;
Thy neighbor's wife desire thou not,
Nor grudge him aught he hath got.
Kyri' Eleison!

May Christ the Lord, aid us to this;
He Who our Mediator is.
With our good acts naught can be done
But earn chastisement alone.
Kyri' Eleison!
— Luther's Hymns, *p. 101.*

X

The Christian and the State

The Christian and the State

※

1. THE TWO ORDERS OF GOVERNMENT

THERE are two kingdoms, one the kingdom of God, the other the kingdom of the world. I have written this so often that I am surprised that there is anyone who does not know it or note it. . . . God's kingdom is a kingdom of grace and mercy, not of wrath and punishment. In it there is only forgiveness, consideration for one another, love, service, the doing of good, peace, joy, etc. But the kingdom of the world is a kingdom of wrath and severity. In it there is only punishment, repression, judgment, and condemnation, for the suppressing of the wicked and the protection of the good. For this reason it has the sword, and a prince or lord is called in Scripture God's wrath, or God's rod (Isaiah xiv). . . . Now he who would confuse these two kingdoms — as our false fanatics do — would put wrath into God's kingdom and mercy into the world's kingdom; and that is the same as putting the devil in heaven and God in hell.

— "*An Open Letter Concerning the Hard Book Against the Peasants*," Works of Martin Luther, *Vol. IV, pp. 265 f.*

To wield the temporal sword belongs to the emperor, to kings, to princes, and to the rulers of this world, and by no means to the spiritual estate, whose sword is not to be of iron, but the sword of the Spirit, which is the Word and commandment of God, as St. Paul says.

— "*A Treatise Concerning the Ban,*" Works of Martin Luther, *Vol. II, pp. 38 f.*

The two powers or governments, God's and Caesar's, or spiritual and temporal kingdoms, must be kept apart, as Christ does here, (Matt. 22:15–22), in a clear and brief declaration, making a distinction not only, but also illustrating finely how each is to be constituted and administered. When he says, " Render unto Caesar the things that are Caesar's," he refers to the relation of subjects to their rulers; the other part, " Render unto God the things that are God's," is especially intended for such as are in authority.

For it is thus ordained of God that subjects must and shall give to their rulers what they need; when he commands them to give, it is implied that these may take; and where we are to give what is due, there we infer that we owe them something, so that the language might be: " to return," rather than simply to render or give. That is something for subjects under civil authority.

On the other hand, there are restrictions placed upon rulers that they govern in the same spirit, and not take from their subjects what is not due them; but remember to give and do also what they are in duty bound to do by virtue of their presiding over countries and nations, so that they may grow and prosper. That is why they were elevated by God to their respective positions of honor, not that they sit there simply as place-thieves, and doing what they like. . . .

Government must also be told how to act toward its subjects. Those in authority also rob and take what is not theirs, and that on the responsibility of their superiors. As when an emperor or prince goes on, plaguing land and people with unnecessary assessments and other burdens. In that situation thou must also hear thy text. If thou desirest the subjects to put into practice their lesson and be honest with thee, thou must also avoid taking from them what is not thine. For Christ does not say here, Render to Caesar that which he wants and likes, but he assigns limits to him, how far he may reach, that is: " The things that are Caesar's," or what he is rightfully entitled to.

Therefore, land, cities, homes, are not to be governed as the one in authority over them may like, as if an employer could treat his employes to suit his notion, contrary to the Lord's justice. Nay, the employe would say, I owe thee what is thine, not what thou mayest desire to have. One might require so much as my head or fist, or he would not pay me wages or food and clothing, and so plunder and plague me as not to leave a rag upon my body. That would be taking the rights from the man-servant, and her property from the maid-servant. . . .

This is a brief statement as to the first estate or government, both in its higher and its lower functions, to show how far we are away from our true position and how full the world is everywhere of thievery. But these matters are worst of all, if one is to expound this passage (render to God what is God's) and speak of the God-thieves in the spiritual government of Christendom, in which I and the likes of me are. For as high as heaven is above the earth so dangerous and difficult is this office in comparison with secular or imperial positions which, indeed, are also dangerous where their occupants do not call upon God for help to discharge their duties properly and without injury to their subjects. But if unfaithful ministers or preachers get into their office they will be, not thieves of bread, meat or clothing, wherewith the body is nourished and with which jurists busy themselves, who teach nothing further than what ministers to the belly and try to check that class of stealing; but those who occupy the office that is to give the bread of eternal life to souls and, instead, cause them everlasting thirst, hunger and nakedness, taking away the word by which man is nourished from death to life, such are not simply belly-thieves, but thieves of God and of the heavenly kingdom.

— *Gospel Sermon, Twenty-third Sunday After Trinity* (Lenker Edition, *Vol. XIV, #27–39*).

God has established magistracy for the sake of the unbelieving, insomuch that even Christian men might exercise the power of the sword, and come under obligation thereby to serve their neighbor and restrain the bad, so that the good might remain in peace among them. And still the command of Christ abides in force, that we are not to resist evil. So that a Christian, although he bears the sword, does not use it for his own sake nor to revenge himself, but only for others; and, moreover, this is a mark of Christian love, that with the sword we support and defend the whole Church, and not suffer it to be injured. Christ teaches those only who, while they believe and love, obey also. But the greater multitude in the world, as it does not believe, obeys not the command. Therefore they must be ruled as unchristian, and their caprice be put under restraint; for if their power was suffered to obtain the upper hand, no one could stand before them.

Thus there are two kinds of government in the world, as there are also two kinds of people, — namely, believers and unbelievers. Christians yield themselves to the control of God's word; they have no need of civil government for their own sake. But the unchristian portion require another government, even the civil sword, since they will not be controlled by the word of God. Yet if all were Christians and followed the Gospel, there would be no more necessity or use for the civil sword and the exercising of authority; for if there were no evil-doers there certainly could be no punishment. But since it is not to be expected that all of us should be righteous, Christ has ordained magistracy for the wicked, that they may rule as they must be ruled. But the righteous He keeps for Himself, and rules them by His mere word.

— Commentary on Peter and Jude, *pp. 127 f.*

We must firmly establish secular law and the sword, that no one may doubt that it is in the world by God's will and ordinance. The passages which establish this are the following: Romans xiii, " Let every soul be subject to power and authority, for there is no power but from God. The power that is everywhere is ordained of God. He then who resists the power resists God's ordinance. But he who resists God's ordinance shall bring himself under condemnation." Likewise, I Peter ii, " Be subject to every kind of human ordinance, whether to the king as supreme, or to the governors, as to those sent of Him for the punishing of the evil and for the reward of the good." . . .

There seems to be a powerful argument on the other side. Christ says, Matthew v, " Ye have heard that it was said to them of old: An eye for an eye, a tooth for a tooth. But I say unto you, That a man shall not resist evil, but if any one strikes thee upon the right cheek, turn to him the other also; and whoever will go to law with thee to take thy coat, let him have the cloak also, and whoever forces thee a mile, with him go two miles." Likewise Paul, Romans xii, "Dearly beloved, defend not yourselves, but give place to God's wrath, for it is written, Vengeance is mine, I will repay saith the Lord." Likewise Matthew v, "Love your enemies, do good to them that hate you." And I Peter iii, "Let no one repay evil with evil, nor railing with railing," etc. These and the like passages truly would make it appear as though in the New Testament there should be no secular sword among Christians. . . .

If all the world were composed of real Christians, that is, true believers, no prince, king, lord, sword, or law would be needed. For what were the use of them, since Christians have in their hearts the Holy Spirit, who instructs them and causes them to wrong no one, to love every one, willingly and cheerfully to suffer injustice and even death from every one. Where every wrong is suffered and every right is done, no quarrel, strife, trial, judge, penalty, law or sword is needed. Therefore, it is not possible for the secular sword and law to find any work to do among Christians, since of themselves they do much more than its laws and doctrines can demand. Just as Paul says in I Timothy i, "The law is not given for the righteous, but for the unrighteous."

Why is this? Because the righteous does of himself all and more than all that all the laws demand. But the unrighteous do nothing that the law demands, therefore they need the law to instruct, constrain, and compel them to do what is good. A good tree does not need any teaching or law to bear good fruit, its nature causes it to bear according to its kind without any law and teaching. A man would be a fool to make a book of laws and statutes telling an apple tree how to bear apples and not thorns, when it is able by its own nature to do this better than man with all his books can define and direct. Just so, by the Spirit and by faith all Christians are throughout inclined to do well and keep the law, much more than any one can teach them with all the laws, and need so far as they are concerned no commandments nor law. . . .

All who are not Christians belong to the kingdom of the world and are under the law. Since few believe and still fewer live a Christian life, do not resist the evil, and themselves do no evil, God has provided for non-Christians a different government outside the Christian estate and God's kingdom, and has subjected them to the sword, so that, even though they would do so, they cannot practice their wickedness, and that, if they do, they may not do it without fear nor in peace and prosperity. Even so a wild, savage beast is fastened with chains and bands, so that it cannot bite and tear as is its wont, although it gladly would do so; whereas a tame and gentle beast does not require this, but without any chains and bands is nevertheless harmless. If it were not so, seeing that the whole world is evil and that among thousands there is scarcely one true Christian, men would devour one another, and no one could preserve wife and child, support himself and serve God; and thus the world would be reduced to chaos. For this reason God has ordained the two governments; the spiritual, which by the Holy Spirit under Christ makes Christians and pious people, and the secular, which restrains the unchristian and wicked so that they must needs keep the peace outwardly, even against their will. So Paul interprets the secular sword, Romans xiii, and says it is not a terror to good works, but to the evil. And Peter says it is for the punishment of evil doers. . . .

It is indeed true that Christians, so far as they themselves are concerned, are subject to neither law nor sword and need neither; but first take heed and fill the world with real Christians before ruling it in a Christian and evangelical manner. This you will never accomplish; for the world and the masses are and always will be unchristian, although they are all baptised and are nominally Christian. Christians, however, are few and far between, as the saying is. Therefore it is out of the question that there should be a common Christian government over the whole world, nay even over one land or company of people, since the wicked always outnumber the good. Hence a man who would venture to govern an entire country or the world with the Gospel would be like a shepherd who should place in one fold wolves, lions, eagles, and sheep together and let them freely mingle with one another and say, Help yourselves, and be good and peaceful among yourselves; the fold is open, there is plenty of food; have no fear of dogs and clubs. The sheep, forsooth, would keep the peace and would allow themselves to be fed and governed in peace, but they would not live long; nor would any beast keep from molesting another. . . .

But perhaps you will say, Since Christians do not need the secular sword and the law, why does Paul say to all Christians, in Romans xiii, " Let all souls be subject to power and authority "? And St. Peter says, " Be subject to every human ordinance," etc., as quoted above. I answer, as I have said, that Christians, among themselves and by and for themselves, need no law or sword, since it is neither necessary nor profitable for them. Since, however, a true Christian lives and labors on earth not for himself, but for his neighbor, therefore the whole spirit of his life impels him to do even that which he need not do, but which is profitable and necessary for his neighbor. Because the sword is a very great benefit and necessary to the whole world, to preserve peace, to punish sin and to prevent evil, he submits most willingly to the rule of the sword, pays tax, honors those in authority, serves, helps, and does all he can to further the government, that it may be sustained and held in honor and fear. Although he needs none of these things for himself and it is not necessary for him to do them, yet he considers what is for the good and profit of others, as Paul teaches in Ephesians v. . . .

Why did not Christ and the apostles bear the sword? Tell me, Why did He not also take a wife, or become a cobbler or a tailor? If an occupation or office is not good because Christ Himself did not occupy it, what would become of all occupations and offices, with the exception of the ministry which alone He exercised? Christ fulfilled His own office and vocation, but thereby did not reject any other. It was not meet that He should bear the sword, for He was to bear only that office by which His kingdom is governed and which properly serves His kingdom. Now it does not concern His kingdom that He should be a married man, a cobbler, a tailor, a farmer, a prince, a hangman or a beadle, neither is the sword or secular law of any concern, but only God's Word and Spirit, by which His people are inwardly governed. This office which He exercised then, and still exercises, always bestows God's Word and Spirit; and in this office the apostles and all spiritual rulers must needs follow Him. For they are kept so busily employed with the spiritual sword, the Word of God, in fulfilling this their calling, that they must indeed neglect the worldly sword, and leave it to those who do not have to preach; although it is not contrary to their calling to use it, as I have said. For every one must attend to his own calling and work.

Therefore, even though Christ did not bear the sword nor prescribe it, it is sufficient that He did not forbid or abolish it, but rather endorsed it; just as it is sufficient that He did not abolish the state of matrimony, but endorsed it, though He Himself took no wife and gave no commandment concerning it. He had to identify Himself throughout with the occupation and work which properly and entirely served the furtherance of His kingdom, so that no occasion and binding example might be made of it, to teach and believe that the kingdom of God cannot exist without matrimony and the sword and such externals (since Christ's examples are binding), when it is only by God's Word and Spirit that it does exist. This was and had to be Christ's peculiar work as the supreme King in this kingdom. Since, however, not all Christians have this same office, though innately it belongs to them, it is meet that they should have some other, external one, by which God may also be served.

From all this we see what is the true meaning of Christ's words in Matthew v, " Resist not evil," etc. It is this, that a Christian should be so disposed that he will suffer every evil and injustice, not avenge himself nor bring suit in court, and in nothing make use of secular power and law for himself. For others, however, he may and should seek vengeance, justice, protection and help, and do what he can toward this. Likewise, the State should, either of itself or through the instigation of others, help and protect him without complaint, application or instigation on his part. When the State does not do this, he ought to permit himself to be robbed and despoiled, and not resist the evil, as Christ's words say. . . .

But you ask further, whether the beadles, hangmen, jurists, advocates, and their ilk, can also be Christians and in a state of salvation. I answer: If the State and its sword are a divine service, as was proved above, that which the State needs in order to wield the sword must also be a divine service. There must be those who arrest, accuse, slay and destroy the wicked, and protect, acquit, defend and save the good. Therefore, when such duties are performed, not with the intention of seeking one's own ends, but only of helping to maintain the laws and the State, so that the wicked may be restrained, there is no peril in them and they may be followed like any other pursuit and be used as one's means of support. For, as was said, love of neighbor seeks not its own, considers not how great or how small, but how profitable and how needful for neighbor or community the works are.

You ask, Why may I not use the sword for myself and for my own cause, with the intention by so doing not of seeking my own interest, but the punishment of evil? I answer, Such a miracle is not impossible, but quite unusual and hazardous. Where there is such affluence of the Spirit it may be done, for so we read of Samson in Judges xv, that he said, " I have done unto them as they did unto me "; yet, on the contrary, Proverbs xxix says, " Say not, I will do unto him as he has done unto me "; and Proverbs xxiv, " Say not thou, I will recompense evil." For Samson was called of God to harass the Philistines and deliver the children of Israel. Though he used them as an occasion to advance his own cause, still he did not do so to avenge himself or to seek his own interests, but to serve others and to punish the Philistines. No one but a real Christian and one who is full of the Spirit will follow this example. If reason also should follow this example, it would indeed pretend not to be seeking its own, but this would be untrue. It cannot be done without grace. Therefore, first become like Samson, and then you can also do as Samson did.

— " Secular Authority: To What Extent It Should Be Obeyed," Works of Martin Luther, *Vol. III, pp. 231–250.*

2. THE CHRISTIAN'S DUTY TO OBEY TEMPORAL RULERS

It is God's will to establish and maintain peace among the children of Adam for their own good; as St. Paul says, in Romans xiii, " It is God's minister to you for good." For where there is no rulership, or where rulers are not held in honor, there can be no peace. Where there is no peace, no one can keep his life, or anything else, in the face of another's outrage, thievery, robbery, violence, and wickedness; much less will there be room to teach God's Word, and to raise children in the fear of God and in discipline. Because, then, God will not have the world desolate and empty, but has made it for men to live in and till the land and fill it, as is written in Genesis i; and because this cannot happen where there is no peace; He is compelled, as a Creator, preserving His own creatures, works, and ordinances, to institute and preserve rulership, and to commit to it the sword and the laws, so that He may slay and punish all those who do not obey it, as men who strive also against God and His ordinance, and are not worthy to live.

But again, as, on the one hand, He keeps down the disorder of the rabble and therefore subjects them to the sword and the laws; so, on the other hand, He keeps down the rulers, that they shall not abuse His majesty and power according to their own self-will, but use them for that peace for which He has appointed and preserves them. Nevertheless, it is not His will to allow the rabble to raise their fist against the rulers or to seize the sword, as if to punish and judge the rulers. No, they must leave that! It is not God's will, and He has not committed this to them. They are not to be judges and revenge themselves, or resort to outrage and violence, but God Himself will punish wicked rulers and impose statutes and laws upon them. He will be judge and master over them. He will find them out, better than anyone else can, as indeed, He has done since the beginning of the world.

— " *An Exposition of the Eighty-second Psalm,*" Works of Martin Luther, *Vol. IV, pp. 290 f.*

Paul teaches, Romans xiii, and Titus iii, and St. Peter, I Peter ii: " Submit yourselves to the king as supreme, and to the princes as his ambassadors, and to all the ordinances of the worldly power." But it is the work of the temporal power to protect its subjects, and to punish thievery, robbery, and adultery, as St. Paul says, Romans xiii: " It beareth not the sword in vain; it serves God with it, to the terror of evil doers, and to the protection of the good."

Here men sin in two ways. First, if they lie to the government, deceive it, and are disloyal, neither obey nor do as it has ordered and commanded, whether with their bodies or their possessions. For even if the government does injustice, as the King of Babylon did to the people of Israel, yet God would have it obeyed, without treachery and deception. Secondly, when men speak evil of the government and curse it, and when a man cannot revenge himself and abuses the government with grumbling and evil words, publicly or secretly.

In all this we are to regard that which St. Peter bids us regard, namely, that its power, whether it do right or wrong, cannot harm the soul, but only the body and property; unless indeed it should try openly to compel us to do wrong against God or men.

— "*Treatise on Good Works*," Works of Martin Luther, *Vol. I, pp. 262 f.*

The world is far too wicked to be worthy of good and pious lords, it must have princes who go to war, levy taxes and shed blood, and it must have spiritual tyrants who impoverish and burden it with bulls and letters and laws. This and other chastisements are rather what it has deserved, and to resist them is nothing else than to resist God's chastisement. As humbly as I conduct myself when God sends me a sickness, so humbly should I conduct myself toward the evil government, which the same God also sends me.

— "*A Treatise Concerning the Ban*," Works of Martin Luther, *Vol. II, p. 51.*

All authority has its roots and warrant in parental authority. Where a father is unable alone to rear his child, he employs a teacher to instruct it; if he is too feeble, he obtains the help of his friends or neighbors; if the parent departs this life, he commits and delegates his authority and responsibility to others appointed for the purpose. He must likewise have domestics — men and maids — under him for the administration of the household. All who are called masters stand in the place of parents and from them must obtain authority and power to command. In the Bible they are all called fathers, because in their government they perform the functions of a father and should possess a fatherly heart toward their people. In the language of the Romans and others of ancient times, masters and mistresses of the household were called *patres et matres familiae*, housefathers and housemothers. So they called their princes and magistrates *patres patriae*, fathers of the country; and it is a shame that we who wish to be Christians do not so call our rulers or, at least, treat and honor them as such. What a child owes to its father and mother, the entire household owes them likewise. . . .

The same may be said of obedience due to civil authority, which authority, as we have said, is all embraced in the estate of fatherhood and extends beyond all other relations. Here the father is not one of a single family, but one of many tenants, citizens or subjects. Through civil rulers, as through our parents, God gives us food, home and land, protection and security. Therefore, since they bear this name and title with all honor as their chief glory, it is our duty to honor them and to esteem them as we would the greatest treasure and the most precious jewel on earth. . . .

In this connection it would not be amiss to advise parents, and others filling their office, as to their treatment of those committed to their authority. . . . God does not propose to bestow the parental office and government upon rogues and tyrants; therefore, he does not give them that honor, namely, the power and authority to govern, merely to receive homage. Parents should consider that they are under obligations to obey God and that, first of all, they are conscientiously and faithfully to discharge all the duties of their office; not only to feed and provide for the temporal wants of their children, servants, subjects, etc., but especially to train them to the honor and praise of God.

— "*Large Catechism*" (Lenker Edition, *Vol. XXIV, pp. 72–77*).

Obedience is the duty of subjects, considerateness that of masters, that they take care to rule their subjects well, deal kindly with them, and do everything whereby they may benefit and help them. That is their way to heaven, and these are the best works they can do on earth; with these they are more acceptable to God than if without these they did nothing but miracles. So says St. Paul, Romans xii: " He that ruleth, let him do it with diligence "; as who should say: " Let him not allow himself to be led astray by what other people or classes of people do; let him not look to this work or to that, whether it be splendid or obscure; but let him look to his own position, and think only how he may benefit those who are subject to him; by this let him stand, nor let himself be torn from it, although heaven stood open before him, nor be driven from it, although hell were chasing him. This is the right road that leads him to heaven."

— "*Treatise on Good Works*," Works of Martin Luther, *Vol. I, p. 270.*

I know that no state is well governed by means of laws. If the magistrate be wise, he will rule more prosperously by natural bent than by laws. If he be not wise, he will but further the evil by means of laws; for he will not know what use to make of the laws nor how to adapt them to the individual case. More stress ought, therefore, to be laid, in civil affairs, on putting good and wise men in office than on making laws; for such men will themselves be the very best laws, and will judge every variety of case with lively justice. And if there be knowledge of the divine law combined with natural wisdom, then written laws will be entirely superfluous and harmful. Above all, love needs no laws whatever.

— "*The Babylonian Captivity of the Church*," Works of Martin Luther, *Vol. II, p. 263.*

Rulers are not instituted in order that they may seek their own profit and self-will, but in order to provide for the best interests of their subjects. Flaying and extortion are, in the long run, intolerable. What good would it do if a peasant's field bore as many *gulden* as stalks or grains of wheat, if that only meant that the rulers would take all the more, and make their splendor all the greater, and squander the property on clothing, eating, drinking, building, and the like, as though it were chaff? The splendor would have to be checked and the expenditure stopped, so that a poor man too could keep something.

— "*Admonition to Peace: A Reply to the Twelve Articles of the Peasants in Swabia*," Works of Martin Luther, *Vol. IV, p. 224.*

The magistracy is a necessary state in the world, and to be held in honor; therefore we ought to pray for magistrates, who may easily be corrupted and spoiled. *Honores mutant mores, numquam in meliores:* Honors alter a man's manners, and seldom for the better. The prince who governs without laws, according to his own brain, is a monster, worse than a wild beast; but he who governs according to the prescribed laws and rights, is like unto God, who is an erector and founder of laws and rights.

— Table-Talk, #*DCCXVI*.

3. CONCERNING THE RIGHT OF REBELLION

Here stands the law, and says, " No one shall fight or make war against his overlord; for a man owes his overlord obedience, honor and fear " (Romans xiii). If one chops over one's head, the chips fall in one's eyes, and as Solomon says, " He who throws stones in the air, upon his head they fall." That is the law in a nut-shell. God Himself has instituted it and men have accepted it, for it does not fit together that men shall both obey and resist, be subject and not put up with their lords.

But we have already said that justice ought to be mistress of law, and where circumstances demand, guide the law, or even command and permit men to act against it. Therefore the question here is whether it can be just, i.e., whether a case can arise in which one can act against this law, be disobedient to rulers and fight against them, depose them or put them in bonds. . . .

The peasants in their rebellion alleged that the lords would not allow the Gospel to be preached and robbed the poor people, and, therefore that they must be overthrown; but I have answered this by saying that although the lords did wrong in this, it would not therefore be just or right to do wrong in return, that is, to be disobedient and destroy God's ordinance, which is not ours. On the contrary, we ought to suffer wrong and if prince or lord will not tolerate the Gospel, then we ought to go into another princedom where the Gospel is preached, as Christ says in Matthew x, " If they persecute you in one city flee into another."

It is just, to be sure, that if a prince, king, or lord goes crazy, he should be deposed and put under restraint, for he is not to be considered a man since his reason is gone. Yes, you say a raving tyrant is crazy, too, or is to be considered even worse than a madman, for he does much more harm. That answer puts me in a tight place, for such a statement makes a great appearance and seems to be in accord with justice. Nevertheless, it is my opinion that the cases of madmen and tyrants are not the same; for a madman can neither do nor tolerate anything reasonable, nor is there any hope for him because the light of reason has gone out. But a tyrant, however much of this kind of thing he does, knows that he does wrong. He has his conscience and his knowledge, and there is hope that he may do better, allow himself to be instructed, and learn, and follow advice, none of which things can be hoped for in a crazy man, who is like a clod or a stone. . . .

Here you will say, perhaps, " Yes, if everything is to be endured from the tyrants, you give them too much and their wickedness only becomes stronger and greater by such teaching. Is it to be endured then that every man's wife and child, body and goods, are to be in danger? Who can start any good thing if that is the way we are to live? " I reply: My teaching is not for you, if you will to do whatever you think good and whatever pleases you. Follow your own notion and slay all your lords, and see what good it does you. My teaching is only for those who would like to do right. To these I say that rulers are not to be opposed with violence and rebellion, as the Romans, the Greeks, the Swiss and the Danes have done; but there are other ways of dealing with them.

In the first place, if they see that the rulers think so little of their soul's salvation that they rage and do wrong, of what importance is it that they ruin your property, body, wife and child? They cannot hurt your soul, and they do themselves more harm than they do you, because they damn their own souls and the ruin of body and property must then follow. Do you think that you are not already sufficiently revenged upon them?

In the second place, what would you do if these rulers of yours were at war and not only your goods and wives and children, but you yourself must be broken, imprisoned, burned and slain for your lord's sake? Would you for that reason slay your lord? . . .

In the third place, if the rulers are bad, what of it? God is there, and He has fire, water, iron, stone and numberless ways of killing. How quickly He has slain a tyrant! He would do it, too, but our sins do not permit it; for He says in Job, " He letteth a knave rule because of the people's sins." It is easy enough to see that a knave rules, but no one is willing to see that he is ruling not because of his knavery, but because of the people's sin. The people do not look at their own sin, and think that the tyrant rules because of his knavery; so blinded, perverse and mad is the world! That is why things go as they went with the peasants in the revolt. They wanted to punish the sins of the rulers, just as though they were themselves pure and guiltless; therefore, God had to show them the beam in their eye in order to make them forget another's splinter.

In the fourth place, the tyrants run the risk that, by God's decree, their subjects may rise up, as has been said, and slay them or drive them out. For we are here giving instruction to those who want to do what is right, and they are very few; the great multitude remain heathen, godless, and unchristian, and these, if God so decrees, set themselves wrongfully against the rulers and create disaster, as the Jews and Greeks and Romans often did. Therefore you have no right to complain that by our doctrine the tyrants and rulers gain security to do evil; nay, they are certainly not secure. . . .

In the fifth place, God has still another way to punish rulers, so that you have no need to revenge yourself. He can raise up foreign rulers, like the Goths against the Romans, the Assyrians against the Jews, etc., so that there is vengeance, punishment, and danger enough hanging over tyrants and rulers, and God does not allow them to be wicked and have peace and joy; He is right behind them, and has them between spurs and under bridle. This agrees, also, with the natural law that Christ teaches, in Matthew vii, "What ye would that people do to you, that do you to them." No father would be driven out by his own family, slain, or ruined because of his misdeeds (especially if the family did it out of disregard of authority and love of violence, in order to revenge themselves and be judges in their own case) without previous complaint to a higher authority. It ought to be just as wrong for any subject to act against his tyrant.

— "*Whether Soldiers, Too, Can Be Saved,*" Works of Martin Luther, *Vol. V, pp. 42–49.*

Insurrection is an unprofitable method of procedure, and never results in the desired reformation. For insurrection is devoid of reason and generally hurts the innocent more than the guilty. Hence no insurrection is ever right, no matter how good the cause in whose interest it is made. The harm resulting from it always exceeds the amount of reformation accomplished, so that it fulfils the saying, " Things go from bad to worse." For this reason temporal powers are ordained and the sword given into their hands that they may punish the wicked and protect the godly, and that insurrection may not be necessary, as St. Paul says in Romans xiii, and also St. Peter in I Peter ii. . . .

My sympathies are and always will be with those against whom insurrection is made, however wrong the cause they stand for, and opposed to those who make insurrection, however much they may be in the right. For there can be no insurrection without the shedding of innocent blood and wrong done to the guiltless.

God has forbidden insurrection, in that He says through Moses, *Quod justum est, juste exequaris,* — " Thou shalt follow justly after that which is just," and " Vengeance is mine, I will repay "; upon which texts is based the true proverb, " He who strikes back is in the wrong," and that other, " No one can be his own judge." Now insurrection is nothing else than being one's own judge and avenger, and that God cannot endure. Hence the only possible result of insurrection is that matters become worse than they were, because insurrection is contrary to God and God will have nothing to do with it.

— " *An Earnest Exhortation for All Christians, Warning Them Against Insurrection and Rebellion,*" Works of Martin Luther, *Vol. III, pp. 211 f.*

Here stands God's Word, and says through the mouth of Christ, " He who takes the sword shall perish by the sword." That means nothing else than that no one, by his own violence, shall arrogate authority to himself; but as Paul says, " Let every soul be subject to the higher powers with fear and reverence."

How can you get over these sayings and laws of God, when you boast that you are acting according to divine law, and yet take the sword in your own hands, and revolt against the " higher powers " that are ordained of God? Do you not think that Paul's judgment in Romans xiii will strike you, " He that withstands the ordinance of God shall receive condemnation "? . . .

. I will . . . give you some illustrations of Christian law. . . .

Look at St. Peter in the garden. He wanted to defend his Lord Christ with the sword, and cut off Malchus' ear. Tell me, had not Peter great right on his side? Was it not an intolerable wrong that they were going to take from Christ, not only His property, but also His life? Nay, they not only took from Him life and property, but in so doing they entirely suppressed the Gospel by which they were to be saved, and thus robbed heaven. Such a wrong you have not yet suffered, dear friends. But see what Christ does and teaches in this case. However great the wrong was, nevertheless He stopped St. Peter, bade him put up his sword, and would not allow him to avenge or prevent this wrong. In addition He passed a judgment of death upon him, as though upon a murderer, and said, " He that takes the sword shall perish with the sword." From this we must understand that it is not enough that anyone has done us wrong, and that we have a good case, and have right on our side, but we must also have the right and power committed to us by God to use the sword and punish wrong. . . .

A second example is Christ himself. What did He do when they took His life on the cross and thereby took away from Him the work of preaching for which He had been sent by God Himself for the blessing of the souls of men? He did just what St. Peter says. He committed the whole matter to Him who judgeth righteously, and He endured this intolerable wrong. More than that, He prayed for His persecutors and said, " Father, forgive them, for they know not what they do."

— " *Admonition to Peace: A Reply to the Twelve Articles of the Peasants in Swabia*," Works of Martin Luther, *Vol. IV, pp. 226– 232.*

According to Scripture, it is in no wise proper for anyone who would be a Christian to set himself against his government, whether it acts justly or unjustly, but a Christian ought to endure oppression and injustice, especially at the hands of his govern- ment. For although his Imperial Majesty may transgress his duty and oath, that does not destroy his imperial sovereignty or the obedience that is due from his subjects so long as the empire and electors recognize him as emperor, and do not depose him. Many an emperor and prince breaks all God's commandments and still

remains emperor and prince, and yet his obligation and oath to God are far higher than to men. If the mere fact that the emperor does wrong were sufficient reason why a subject should set himself against him, then there would be a reason for resisting him every time he does anything against God; that would mean that there would be no government and no obedience in the world, for every subject could allege that his ruler was acting against God.
— Luther's Correspondence, *Vol. II, #870, pp. 519 f.*

If it should happen, as it often does, that the temporal power and authorities, as they are called, should urge a subject to do contrary to the Commandments of God, or hinder him from doing them, there obedience ends, and that duty is annulled. Here a man must say as St. Peter says to the rulers of the Jews: " We ought to obey God rather than men." He did not say: " We must not obey men "; for that would be wrong; but he said: " God rather than men." Thus, if a prince desired to go to war, and his cause was manifestly unrighteous, we should not follow nor help him at all; since God has commanded that we shall not kill our neighbor, nor do him injustice. Likewise, if he bade us bear false witness, steal, lie or deceive and the like. Here we ought rather give up goods, honor, body, and life, that God's Commandments may stand.
— " *Treatise on Good Works,*" Works of Martin Luther, *Vol. I, p. 271.*

When a prince is in the wrong, are his people bound to follow him then too? I answer, No, for it is no one's duty to do wrong; we ought to obey God Who desires the right, rather than men. How is it, when the subjects do not know whether the prince is in the right or not? I answer, As long as they cannot know, nor find out by any possible means, they may obey without peril to their souls. For in such a case one must apply the law of Moses, when he writes in Exodus xxi, that a murderer who has unknowingly and involuntarily killed a man shall be delivered by fleeing to a city of refuge and by the judgment of the congregation. For whichever side is defeated, whether it be in the right or in the wrong, must accept it as a punishment from God; but whichever side wars and wins, in such ignorance, must regard their battle as though one fell from the roof and killed another, and leave the matter to God. For it is the same to God whether He deprives you of goods and life by a just lord or by an unjust. You are His creature, and He can do with you as He will — if only your conscience is clear. God Himself thus excuses Abimelech in Genesis xx, when he took Abraham's wife, not because he had done right, but because he had not known that she was Abraham's wife.

— *" Secular Authority: To What Extent It Should Be Obeyed,"* Works of Martin Luther, *Vol. III, p. 270.*

> In these our days so perilous,
> Lord, peace in mercy send us;
> No God but thee can fight for us,
> No God but thee defend us;
> Thou our only God and Saviour.
>
> Grant our king and all in authority
> Peace and a proficient rule;
> That we may lead a quiet and peaceable life,
> In all godliness and honesty.

— Luther's Hymns, *p. 110.*

XI

Eschatology

Eschatology

1. THE CHRISTIAN HOPE

WHAT have the most exalted minds among the nations thought of a future life, and of the resurrection? Has it not been, that the more exalted they were in mind, the more ridiculous the resurrection and eternal life have appeared to them? Unless you mean to say, that those philosophers and Greeks at Athens, who, (Acts xvii. 18,) called Paul, as he taught these things, a " babbler " and a " setter forth of strange gods," were not of exalted minds. Portius Festus, (Acts xxvi. 24,) calls out that Paul is " mad," on account of his preaching eternal life. What does Pliny bark forth, Book vii? What does Lucian also, that mighty genius? Were not they men wondered at? Moreover to this day there are many, who, the more renowned they are for talent and erudition, the more they laugh at this article; and that openly, considering it a mere fable. And certainly, no man upon earth, unless imbued with the Holy Spirit, ever secretly knows, or believes in, or wishes for, eternal salvation, how much soever he may boast of it by his voice and by his pen.

— *Bondage of the Will, #XLIII, pp. 126 f.*

God so governs this corporal world in external things, that, according to human reason and judgment, you must be compelled to say, either that there is no God, or that God is unjust: as a certain one saith, " I am often tempted to think there is no God." For see the great prosperity of the wicked, and on the contrary the great adversity of the good; according to the testimony of the proverbs, and of experience the parent of all proverbs. The more abandoned men are, the more successful! " The tabernacles of robbers (saith Job) prosper." And Psalm lxxiii. complains, that the sinners of the world abound in riches. Is it not, I pray you, in the judgment of all, most unjust, that the evil should be prosperous, and the good afflicted? Yet so it is in the events of the world. And here it is, that the most exalted minds have so fallen, as to deny that there is any God at all; and to fable, that fortune disposes of all things at random: such were Epicurus and Pliny. And Aristotle, in order that he might make his " First-cause Being " free from every kind of misery, is of opinion, that he thinks of nothing whatever but himself; because he considers, that it must be most irksome to him, to see so many evils and so many injuries.

But the Prophets themselves, who believed there is a God, were tempted still more concerning the injustice of God, as Jeremiah, Job, David, Asaph, and others. And what do you suppose Demosthenes and Cicero thought, who, after they had done all they could, received no other reward than a miserable death? And yet all this, which is so very much like injustice in God, when set forth in those arguments which no reason or light of nature can resist, is most easily cleared up by the light of the Gospel, and the knowledge of grace: by which, we are taught, that the wicked flourish *in their bodies,* but lose *their souls!* And the whole of this insolvable question is solved in one word — There is a life after this life: in which will be punished and repaid, every thing that is not punished and repaid here: for this life is nothing more than an entrance on, and a beginning of, the life which is to come!

— Bondage of the Will, *#CLXVI, pp. 387 f.*

Looking at the Christian community with the eye of human reason and reflection, no more wretched, tormented, persecuted, unhappy people are in evidence on earth than those who confess and glory in Christ the crucified. In the world they are continually persecuted, tormented and assailed by the devil with all manner of wretchedness, misfortune, distress and death. Even to their own perceptions, it seems as if they surely are forgotten and forsaken by God in the sight of mankind. For he allows them to remain prostrate under the weight of the cross, while others in the world, particularly their persecutors, live in the enjoyment of honor and fortune, of happiness, power and riches, with everything moving to the fulfilment of their desires. The Scriptures frequently deplore this condition of things, especially the Psalms, and Paul in First Corinthians 15:19 confesses: " If we have only hoped in Christ in this life, we are of all men most pitiable."

Now, assuredly this state of affairs cannot continue without end; it cannot be God's intention to permit Christians thus to suffer continually while they live, to die because of it and remain dead. It would be incompatible with his eternal, divine truth and honor manifest in his Word. For there he declares he will be the God of the pious, of them who fear and trust him, and gives them unspeakable promises. Necessarily, then, he has planned a future state for Christians and for non-Christians, in either instance unlike what they know on earth. Possibly one of the chief reasons why God permits Christians to suffer on earth is to make plain the distinction between their reward and that of the ungodly. In the sufferings of believing Christians, and in the wickedness, tyranny, rage, and persecution directed by the unrighteous against the godly, is certain indication of a future life unlike this and a final judgment of God in which all men, godly and wicked, shall be forever recompensed.

— *Epistle Sermon, Twenty-sixth Sunday After Trinity* (Lenker Edition, *Vol. IX, #2–3*).

The science of alchymy I like very well, and, indeed, 'tis the philosophy of the ancients. I like it not only for the profits it brings in melting metals, in decocting, preparing, extracting, and distilling herbs, roots; I like it also for the sake of the allegory and secret signification, which is exceedingly fine, touching the resurrection of the dead at the last day. For, as in a furnace the fire extracts and separates from a substance the other portions, and carries upward the spirit, the life, the sap, the strength, while the unclean matter, the dregs, remain at the bottom, like a dead and worthless carcass; even so God, at the day of judgment, will separate all things through fire, the righteous from the ungodly. The Christians and

righteous shall ascend upward into heaven, and there live everlastingly, but the wicked and the ungodly, as the dross and filth,
shall remain in hell, and there be damned.

— Table-Talk, #*DCCLXI.*

There are two ways of viewing things, — one for God, the other
for the world. So also this present life and that to come are twofold. This life cannot be that, since none can reach that but by
death, — that is, by ceasing from *this* life. This life is just to eat,
drink, sleep, endure, bring up children, etc., in which all moves
on successively, hours, day, year, one after another: if you wish
now to apprehend that life, you must banish out of your mind the
course of this present life; you must not think that you can so apprehend it, where it will all be one day, one hour, one moment.

Since then in God's sight there is no reckoning of time, a thousand years must be before him, as it were, a day. Therefore the
first man, Adam, is just as near to him as he who shall be last
born before the last day. For God sees not time lengthwise but
obliquely, just as when you look at right-angles to a long tree
which lies before you, you can fix in your view both place and
parts at once, — a thing you cannot do if you only look at it
lengthwise. We can, by our reason, look at time only according to
its duration; we must begin to count from Adam, one year after
another, even to the last day. But before God it is all in one heap;
what is long with us is short with him, — and again, here there is
neither measure nor number. So when man dies, the body is buried
and wastes away, lies in the earth and knows nothing; but when
the first man rises up at the last day, he will think he has lain
there scarcely an hour, while he will look about himself and become assured that so many people were born of him and have come
after him, of whom he had no knowledge at all.

— Commentary on Peter and Jude, *pp. 312 f.*

St. Paul writes to those at Thessalonica (I Thess. 4:13), that
they should not sorrow over the dead as the others who have no
hope, but that they should comfort themselves with God's Word, as
those who possess sure hope of eternal life and the resurrection of
the dead. For it is no wonder that those who have no hope grieve;

nor can they be blamed for this. Since they are beyond the pale of the faith in Christ they either must cherish this temporal life alone and love it and be unwilling to lose it, or store up for themselves, after this life, eternal death and the wrath of God in hell, and go there unwillingly. But we Christians, who have been redeemed from all this through the precious blood of God's Son, should train and accustom ourselves in faith to despise death and regard it as a deep, strong, sweet sleep; to consider the coffin as nothing other than our Lord Jesus' bosom or Paradise, the grave as nothing other than a soft couch of ease or rest. As verily, before God, it truly is just this; for he testifies, John 11:21: Lazarus, our friend sleeps; Matthew 9:24: The maiden is not dead, she sleeps. Thus, too, St. Paul, in I Corinthians 15, removes from sight all hateful aspects of death as related to our mortal body and brings forward nothing but charming and joyful aspects of the promised life. He says there (vv. 42 ff): It is sown in corruption and will rise in incorruption; it is sown in dishonor (that is, a hateful, shameful form) and will rise in glory; it is sown in weakness and will rise in strength; it is sown a natural body and will rise a spiritual body.

— " Christian Songs, Latin and German, for Use at Funerals," Works of Martin Luther, *Vol. VI, pp. 287 f.*

If we are, at the last day, to rise bodily, in our flesh and blood, to eternal life, we must have had a previous spiritual resurrection here on earth. Paul's words in Romans 8:11 are: " But if the Spirit of him that raised up Jesus from the dead dwelleth in you, he that raised up Christ Jesus from the dead shall give life also to your mortal bodies through his Spirit that dwelleth in you." In other words: God having quickened, justified and saved you spiritually, he will not forget the body, the building or tabernacle of the living spirit; the spirit being in this life risen from sin and death, the tabernacle, or the corruptible flesh-and-blood garment, must also be raised; it must emerge from the dust of earth, since it is the dwelling-place of the saved and risen spirit, that the two may be reunited unto life eternal.

— *Epistle Sermon, Easter Wednesday* (Lenker Edition, *Vol. VIII, #5).*

Those who are not Christians will find small comfort, amid their evils, in the contemplation of future blessings; since for them all these things are uncertain. Although much ado is made here by that famous emotion called hope, by which we call on each other, in words of human comfort, to look for better times, and continually plan greater things for the uncertain future, yet are always deceived. Even as Christ teaches concerning the man in the Gospel, Luke xii, who said to his soul, " I will pull down my barns, and build greater; and will say to my soul, Soul, thou hast much goods laid up for many years; take thine ease, eat, drink, and be merry. But God said unto him, Thou fool, this night thy soul shall be required of thee; and then whose shall those things be which thou hast provided? So is he that layeth up treasure for himself, and is not rich toward God."

Nevertheless, God has not so utterly forsaken the sons of men that He will not grant them some measure of comfort in this hope of the passing of evil and the coming of good things. Though they are uncertain of the future, yet they hope with certain hope, and hereby they are meanwhile buoyed up, lest falling into the further evil of despair, they should break down under their present evil, and do some worse thing. Hence, even this sort of hope is the gift of God; not that He would have them lean on it, but that He would turn their attention to that firm hope, which is in Him alone. . . .

But Christians have . . . the very greatest future blessings certainly awaiting them; yet only through death and suffering. Although they, too, rejoice in that common and uncertain hope that the evil of the present will come to an end, and that its opposite, the blessing, will increase; still, that is not their chief concern, but rather this, that their own particular blessing should increase, which is the truth as it is in Christ, in which they grow from day to day, and for which they both live and hope. But beside this they have, as I have said, the two greatest future blessings in their death. The first, in that through death the whole tragedy of this world's ills is brought to a close; as it is written, " Precious in the sight of the Lord is the death of His saints "; and again, " I will lay me down in peace and sleep "; and, " Though the righteous be prevented with death, yet shall he be at rest." But to the ungodly death is the beginning of evils; as it is said, " The death of the wicked is very evil," and, "Evil shall catch the unjust man unto destruction." Even so Lazarus, who received his evil things in his lifetime, is comforted, while the rich glutton is tormented, because he received his good things here. So that it is always well with the Christian, whether he die or live; so blessed a thing is it to be a Christian and to believe in Christ. Wherefore Paul says, "To me to live is Christ, and to die is gain," and, in Romans xiv, "Whether we live, we live unto the Lord; and whether we die, we die unto the Lord; whether we live therefore, or die, we are the Lord's." . . .

The other blessing of death is this, that it not only concludes the pains and evils of this life, but (which is more excellent) makes an end of sins and vices. And this renders death far more desirable to believing souls, as I have said above, than the former blessing; since the evils of the soul, which are its sins, are beyond comparison worse evils than those of the body. This alone, did we but know it, should make death most desirable. But if it does not, it is a sign that we neither feel nor hate our sin as we should. For this our life is so full of perils — sin, like a serpent, besetting us on every side — and it is impossible for us to live without sinning; but fairest death delivers us from these perils, and cuts our sin clean away from us.

— *"The Fourteen of Consolation,"* Works of Martin Luther, *Vol. I, pp. 146–149.*

It is true that souls hear, perceive, and see after death; but how it is done, we do not understand. . . . If we undertake to give an account of such things after the manner of this life, then we are fools. Christ has given a good answer; for his disciples also were without doubt just as curious. "He that believeth in me, though he were dead, yet shall he live," (John xi. 25); likewise: "Whether we live, or whether we die, we are the Lord's," (Rom. xiv. 8). . . . Abraham lives. God is the God of the living. If now one would say: "The soul of Abraham lives with God, his body lies here dead," it would be a distinction which to my mind is mere rot! I will dispute it. One must say: "The whole Abraham, the entire man, lives!"

— Conversations with Luther, *pp. 122 f.*

You must not calculate how far life and death are apart, or how many years may pass while the body is wasting in the grave, and how one after another dies, but endeavor to grasp the thought of Christ with reference to the conditions apart from this time and hour. For he does not calculate time by tens, hundreds or thousands of years, nor measure the years consecutively, the one preceding, the other following, as we must do in this life; but he grasps everything in a moment, the beginning, middle and end of the whole human race and of all time. And what we regard and measure according to time, as by a long drawn out rule, all this he sees as at a glance, and thus both the death and life of the last as well as of the first man are to him as only a moment of time.

Thus we should learn to view our death in the right light, so that we need not become alarmed on account of it, as unbelief does; because in Christ it is indeed not death, but a fine, sweet and brief sleep, which brings us release from this vale of tears, from sin and from the fear and extremity of real death and from all the misfortunes of this life, and we shall be secure and without care, rest sweetly and gently for a brief moment, as on a sofa, until the time when he shall call and awaken us together with all his dear children to his eternal glory and joy. For since we call it a sleep, we know that we shall not remain in it, but be again awakened and live, and that the time during which we sleep, shall seem no longer than if we had just fallen asleep. Hence, we shall censure ourselves that we were surprised or alarmed at such a sleep in the hour of death, and suddenly come alive out of the grave and from decomposition, and entirely well, fresh, with a pure, clear, glorified life, meet our Lord and Savior Jesus Christ in the clouds. . . .

Scripture everywhere affords such consolation, which speaks of the death of the saints, as if they fell asleep and were gathered to their fathers, that is, had overcome death through this faith and comfort in Christ, and awaited the resurrection, together with the saints who preceded them in death. Therefore the early Christians (undoubtedly from the Apostles or their disciples) followed the custom of bringing their dead to honorable burial and wherever possible interned them in separate places, which they called, not places of burial or graveyards, but *coemeteria*, sleeping-chambers, *dormitoria*, houses of sleep, names that have remained in use until our time.

— *Gospel Sermon, Twenty-fourth Sunday After Trinity* (Lenker Edition, *Vol. XIV, #35–39*).

Augustine, Ambrose, and Jerome held nothing at all of purgatory. Gregory, being in the nighttime deceived by a vision, taught something of purgatory, whereas God openly commanded that we should search out and inquire nothing of spirits, but of Moses and the prophets.

Therefore we must not admit Gregory's opinion on this point; the day of the Lord will show and declare the same, when it will be revealed by fire.

This sentence, " And their works do follow them," must not be understood of purgatory, but of the doctrine of good works, or of godly and true Christians, and of heretics. Arius, the heretic, has had his judgment; the fire of faith has declared it. For the last day will discover and declare all things.

God has, in his Word, laid before us two ways; one which by faith leads to salvation, — the other, by unbelief, to damnation.

As for purgatory, no place in Scripture makes mention thereof, neither must we any way allow it; for it darkens and undervalues the grace, benefits, and merits of our blessed, sweet Saviour Christ Jesus.

The bounds of purgatory extend not beyond this world; for here in this life the upright, good, and godly Christians are well and soundly scoured and purged.

— Table-Talk, *#DXV*.

Shall we pray for the dead? . . . We have no command from God to pray for the dead; therefore no one sins by not praying for them; for what God does not bid or forbid to do, in that no one can sin. Yet, on the other hand, since God has not permitted us to know, how it is with the souls of the departed and we must continue uninformed, as to how he deals with them, we will not and cannot restrain them, nor count it as sin, if they pray for the dead. For we are ever certain from the Gospel, that many have been raised from the dead, who, we must confess, did not receive nor did they have their final sentence; and likewise we are not assured of any other, that he has his final sentence.

Now since it is uncertain and no one knows, whether final judgment has been passed upon these souls, it is not sin if you pray for them; but in this way, that you let it rest in uncertainty and speak thus: Dear God, if the departed souls be in a state that they may yet be helped, then I pray that thou wouldst be gracious. And when you have thus prayed once or twice, then let it be sufficient and commend them unto God. For God has promised that when we pray to him for anything he would hear us. Therefore when you have prayed once or twice, you should believe that your prayer is answered, and there let it rest, lest you tempt God and mistrust him.

— *Gospel Sermon, First Sunday After Trinity* (Lenker Edition, *Vol. XIII, #28–29*).

2. THE LAST DAY

The prophets spoke and preached of the second coming of Christ as we do now; we know that the last day will come, yet we know not what and how it will be after this life, but only in general, that we, who are true Christians, shall have everlasting joy, peace, and salvation. The prophets held likewise, that soon after the coming of Christ, the last day would appear. First, they named the day of the Messiah the last day. Secondly, they set the signs of the first and second coming both together, as if they would happen at one time. Thirdly, in the Epistle to the Corinthians, they demanded of St. Paul, if the last day would appear while they lived. Fourthly, Christ himself related that these signs should come together.

— Table-Talk, #CCV.

It is my firm belief that the angels are getting ready, putting on their armor and girding their swords about them, for the last day is already breaking, and the angels are preparing for the battle, when they will overthrow the Turks and hurl them along with the pope, to the bottom of hell. The world will perish shortly. Among us there is the greatest ingratitude and contempt for the

Word. . . . As things are beginning to go, the last day is at the door, and I believe that the world will not endure a hundred years. For the light of the gospel is now dawning. That day will follow with thunder and lightning, for the voice of the Lord and of the trumpet are conveyed in the thunder. It will come from the east, and the earth will be severely shaken by the crash with such horror, that men will die of fear. I believe that the last day is not far off, for this reason: the gospel is now making its last effort, and it is just the same as with a light which, when it is about to go out, gives forth a great flash at the end as if it intended to burn a long time yet, and then it is gone. So it appears to be in the case of the gospel, which seems on the point of widely extending itself, but I fear that it also will go out in a flash, and that the last day will then be at hand. It is just so with a sick man: when he is about to die he often appears most refreshed, and in a trice he has departed.
— Conversations with Luther, *pp. 250 f.*

I hope that the day is near at hand when the advent of the great God will appear, for all things everywhere are boiling, burning, moving, falling, sinking, groaning.
— Luther's Correspondence, *Vol. II, #741, p. 381.*

The world runs and hastens so diligently to its end that it often occurs to me forcibly that the last day will break before we can completely turn the Holy Scriptures into German. For it is certain from the Holy Scriptures that we have no more temporal things to expect. All is done and fulfilled: the Roman Empire is at an end; the Turk has reached his highest point; the pomp of the papacy is falling away and the world is cracking on all sides almost as if it would break and fall apart entirely. It is true that this same Roman Empire now under our Emperor Charles is coming up a bit and is becoming mightier than it has been for a long time, but I think that that shows it is the last phase, and that before God it is just as when a light or wisp of straw is burnt up and about to go out, then it gives forth a flame as if it was going to burn brightly and even at the same moment goes out: — even so Christendom now does with the light of the Gospel.

Moreover all prophets in and out of the Bible write that after this time, namely, after the present year of 1530, things will go well again. That which they so rightly point to and prophesy will be, I hope, the last day, which will free us from all evil and help us to everlasting joy. So I reckon this epoch of the Gospel light as none other than the time in which God shortens and restrains tribulation by means of the Gospel, as Christ says in Matthew xxiv: " If the Lord shortened not these days, no man would be saved." For if the world had to stand longer as it has hitherto stood, the whole world would become Mohammedan or skeptical, and no Christian would be left, as Christ says (Luke 18:8) : " When the Son of man cometh, shall He find faith on the earth? " And, in fact, there was no more right understanding nor doctrine in the Christian faith present, but mere error, darkness and super-stition with the innumerable multitude.

— Luther's Correspondence, *Vol. II, #869, pp. 516 f.*

I do not wish to force any one to believe as I do; neither will I permit anyone to deny me the right to believe that the last day is near at hand. These words and signs of Christ, (Luke 21:25–36), compel me to believe that such is the case. For the history of the centuries that have passed since the birth of Christ nowhere re-veals conditions like those of the present. There has never been such building and planting in the world. There has never been such gluttonous and varied eating and drinking as now. Wearing ap-parel has reached its limit in costliness. Who has ever heard of such commerce as now encircles the earth? There have arisen all kinds of art and sculpture, embroidery and engraving, the like of which has not been seen during the whole Christian era.

In addition men are so delving into the mysteries of things that today a boy of twenty knows more than twenty doctors formerly knew. There is such a knowledge of languages and all manner of wisdom that it must be confessed, the world has reached such great heights in the things that pertain to the body, or as Christ calls them, " cares of life," eating, drinking, building, planting, buy-ing, selling, marrying and giving in marriage, that every one must see and say either ruin or a change must come. It is hard to see how a change can come. Day after day dawns and the same condi-tions remain. There was never such keenness, understanding and judgment among Christians in bodily and temporal things as now — I forbear to speak of the new inventions, printing, fire-arms, and other implements of war.

But not only have such great strides been made in the world of commerce, but also in the spiritual field have there been great changes. Error, sin, and falsehood have never held sway in the world as in these last centuries. The Gospel has been openly condemned at Constance, and the false teachings of the Pope have been adopted as law though he practiced the greatest extortion. Daily mass is celebrated many hundred thousand times in the world, and thereby the greatest sin is committed. By confession, sacrament, indulgence, rules and laws, so many souls are driven to condemnation that it seems God has given the whole world over to the devil. In short it is not possible that there should be greater falsehood, more heinous error, more dreadful blindness, and more obdurate blasphemy than have ruled in the church through the bishops, cloisters, and universities. As a result Aristotle, a blind heathen, teaches and rules Christians more than does Christ.

— *Gospel Sermon, Second Sunday in Advent* (Lenker Edition, *Vol. X, #5–7*).

The world has come to its end; the Roman Empire is almost gone and torn to bits; it stands as the kingdom of the Jews stood when Christ's birth was near; the Jews had scarcely anything of their kingdom, Herod was the token of farewell. And so, I think, now that the Roman Empire is almost gone, Christ's coming is at the door, and the Turk is the Empire's token of farewell, a parting gift to the Roman Empire.

— *" On War Against the Turk,"* Works of Martin Luther, *Vol. V, p. 118.*

Christ is at present not manifest in person, but on the day of judgment he will appear in effulgent splendor, in undimmed honor; a splendor and honor eternally manifest to all creatures. The last day will be an eternal day. Upon the instant of its appearing every heart and all things will stand revealed. . . . Then there will be neither preaching nor faith. To all men everything will be manifest by experience, and by sight as in a clear sky. . . .

God has reserved unto the last day the displaying of his greatness and majesty, his glory and effulgence. We behold him now in the Gospel and in faith — a narrow view of him. Here he is not great because but slightly comprehended. But in the last appearing he will permit us to behold him in his greatness and majesty.

— *Epistle Sermon, First Christmas Sermon* (Lenker Edition, *Vol. VII, #36*).

In the life to come we shall no more have need of faith, (I Cor. xiii. 12). For then we shall not see darkly through a glass (as we now do) but we shall see face to face: that is to say, there shall be a most glorious brightness of the eternal majesty, in which we shall see God even as he is. There shall be a true and a perfect knowledge and love of God, a perfect light of reason and a good will.

— Commentary on Galatians, *p. 210.*

When at the last day we shall live again, we shall blush for shame, and say to ourselves: " fie on thee, in that thou hast not been more courageous, bold, and strong to believe in Christ, and to endure all manner of adversities, crosses, and persecutions, seeing his glory is so great. If I were now in the world, I would not stick to suffer ten thousand times more."

— Table-Talk, *#CCCX.*

> Christ was laid in Death's strong bands,
>   For our transgressions given.
> Risen, at God's right hand he stands
>   And brings us life from heaven.
> Therefore let us joyful be
> Praising God right thankfully
>   With loud songs of Hallelujah!
>   Hallelujah!
>
> None o'er Death could victory win;
>   O'er all mankind he reigned.
> 'Twas by reason of our sin;
>   There was not one unstained.

Thus came Death upon us all,
Bound the captive world in thrall,
   Held us 'neath his dread dominion.
      Hallelujah!

Jesus Christ, God's only Son,
   To our low state descending,
All our sins away hath done
   Death's power forever ending.
Ruined all his right and claim
Left him nothing but the name,
   For his sting is lost forever.
      Hallelujah!

Strange and dreadful was the fray,
   When Death and Life contended;
But 'twas Life that won the day,
   And Death's dark sway was ended.
Holy Scripture plainly saith,
Death is swallowed up of Death,
   Put to scorn and led in triumph.
      Hallelujah!
— Luther's Hymns, *p. 94.*

INDEX